Lecture Notes in Artificial Intelligence 4369

Edited by J. G. Carbonell and J. Siekmann

Subseries of Lecture Notes in Computer Science

Masanobu Umeda Armin Wolf
Oskar Bartenstein Ulrich Geske
Dietmar Seipel Osamu Takata (Eds.)

Declarative Programming
for Knowledge Management

16th International Conference on Applications
of Declarative Programming and Knowledge Management, INAP 2005
Fukuoka, Japan, October 22-24, 2005
Revised Selected Papers

 Springer

Series Editors

Jaime G. Carbonell, Carnegie Mellon University, Pittsburgh, PA, USA
Jörg Siekmann, University of Saarland, Saarbrücken, Germany

Volume Editors

Masanobu Umeda
Kyushu Institute of Technology
680-4 Kawazu, Iizuka, Fukuoka 820-8502, Japan
E-mail: umerin@ci.kyutech.ac.jp

Armin Wolf
Ulrich Geske
Fraunhofer FIRST
Kekuléstraße 7, 12489 Berlin, Germany
E-mail: {armin.wolf,ulrich.geske}@first.fraunhofer.de

Oskar Bartenstein
IF Computer Japan
5-28-2 Sendagi, Bunkyo-ku, Tokyo 113-0022, Japan
E-mail: oskar@ifcomputer.co.jp

Dietmar Seipel
Universität Würzburg
Am Hubland, 97074 Würzburg, Germany
E-mail: seipel@informatik.uni-wuerzburg.de

Osamu Takata
Kyushu Institute of Technology
680-4 Kawazu, Iizuka, Fukuoka 820-8502, Japan
E-mail: takata@ci.kyutech.ac.jp

Library of Congress Control Number: 2006938800

CR Subject Classification (1998): I.2.4, I.2, D.1.6

LNCS Sublibrary: SL 7 – Artificial Intelligence

ISSN   0302-9743
ISBN-10   3-540-69233-9 Springer Berlin Heidelberg New York
ISBN-13   978-3-540-69233-1 Springer Berlin Heidelberg New York

Springer is a part of Springer Science+Business Media

springer.com

© Springer-Verlag Berlin Heidelberg 2006
Printed in Germany

Typesetting: Camera-ready by author, data conversion by Scientific Publishing Services, Chennai, India
Printed on acid-free paper   SPIN: 11963578   06/3142   5 4 3 2 1 0

Preface

Knowledge means power – but only if it is available at the right time, the right place, and in the hands of the right people. Structured, engineered, repeatable methods to gather, transport, and apply knowledge are collectively called *knowledge management*.

Declarative programming strives for the ideal of programming by wish: the user states what he or she wants, and the computer figures out how to achieve it. Thus, declarative programming splits into two separate parts: methods for humans on how to write wishes, and algorithms for computers that fulfil these wishes.

Knowledge management is now recognized as an economic key factor. Declarative programming has matured far beyond the research stage of a merely interesting formal logic model to one of the powerful tools in computer science. Nowadays, no professional activity is thinkable without knowledge management, and companies increasingly need to document their business processes. Here, declarative programming carries the promise to be a shortcut to not only documenting but also implementing knowledge-based enterprises.

This volume presents a selection of papers presented at the 16th International Conference on Applications of Declarative Programming and Knowledge Management, INAP 2005, held in October 2005 at Waseda University, Fukuoka, Japan. These papers reflect a snapshot of ongoing research and current applications in knowledge management and declarative programming. Further, they provide reality checks and many pointers for readers who consider introducing related technologies into their products or working environments.

Skimming through the table of contents, technology managers as well as implementors will be surprised on the wide scope covered by this selection of papers. If you think of knowledge streams as supply, manufacturing, or distribution chains, you will see that it all fits together.

The papers have been selected for their thought-provoking value, the authors are aware that their readers have diverse backgrounds. We sincerely hope that this book is stimulating reading, applying and conducting further research in declarative programming and knowledge management.

Japan/Germany 2006

Masanobu Umeda
Armin Wolf
Oskar Bartenstein
Ulrich Geske
Dietmar Seipel
Osamu Takata
(Editors)

Organization

INAP 2005 was organized by IF Computer, Japan, the Kyushu Institute of Technology, Japan, Fraunhofer FIRST, Germany, University of Würzburg, Germany, and Waseda University, Japan.

Executive Committee

Conference Chair:	Oskar Bartenstein
	IF Computer, Japan
Program Co-chair:	Masanobu Umeda
	Kyushu Institute of Technology, Japan
Program Co-chair:	Armin Wolf
	Fraunhofer FIRST, Germany
Constraints Track Chair:	Ulrich Geske
	Fraunhofer FIRST, Germany
Knowledge Management Track Chair:	Dietmar Seipel
	University of Würzburg, Germany
Applications Track Chair:	Osamu Takata
	Kyushu Institute of Technology, Japan
Local Arrangement Chair:	Osamu Yoshie
	Waseda University, Japan

Program Committee

Masanobu Umeda, Kyushu Institute of Technology, Japan
Armin Wolf, Fraunhofer FIRST, Germany
Oskar Bartenstein, IF Computer, Japan
Ulrich Geske, Fraunhofer FIRST, Germany
Dietmar Seipel, University of Würzburg, Germany
Osamu Yoshie, Waseda University, Japan
Osamu Takata, Kyushu Institute of Technology, Japan
Kouichi Shibao, AIE Research, Japan
Virginia Dignum, Utrecht University, Netherlands
Petra Hofstedt, Technical University of Berlin, Germany
Neng-Fa Zhou, The City University of New York, USA
Sergio A. Alvarez, Boston College, USA
Joachim Baumeister, University of Würzburg, Germany
Carolina Ruiz, Worcester Polytechnic Institute, USA

External Referees

Masaaki Hashimoto, Kyushu Institute of Technology, Japan
Hidenobu Kunichika, Kyushu Institute of Technology, Japan
Keiichi Katamine, Kyushu Institute of Technology, Japan
Naoyasu Ubayashi, Kyushu Institute of Technology, Japan
Taketoshi Ushiama, Kyushu University, Japan
Andreas Böhm, University of Würzburg, Germany
Marbod Hopfner, University of Würzburg, Germany

Supporting Institutions

IF Computer, Tokyo, Japan
Waseda University, Graduate School of Information, Production and Systems, Japan

Table of Contents

Frontier Technologies

Prolog Cafe: A Prolog to Java Translator System 1
Mutsunori Banbara, Naoyuki Tamura, and Katsumi Inoue

TURTLE++ – A CIP-Library for C++ 12
Petra Hofstedt and Olaf Krzikalla

Constraint Solving for Sequences in Software Validation and
Verification 25
Nikolai Kosmatov

Using a Logic Programming Language with Persistence and Contexts ... 38
Salvador Abreu and Vitor Nogueira

On a Rough Sets Based Data Mining Tool in Prolog: An Overview 48
Hiroshi Sakai

Not-First and Not-Last Detection for Cumulative Scheduling
in $\mathcal{O}(n^3 \log n)$ 66
Andreas Schutt, Armin Wolf, and Gunnar Schrader

Calc/Cream: OpenOffice Spreadsheet Front-End for Constraint
Programming.. 81
Naoyuki Tamura

$\mathcal{O}(n \log n)$ Overload Checking for the Cumulative Constraint and Its
Application 88
Armin Wolf and Gunnar Schrader

Inductive Logic Programming: Yet Another Application of Logic 102
Akihiro Yamamoto

Industrial Case Studies

Railway Scheduling with Declarative Constraint Programming 117
Ulrich Geske

User Profiles and Matchmaking on Mobile Phones.................... 135
Thomas Kleemann and Alex Sinner

A Design Product Model for Mechanism Parts by Injection Molding   148
    Tatsuichiro Nagai, Isao Nagasawa, Masanobu Umeda,
    Tatsuji Higuchi, Yasuyuki Nishidai, Yusuke Kitagawa,
    Tsuyoshi Tsurusaki, Masahito Ohhashi, and Osamu Takata

A Knowledge-Based System for Process Planning in Cold Forging
Using the Adjustment of Stepped Cylinder Method   161
    Osamu Takata, Yuji Mure, Yasuo Nakashima, Masuharu Ogawa,
    Masanobu Umeda, and Isao Nagasawa

Business Integration

An Overview of Agents in Knowledge Management   175
    Virginia Dignum

ubiCMS – A Prolog Based Content Management System   190
    Oskar Bartenstein

Multi-threading Inside Prolog for Knowledge-Based Enterprise
Applications   200
    Masanobu Umeda, Keiichi Katamine, Isao Nagasawa,
    Masaaki Hashimoto, and Osamu Takata

A Meta-logical Approach for Multi-agent Communication of Semantic
Web Information   215
    Visit Hirankitti and Vuong Xuan Tran

Author Index   229

Prolog Cafe: A Prolog to Java Translator System

Mutsunori Banbara[1], Naoyuki Tamura[1], and Katsumi Inoue[2]

[1] Information Science and Technology Center, Kobe University
1-1 Rokkodai, Nada, Kobe 657-8501, Japan
{banbara, tamura}@kobe-u.ac.jp
[2] National Institute of Informatics
2-1-2 Hitotsubashi, Chiyoda-ku, Tokyo 101-8430, Japan
ki@nii.ac.jp

Abstract. We present the Prolog Cafe system that translates Prolog into Java via the WAM. Prolog Cafe provides multi-threaded Prolog engines. A Prolog Cafe thread seems to be conceptually an independent Prolog evaluator and communicates with each other through shared Java objects. Prolog Cafe also has the advantages of portability, extensibility, smooth interoperation with Java, and modularity. In performance, our translator generates faster code for a set of classical Prolog benchmarks than an existing Prolog-to-Java translator jProlog.

1 Introduction

Recent development of Prolog in Java suggests a successful direction to extend not only Prolog to be more networked and mobile, but also Java applications to be more intelligent. We aim to develop a Java-conscious Prolog system that has the advantages of portability, extensibility, interoperability, parallelism, and modularity.

In the implementation of Prolog, the Warren Abstract Machine (WAM) [1,2] has became a *de facto* standard. WAM is flexible enough for several extensions such as higher-order, concurrent, constraint, and linear logic programming. WAM has been also a basis for compiling Prolog into C [3], C++, Java, C#.

We present the Prolog Cafe system that translates Prolog into Java. The execution model of translated Java classes is based on the WAM. Main features of Prolog Cafe are as follows:

- *Portability*
  Prolog Cafe is a 100% pure Java implementation and is portable to any platform supporting a Java compiler.
- *Extensibility*
  The output of Prolog Cafe translator can be well structured and readable. Prolog Cafe is therefore easily expandable with increasing Java class libraries.
- *Interoperability*
  From the Java side, the translated code of Prolog Cafe can be easily embedded into Java applications such as Applets and Servlets. From the Prolog side, any Java object can be represented as a Prolog term, and its methods and fields can be exploited from Prolog.

M. Umeda et al. (Eds.): INAP 2005, LNAI 4369, pp. 1–11, 2006.

– *Parallelism*
  Prolog Cafe provides multi-threaded Prolog engines. A Prolog Cafe thread seems to be conceptually an independent Prolog evaluator, in which a Prolog goal runs on a local runtime environment. Prolog Cafe threads communicate with each other through shared Java objects.
– *Modularity*
  Prolog modules are translated into separate Java packages that can be imported from each other.

In performance, our translator generates faster code for a set of classical Prolog benchmarks than an existing Prolog-to-Java translator jProlog. Main differences from the previous version of Prolog Cafe [4] are new features of interoperability, parallelism, and modularity listed above.

Usefulness of Prolog Cafe has been shown through several applications: P# [5], Multisat [6], Maglog [7], Holoparadigm [8], and CAWOM [9]. Among these applications, we give a brief introduction to the Multisat system, a parallel execution system of SAT solvers.

The reminder of this paper is organized as follows. After showing the translation method of existing Prolog to Java translators in Section 2, Section 3 presents the Prolog Cafe system in detail. Related work is discussed in Section 4, and the paper is concluded in Section 5.

2   Existing Prolog to Java Translator Systems

In this section, we present how jProlog and LLPj translate Prolog into Java. Due to space limitations, we use the following simple example:

```
p :- q, r.
q.
```

2.1   jProlog

The jProlog [10] system, developed by B. Demoen and P. Tarau, is a first generation Prolog to Java translator via the WAM. jProlog is based on *binarization transformation* [11], a continuation passing style compilation used in BinProlog.

In jProlog approach, each clause is first translated into a binary clause by binarization and then translated into one Java class. Each predicate with the same name/arity is translated a set of classes; there is one class for direct entry point, and other classes for clauses. Each continuation goal is translated into a term object, that is executed by referring to the hash table to transform it into its corresponding predicate object.

Our example is first translated into the following binary clauses where Cont represents a continuation goal:

```
p(Cont) :- q(r(Cont)).
q(Cont) :- call(Cont).
```

and then each of them is translated into the following Java classes:

```
public class pred_p_0 extends Code { % entry point of p/0
    static Code cl1 = new pred_p_0_1();
    static Code q1cont;
    void init(PrologMachine mach) {
        q1cont = mach.LoadPred("q",0); % get continuation goal q/0
    }
    Code Exec(PrologMachine mach) {
        return cl1.Exec(mach); % call the clause p(Cont) :- q(r(Cont))
    }
}
class pred_p_0_1 extends pred_p_0 { % p(Cont) :- q(r(Cont)).
    Code Exec(PrologMachine mach) {
        PrologObject continuation = mach.Areg[0]; % get Cont
        mach.Areg[0] = new Funct("r".intern(), continuation); % create r(Cont)
        mach.CUTB = mach.CurrentChoice;
        return q1cont; % call q/0
    }
}
public class pred_q_0 extends Code { % entry point of q/0
    static Code cl1 = new pred_q_0_1();
    Code Exec(PrologMachine mach) {
        return cl1.Exec(mach); % call the clause q(Cont) :- call(Cont).
    }
}
class pred_q_0_1 extends pred_q_0 { % q(Cont) :- call(Cont).
    Code Exec(PrologMachine mach) {
        mach.CUTB = mach.CurrentChoice;
        return UpperPrologMachine.Call1; % call Cont
    }
}
```

The PrologMachine class represents a Prolog engine and has a runtime environment such as argument registers ($\mathtt{Areg[1]} - \mathtt{Areg[n]}$), cut register (CUTB), choice point stack, trail stack, and so on. The Code class is a common superclass of all predicates. This class has the Exec method, and its argument is an object of currently activated Prolog engine. Continuation goal is always stored in Areg[0] at term level. Prolog cut (!) is implemented by the traditional way used in usual WAM-based Prolog systems. Translated code is executed in the following supervisor function:

```
code = goal predicate;
while (ExceptionRaised == 0) {
    code = code.Exec(this) ;    % this indicates Prolog engine
}
```

This function iteratively invokes the Exec method until the failure of all trials. The Exec method does certain actions referring to a Prolog engine and returns a continuation goal.

jProlog provides a simple and sound basis for translating Prolog into Java. It also supports intuitionistic assumption, backtrackable destructive assignment, and delayed execution. However, there are some points that can be improved since jProlog is an experimental system. For example, jProlog has no support for multi-threaded execution and does not incorporate well-known optimizations such as indexing and specialization of head unification.

2.2 LLPj

LLPj [12] is a Java implementation of a linear logic programming language. LLPj takes a different approach from jProlog for translating Prolog into Java.

In LLPj approach, each predicate with the same name/arity is translated into only one class, in which each clause is translated into one method. Each continuation goal is translated into a predicate object rather than a term. The previous example is translated as follows:

```
public class PRED_p_0 extends Predicate {
    public PRED_p_0 ( Predicate cont) {
        this.cont = cont;          % get Cont
    }
    public void exec() {
        if(clause1()) return;      % call the clause p(Cont) :- q(r(Cont))
    }
    private boolean clause1() {    % p(Cont) :- q(r(Cont)).
        try {
            Predicate new_cont = new PRED_r_0(cont);   % create r(Cont)
            (new PRED_q_0(new_cont)).exec();           % call q/0
        } catch (CutException e) {
            if(e.id != this) throw e;
            return true;
        }
        return false;
    }
}
public class PRED_q_0 extends Predicate {
    public PRED_q_0 ( Predicate cont) {
        this.cont = cont;          % get Cont
    }
    public void exec() {
        if(clause1()) return;      % call the clause q(Cont) :- call(Cont).
    }
    private boolean clause1() {    % q(Cont) :- call(Cont).
        try {
            cont.exec();           % call Cont
        } catch (CutException e) {
            if(e.id != this) throw e;
            return true;
        }
        return false;
    }
}
```

The `Predicate` class is a common superclass of all predicates that has the `exec` method and the `cont` and `trail` fields. These two fields are used to store a continuation goal and a trail stack respectively. The `exec` method invokes, in order, the methods corresponding to clauses. Thus, everything we need at runtime is maintained in each predicate locally, and there is no implementation of Prolog engine such as `PrologMachine` in jProlog. Prolog cut (!) is implemented by using Java's exception handlers `try` and `catch` block. Translated code is executed by invoking the `exec` method:

```
code = goal predicate;
code.exec();
```

LLPj is comparable in performance to jProlog for some Prolog benchmarks used in Section 3.4. The weakness of this approach is that the invocation of `exec` will invoke other nested `exec` methods, and never return until the system reaches the first solution. This leads to a memory overflow for large programs.

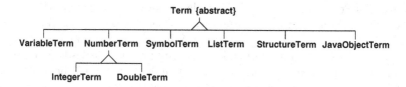

Fig. 1. Term Structure of Prolog Cafe

3   Prolog Cafe

In this section, we present the Prolog Cafe system, especially its translation method and new features of interoperability and parallelism. In performance, we compare Prolog Cafe with jProlog for a set of classical Prolog benchmarks. We also give a brief introduction to the Multisat system.

3.1   Translating Prolog into Java

Each term is translated into a Java object of classes in Figure 1: `VariableTerm`, `IntegerTerm`, `DoubleTerm`, `SymbolTerm`, `ListTerm`, and `StructureTerm`. The `Term` class, which has an abstract method `unify`, is a common superclass of these classes. The `JavaObjectTerm` class is used to represent any Java object as a Prolog term.

The Prolog Cafe translator is based on the jProlog approach with featuring LLPj. Prolog Cafe incorporates the optimization of indexing (only first level) and specialization of head unification. Basically, each predicate is translated into a set of classes; one class is for an entry point of a predicate, and the other classes are for clauses and choice instructions [1]. Each continuation goal is translated into a predicate object rather than a term. Our previous example is translated as follows:

```
import jp.ac.kobe_u.cs.prolog.lang.*;
public class PRED_p_0 extends Predicate {
    public PRED_p_0(Predicate cont) {
        this.cont = cont;                      % get Cont
    }
    public Predicate exec(Prolog engine) {     % p(Cont) :- q(r(Cont)).
        engine.setB0();
        Predicate p1 = new PRED_r_0(cont);     % create r(Cont)
        return new PRED_q_0(p1);               % call q/0
    }
}
public class PRED_q_0 extends Predicate {
    public PRED_q_0(Predicate cont) {          % get Cont
        this.cont = cont;
    }
    public Predicate exec(Prolog engine) {     % q(Cont) :- call(Cont).
        return cont;                           % call Cont
    }
}
```

---

[1] It is noted that a predicate is translated into only one class in the deterministic case such as a predicate consisting in only one clause.

The output of Prolog Cafe consists of two classes and is smaller than that of jProlog. Translating continuations into predicate objects makes it possible to avoid the overhead of referring to the hash table. We can also avoid memory overflow occurred in LLPj since translated code is executed by a supervisor function.

Besides static predicates, Prolog Cafe can handle dynamic predicates and has provided a small Prolog interpreter. An implementation of `assert` and `retract` was discussed in the paper [4].

3.2   Interoperation with Java

It is possible to represent any Java object as a Prolog term, invoke its methods, and access to its fields by using the following built-in predicates:

- `java_constructor(+Class, ?Object)`
- `java_method(+Object, +Method, ?Return)`
- `java_get_field(+Object, +Field, ?Value)`
- `java_set_field(+Object, +Field, +Value)`

Object creation is performed by calling `java_constructor/2` where the first argument is an atom or compound term. A call to `java_constructor(f(a_1,...,a_n), O)` creates an object with the class name f and the argument objects $a'_1, ..., a'_n$. The created object is wrapped by `JavaObjectTerm` as a Prolog term and then unified with O. Each argument a_i is converted to a certain java object a'_i by the mapping that supports Java widening conversion. We omit the detail of data conversion here. Method invocation is performed by calling `java_method/3` where the first argument is an atom or Java object. It is noted that the second argument represents a static method when the first argument is an atom. A call to `java_method(O, g(b_1,...,b_n), R)` invokes a method with the method name g and the argument objects $b'_1, ..., b'_n$. The return value is wrapped by `JavaObjectTerm` as a Prolog term and then unified with R. Each argument b_i is converted to a certain Java object b'_i. Field access is performed by calling `java_get_field/3` and `java_set_field/3` in the similar way.

```
main :-
    java_constructor('java.awt.Frame', X),
    java_method(X, setSize(400,300), _),
    java_get_field('java.lang.Boolean', 'TRUE', True),
    java_method(X, setVisible(True), _).
```

For example, a call to `main` in the above code shows an empty frame on your screen.

3.3   Explicit Parallelism

Prolog Cafe provides multi-threaded Prolog engines. A Prolog Cafe thread seem to be conceptually an independent Prolog evaluator, in which a Prolog goal runs on a local runtime environment. The `PrologControl` class is an implementation of Prolog Cafe thread and provides several methods for the control such as `start`, `stop`, and `join`. From the Prolog side, the control of thread can be programmed as follows:

```
start(Goal, Engine) :-
    java_constructor('PrologControl', Engine),
    copy_term(Goal, G0),
    java_wrap_term(G0, G),
    java_method(Engine, setPredicate(G), _),
    java_method(Engine, start, _).
stop(Engine)  :- java_method(Engine, stop, _).
join(Engine)  :- java_method(Engine, join, _).
sleep(Wait)   :- java_method('java.lang.Thread', sleep(Wait), _).
```

Creating thread is performed by call start/2. This predicate is similar to the launch_goal/2 of Ciao Prolog [13] and the new_engine/3 of Jinni [14]. A call to start(Goal, Engine) first creates a thread object and unifies it with Engine by using java_constructor/2, and it sets a copy of Goal to Engine, and then invokes the method start of thread object. Execution of Goal is thus proceeds on the new thread in an independent runtime environment. A call to join waits for the thread until the assigned goal succeeds or fails. The stop/1 predicate is used to kill the thread. Calling the sleep/1 causes the currently executing thread to sleep for the specified number of milliseconds.

Each goal, which runs separately on a thread, communicates through a shared Java object as a Prolog term. Synchronization can be done by the built-in predicate synchronized/2. A call to synchronized(+Object, +Goal) locks the Object and then execute Goal. This predicate is implemented by using the synchronized block of Java.

3.4   Experiments

We compare Prolog Cafe with jProlog. Table 1 shows the performance results of a set of classical Prolog benchmarks. A time of "?" in jProlog means that we met some errors during the compilation of generated Java code because of few built-in predicates. All times in millisecond were collected on Linux system (Xeon 2.8GHz, 2G memory) with JDK 1.5.0.

Prolog Cafe generates 2.7 times faster code than jProlog in average. This speedup is due to indexing, specialization of head unification, and first-call-optimization. For the purpose of reference, we add the execution time of SWI-Prolog to Table 1. SWI-Prolog is an efficient Prolog compiler system that compile Prolog into WAM. Compared with SWI-Prolog with -O option, Prolog Cafe is only 1.3 times slower for the queens_10 (all solutions) and is about 3 times slower in average. It is noted that Prolog Cafe is about 10 times faster for the tak than SWI-Prolog without -O option.

Prolog Cafe is disadvantageous in performance compared with SWI-Prolog, but still has some possibilities for speedup. This is because Prolog Cafe is a simple implementation and does not incorporate well-known optimizations, such as register allocation, last-call-optimization, and global analysis.

Table 1. Comparison for Prolog Cafe vs jProlog vs SWI-Prolog

Prolog Programs	Runs Avg.	Prolog Cafe 0.9.3	jProlog 0.1	SWI-Prolog 5.0
browse	10	441.1	3011.8	218.0
ham	10	556.4	741.6	135.0
nrev(300 elem.)	10	34.1	115.3	15.0
tak	10	229.0	302.6	47.0
zebra	10	61.8	62.2	6.0
cal	10	223.7	?	36.0
poly_10	10	224.3	?	10.0
queens_10 (all sol.)	10	462.9	?	344.0
sendmore	10	66.6	?	18.0
Average of Ratio	10	1.00	2.77	0.30

3.5 Multisat: A Parallel Execution System of SAT Solvers

Multisat [6] is a heterogeneous SAT solver integrating both systematic and stochastic algorithms, and includes solvers reimplemented in Java: Satz [15], Walksat [16], and Chaff [17]. In Multisat, multiple solvers run in parallel on Prolog Cafe threads.

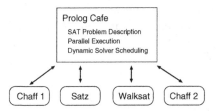

Fig. 2. A Multisat architecture

Each solver can be dynamically created and killed from Prolog Cafe. Figure 2 shows a situation that Satz, Walksat and two Chaffs are created from Multisat. Main features of Multisat are as follows:

1. *Competitive Mode*
   Running multiple solvers in parallel, solvers compete with each other and share resources. No control is performed at all so that threads are processed equally. In the competitive mode, a solver that most fits the given problem firstly returns the output. Hence, solvers' strength and weakness for each SAT problem can be observed in this mode.

2. *Cooperative Mode*
   In the cooperative mode, solvers exchange derived clauses. Here, Chaff generates a new clause called a *lemma* when the current assignment leads to a conflict. Such a lemma is utilized to avoid the same conflict. However, unrestricted incorporation of lemmas involves a memory explosion. Here, we further use these lemmas in other solvers that are running in parallel.

3. *Dynamic Preference*

In Multisat, solvers run in parallel on Prolog Cafe threads. The status of each thread is either active or suspended. In default, each active solver is given the same amount of resources. In the scheduling system, active threads become suspended by method calls like `sleep()` and `wait()` or by input-output and synchronized blocks. On the other hand, scheduling threads is also possible according to their priorities using `setPriority` method.

Effectiveness of Multisat has been shown through applications to SATLIB problems [18], SAT planning [19], and job-shop scheduling [20]. Multisat has solved SATLIB problems efficiently in average compared with single solvers. Multisat is particularly useful for SAT planning and job-shop scheduling because this type of problem suite should alternately handle satisfiable and unsatisfiable problems. Detailed experiment results of Multisat are shown in the paper [6].

4   Related Work

In addition to jProlog, LLPj, and Prolog Cafe, a number of Prolog in Java have been recently developed: MINERVA, Jinni, W-Prolog, tuProlog, PROLOG+CG, JIProlog, JavaLog, DGKS Prolog, JLog, and XProlog. MINERVA [21] and Jinni [14] are commercial Prolog systems which compile Prolog into their own virtual machines that are executed in Java. W-Prolog [22] and others are implemented as interpreter systems. Each system has strength and weakness for our requirements. MINERVA and Jinni might be more efficient but are not possible to produce standalone executables. MINERVA has also no support for multi-threaded execution. Prolog Interpreters such as W-Prolog might be simpler but does not give nice performances. We thus decided to adopt the approach of translating Prolog into Java. This approach has the advantage of giving comparatively nice speedup in performance and producing standalone executables.

5   Conclusion

In this paper, we have presented the Prolog Cafe system, a Prolog-to-Java source-to-source translator system via the WAM. We have shown how Prolog Cafe translate Prolog into Java and new features of smooth interoperation with Java and explicit parallelism. In performance, our translator generates 2.7 times faster code for a set of classical Prolog benchmarks than an existing Prolog-to-Java translator jProlog. We have also given a brief introduction to the Multisat system as an application of Prolog Cafe. Hence, we conclude that Prolog Cafe can be well suited to develop Java-based intelligent applications such as mobile agent programs. Prolog Cafe is distributed as open source software under GPL license. The newest package (version is 0.9) is available from

http://kaminari.istc.kobe-u.ac.jp/PrologCafe/

There are some important future topics. Supporting ISO Prolog is necessary. Eclipse plug-in for Prolog Cafe can be a promising tool for improving usability.

References

1. Aït-Kaci, H.: Warren's Abstract Machine. MIT Press (1991)
2. Warren, D.H.D.: An abstract Prolog instruction set. Technical Report Technical Note 309, SRI International, Menlo Park, CA (1983)
3. Codognet, P., Diaz, D.: WAMCC: Compiling Prolog to C. In Sterling, L., ed.: Proceedings of International Conference on Logic Programming, The MIT Press (1995) 317–331
4. Banbara, M., Tamura, N.: Translating a linear logic programming language into Java. In: Proceedings of the ICLP'99 Workshop on Parallelism and Implementation Technology for (Constraint) Logic Programming Languages. (1999) 19–39
5. Cook, J.J.: P#: a concurrent prolog for the .net framework. Software: Practice and Experience **34** (2004) 815–845
6. Inoue, K., Sasaura, Y., Soh, T., Ueda, S.: A competitive and cooperative approach to propositional satisfiability. Discrete Applied Mathematics (2006)
7. Kawamura, T., Kinoshita, S., Sugahara, K.: Implementation of a mobile agent framework on java environment. In Gonzalez, T., ed.: Proceedings of the IASTED International Conference Parallel and Distributed Computing and Systems. (2004) 589–593 MIT, Cambridge, USA.
8. Barbosa, J.L.V., Yamin, A.C., Augustin, I., Vargas, P.K., Geyer, C.F.R.: Holoparadigm: a multiparadigm model oriented to development of distributed systems. In: Proceedings of the International Conference on Parallel and Distributed Systems (ICPADS 2002). (2002) 6 pages
9. Wohlstadter, E., Jackson, S., Devanbu, P.T.: Generating wrappers for command line programs: The cal-aggie wrap-o-matic project. In: Proceedings of International Conference on Software Engineering. (2001) 243–252
10. Demoen, B., Tarau, P.: jProlog home page (1996) http://www.cs.kuleuven.ac.be/~bmd/PrologInJava/.
11. Tarau, P., Boyer, M.: Elementary Logic Programs. In: Proceedings of Programming Language Implementation and Logic Programming. Number 456 in Lecture Notes in Computer Science, Springer (1990) 159–173
12. Banbara, M., Tamura, N.: Java implementation of a linear logic programming language. In: Proceedings of the 10th Exhibition and Symposium on Industrial Applications of Prolog. (1997) 56–63
13. Carro, M., Hermenegildo, M.V.: Concurrency in prolog using threads and a shared database. In Schreye, D.D., ed.: Proceedings of the 15th International Conference on Logic Programming (ICLP'99). (1999) 320–334
14. Tarau, P.: Jinni: a lightweight java-based logic engine for internet programming. In Sagonas, K., ed.: Proceedings of JICSLP'98 Implementation of LP languages Workshop. (1998) invited talk.
15. Li, C.M., Anbulagan: Heuristics based on unit propagation for satisfyability problems. In: Proceedings of the Fifteenth International Joint Conference on Artificial Intelligence (IJCAI 1997). (1997) 366–371
16. B.Selman, H.Kautz, B.Cohen: Local search strategies for satisfiability testing. In D.S.Johnson, M, A., eds.: Cliques, Coloring and Satisfiability: Second DIMACS Implementation Challenge. Volume 26 of DIMACS Series in Discrete Mathematics and Theoretical Computer Science. American Mathematical Society (1996) 521–531
17. Moskewicz, M.W., Madigan, C.F., Zhao, Y., Zhang, L., Malik, S.: Chaff: Engineering an efficient sat solver. In: Proceedings of the 38th Design Automation Conference (DAC 2001), ACM (2001) 530–535

18. Hoos, H.H., Stutzle, T.:   SATLIB: An online resource for research on sat. In I.P.Gent, H.v.Maaren, T., ed.: SAT 2000.   IOS Press (2000) 283–292 http://www.satlib.org/.
19. Kautz, H., Selman, B.: Unifying sat-based and graph-based planning. In: Proceedings of the 16th International Joint Conference on Artificial Intelligence. (1999) 318–325
20. M.R.Garey, D.S.Johnson, R.Sethi: The complexity of flowshop and jobshop scheduling. Mathematics Operation Research 1 (1976) 117–129
21. IF Computer: MINERVA home page (1996) http://www.ifcomputer.com/ MINERVA/.
22. Winikoff, M.: W-Prolog home page. http://goanna.cs.rmit.edu.au/~winikoff/ wp/ (1996)

TURTLE++ – A CIP-Library for C++

Petra Hofstedt and Olaf Krzikalla

Technical University of Berlin
ph@cs.tu-berlin.de, krzikalla@gmx.net

Abstract. This article introduces the TURTLE++ library which combines constraint-based and imperative paradigms and enables in this way *constraint imperative programming* (CIP) with C++. Integrating CIP into C++ allows to exploit the powerful expressiveness of the CIP paradigm within a language widely used and accepted in practice. We discuss the main concepts and implementation and illustrate programming with TURTLE++ by means of typical examples.

1 Introduction

Using *imperative* programming languages the user describes the precise steps to compute a solution for a given problem. In contrast, in *declarative* languages the programmer simply gives a problem specification, while the computation mechanism of the language is responsible to provide solutions. In constraint programming – as a member of the declarative paradigm – constraints, i.e. formulae of first order predicate logic, are used for the problem description, specifying the problem variables, their properties and relationships. These constraints are handled by constraint solvers provided by the languages to obtain solutions.

The imperative and the constraint-based paradigm are qualified for different tasks: Temporal orders of events are best specified using imperative concepts, while constraints are better suited for search problems or partially unspecified tasks. *Constraint imperative programming (CIP)* [4] allows to combine both paradigms and thus to use their concepts simultaneously within one language.

The following example origins from [8]. Program 1.1 uses a pure imperative approach to describe a graphical element, e.g. in a user interaction, which can be dragged with the mouse inside certain borders. Pressing a mouse-button the vertical coordinate y of the graphical element is adapted within a minimum and a maximum range. This description cleanly reflects the temporal – i.e. imperative – behaviour but requires also declarative properties, like the range restrictions, to be expressed imperatively. They are ensured by explicit tests which must be performed in each pass within a while-loop as long as the button is pressed.

In contrast, Program 1.2 gives an according CIP implementation, already in the syntax of TURTLE++. The initial instantiation of y by a so-called preferred value (cf. Sect. 2.3) mouse.y gives an orientation for the optimization wrt. the required constraints. It will be overwritten by border.min resp. border.max in case the mouse exceeds a border. Program 1.2 is not only shorter, but expresses

M. Umeda et al. (Eds.): INAP 2005, LNAI 4369, pp. 12–24, 2006.

Program 1.1. A user interface example in the imperative style

---

```
while (mouse.pressed)
{                                // message processing is left out
    int y = mouse.y;
    if (y > border.max)
        y = border.max;
    if (y < border.min)
        y = border.min;
    draw_element (fix_x , y, graphic);
}
```

Program 1.2. The user interface example using CIP

```
while (mouse.pressed)
{
    constrained<int> y = mouse.y;
    require (y >= border.min && y <= border.max);
    draw_element (fix_x , y(), graphic);
}
```

---

the relationship between the border-object and the y-coordinate in exactly the way a programmer would think about it.

TURTLE++ [7] is a C++ *library* which inherited the main ideas of the *language* Turtle[1] [5] but was extended for smooth integration into C++. Meanwhile TURTLE++ has been refined and extended by new constructs for a more convenient handling of value assignment (fixing/unfixing, cf. Sect. 2.4) and by a boolean solver the two of which together allow to nicely express new kinds of problem descriptions as demonstrated later on.

We think that the development of TURTLE++ may support both the spreading and further development of the CIP approach since C++ is a widely used and in practice accepted language whose semantics remain untouched by TURTLE++, while the application programmer is allowed to use the benefits of constraint programming in his or her professional work.

This paper deals with the TURTLE++ approach of integrating constraints and constraint solvers with imperative language concepts. In Sect. 2 we introduce and explain the main concepts of TURTLE++ and shortly touch its implementation. Section 3 is dedicated to programming with our library. We draw a conclusion and discuss related and future work in Sect. 4.

2   The Main Concepts of TURTLE++

The main concepts of the C++ *library* TURTLE++ are *constrainable variables*, *constraint statements* and *user-defined constraints*.

---

[1] A CIP language as well developed at the Technical University of Berlin.

Program 2.1. Variables and a constraint statement

```
int x = 0;              // a normal variable
constrained<int> y;     // a constrainable variable
require (y <= x);       // a constraint statement
```

2.1   Constrainable Variables

These are variables whose values can be determined by placing constraints on them. A constrainable variable is declared by giving it a constrained type. In Program 2.1 y is a constrainable variable, while x is a normal one.

Most of the time a constrainable variable acts like a normal variable: it can be used in expressions and as a function argument. Only in a constraint statement they differ from their normal counterparts. A normal (or imperative) variable is treated like a constant, but a constrainable (or declarative) variable acts like a variable in the mathematical sense, and the constraint solver may change its value in order to satisfy all invoked constraints.

2.2   Constraint Statements

Whenever declarative and imperative languages are combined, one of the main issues is the interaction of the integrated declarative concepts with the imperative model of time. In TURTLE++ this is solved by introducing a lifetime for constraints using the keyword require as shown in Program 2.1.

During program execution the run-time system manages a constraint store which contains the currently required constraints. When a require is reached during the execution of the program, the given constraint is added to this store and taken into account for further computations - its lifetime starts.

The require-statement returns a handle to manage the constraints lifetime. If the return value is ignored (as e.g. in Program 2.1), the imposed constraint exists as long as all its constrainable variables. Otherwise, the lifetime of the constraint is also limited to the lifetime of the returned constraint handle. Constraint handles are, thus, useful especially when imperative execution flow elements (e.g. loops) and constraints are used together, as shown in Program 2.2. Here, after every pass through the **while**-loop the constraint (a >= b) is removed. If we had instead foregone the handle and simply used a single require-statement, then each pass i of the **while**-loop would add a new constraint $a >= b_i$ to the store.

Besides, constraint handles allow to explicitly overwrite a constraint (as will be shown in Program 3.1) and to manipulate its strength. Constraints can be labelled with strengths in constraint hierarchies which are taken into consideration during the solving process and which allow to deal with over- and underconstrained problems. When a constraint is annotated with a strength, e.g. strong or weak, it is added to the store with the given strength, otherwise with the strongest strength mandatory.

Program 2.2. A handle restricting the lifetime of its constraint a $>=$ b

```
constrained <int> a;
... // setup some initial constraints over a
while (not_done())
{
    int b = compute_something();
    constraint_handle <int> z = require (a >= b);
    ...
// leaving the scope of z removes (a >= b) from the store
}
```

The run-time system actually does not handle a single constraint store but several sub-stores. This allows not just search over constraint disjunctions (which may appear in require statements as well as conjunctions, see [7]) but a more appropriate and convenient handling of independent sets of constraints. A constraint sub-store is the set of all constraints over a set of constrainable variables, which are linked. Two variables x and y are linked, if they either both appear in one constraint or if x appears in a constraint containing a constrainable variable linked to y. This allows to maintain independent sets of variables.

2.3 Obtaining Values from Constrainable Variables

The function call operator **operator()() const** is overloaded to obtain a constrainable variable value conveniently. When this operator is invoked, e.g. by

```
std :: cout << a();
```

the constraint solver is started to determine a value of the appropriate variable, here a, satisfying all constraints over a. When the store is overconstrained and no value can be determined, an exception of type overconstrained_error (derived from std :: logic_error) is raised.

But more often underconstrained situations occur. For this purpose TURTLE++ supports a preferred value which can be assigned to a constrainable variable. If it turns out that, while solving a store, more than one solution exists for a certain constrainable variable, a solution closest to the preferred value (if possible for the domain under consideration) is taken. An example is given by Program 2.3: For the variable a there exist infinitely many solutions. Thus, the value 2.5 is chosen which is closest to the preferred value 3 wrt. the linear constraint (a $<=$ 2.5).

Even if a preferred value can be seen as a weakest constraint to a certain degree, it actually isn't. It does neither impose any constraint nor influence calculations inside the constraint store in any other way. The concept of preferred values was mainly introduced to make programs easier and more intuitively predictable by providing a means to define the result of a transfer from a non-deterministic constrained variable to a deterministic imperative variable. In addition the concept is useful to formulate optimization problems as shown in Sect. 3.3.

Program 2.3. Obtaining a value

```
constrained<double> a (3); // assigns a preferred value
require (a <= 2.5);
std :: cout << a(); // prints 2.5
```

Program 2.4. When computing a value for b variable a is *implicitly fixed*

```
constrained<int> a (2), b (0);
require (a == b);
std :: cout << a(); // prints 2
std :: cout << b(); // also prints 2
```

2.4 Implicit Fixing

TURTLE++ delays the computation of a value for a constrainable variable until a read-action to the variable occurs. Once a value is determined for a constrainable variable, this value must be taken into account for further calculations to ensure consistency of the imposed constraints.

Consider e.g. Program 2.4. The output of a forces the computation of a value for this constrainable variable. This assignment must be taken into consideration in the following computation and, thus, TURTLE++ adds *implicitly* a new constraint a == 2 to the store. This implicit addition of a constraint variable == value to the store with the aim to ensure consistency for further calculations is called *implicit fixing*.

Without implicit fixing the value of b would be evaluated to 0 and hence violate the required constraint a == b. Due to this important side effect the evaluation order of constrainable variables must be carefully considered, e.g. if the third and fourth lines were exchanged, both would print 0.

An implicit fix is not immediately added to the constraint sub-store but kept in a delay store inside the sub-store. If only one implicit fix exists in a sub-store, and the same variable is evaluated again, the fix is erased before the re-evaluation (and later in this process a new fix is added). E.g. in Program 2.5 in each pass of the **for**-loop the just entered value of j is assigned as the preferred value of a and is finally printed. While a gets implicitly fixed to j, b remains "untouched". Thus, the implicit fix of a can be removed in the next iteration and eventually the next value entered for j is printed.

If more than one implicit fix exists, always all must be taken into account.

Sometimes, one wants to fix a constrainable variable *explicitly*, which is possible just by the simple statement require (variable == value).

Implicit fixes must be considered carefully, especially if more than one variable is evaluated inside a loop. That's why a constrainable variable can be unfixed explicitly via the member function unfix() for one variable and unfix_all () for all variables in a sub-store, resp. (see also Program 3.1).

Program 2.5. Implicit fixing and unfixing

```
constrained<int> a (2), b (0);
require (a == b);
for (int i = 0; i < 3; ++i)
{
  int j;
  std :: cin >> j;
  a = j;
  std :: cout << a();    // prints j
}
```

Program 2.6. User-defined domain constraint

```
typedef constrained<int> int_c;

constraint_solver<int >:: expr dom (const int_c& x, int l, int r)
{
  return build_constraint (x >= l && x <= r);
}

int_c a, b;
require (dom (a, 0, 9));
require (dom (b, −1, 1));
```

2.5 User-Defined Constraints and Dynamic Expressions

Often the declarative power of expression templates is sufficient to express the constraints in a compact and readable manner. But some constraints are so common that they deserve their own name. Such user-defined constraints can be generated using the function template build_constraint , which takes a constraint just like require, but only builds the internal representation of the given expression without adding it to the constraint store. The naming of complex static expressions enhances the readability of a program. Program 2.6[2] shows the definition and usage of a domain constraint.

Besides this, it is often required to create constraints dynamically. Therefore TURTLE++ provides a generic class dynamic_expr, which can be assigned an expression and which itself can be part of an expression. In the latter case the dynamic expression expands to its contents.

An example is given by Program 2.7. The constraint order is *dynamically* generated over a vector v during a **for**-loop where the dynamic expression expr is stepwise extended expanding its previous contents by new expressions.

Dynamic expressions are very useful for establishing constraints over a previously unknown number of constrained variables as in this example. Note, that

---

[2] In upcoming examples we will rely on the definition of int_c as displayed here without explicitly repeating it again.

Program 2.7. An ordered array using dynamic expressions

```cpp
dynamic_expr<int> order (std::vector<int_c>& v)
{
   dynamic_expr<int> expr = (true);
   for (int i = 1; i < v.size(); ++i)
     expr = (expr && v[i-1] <= v[i]);
   return expr;
}

int main()
{
   std::vector<int_c> v;
   // ... populate v
                                  // declarative style:
   require (order (v));      // order is a constraint
}
```

---

this particular example could be expressed as well imperatively by a sequence of require-statements as shown in Program 2.8. While this is possible because we express a *conjunction* of constraints, other kinds of logic operations like *disjunction* or *implication* actually require the usage of dynamic expressions. I. e., Program 2.9 demonstrates the dynamic generation of a disjunction of constraints which ensures that at least one variable of the vector v is equal to 1.

Comparing Program 2.7 and Program 2.8 again, we think, that moreover, the usage of dynamic expressions improves the declarative expressiveness of the source code.

2.6   Constraint Solvers

TURTLE++ currently comes with two solvers: a solver for linear arithmetics based on the simplex method and a simple search-based boolean solver. Their usage is demonstrated in Sect. 3 by means of examples. Furthermore, the user can extend TURTLE++ by new solvers as described at [1].

Since the interface enables the implementation of a constraint solver responsible for more than one value type, hybrid domains are possible. Even if there is no solver for hybrid constraints available, user-defined constraints may nonetheless be hybrid (i.e. they may contain variables and operations of several domains). In this case, within their definition user-defined constraints must separate homogeneous parts, which are then forwarded to the respective solvers.

2.7   Implementation of TURTLE++ as a Library for C++

Thanks to a lot of developments in the field of generic and template programming resp. in the last decade, it became possible to define and use completely new syntactic constructs in TURTLE++ while maintaining compatibility with the original C++ language.

Program 2.8. An ordered array without dynamic expressions

```
void require_order (std :: vector<int_c>& v)
{
  for (int i = 1; i < v.size (); ++i)
    require (v[i−1] <= v[i]);
}

int main ()
{
  std :: vector<int_c> v;
  // ... populate v
                              // imperative style :
  require_order (v);          // require_order is a function
}
```

Program 2.9. A disjunctive dynamic constraint

```
dynamic_expr<int> contains (std :: vector<int_c>& v, int x)
{
  dynamic_expr<int> expr = (false );
  for (int i = 0; i < v.size (); ++i)
    expr = (expr || v[i] == x);
  return expr;
}

int main ()
{
  std :: vector<int_c> v;
  // ... populate v
  require (contains (v, 1));
}
```

TURTLE++ uses the features of generic programming in C++ to a wide extent. By utilizing template mechanisms and operator overloading constraints can be used in an intuitive declarative manner. The require statement is implemented as a function template which simply expects an expression object, which can contain a nearly arbitrarily complex expression. The expression object is created from the expression and both can be treated separately. So the user can either write down expressions and formulae in the usual intuitive way or build them dynamically during program execution.

Furthermore, the pure generic interface enables the user to add or adapt constraint solvers at will. This is especially important for user-defined domains and offers a wide application field for TURTLE++.

3   CIP with TURTLE++

In this section we illustrate constraint imperative programming with TURTLE++ by means of three small but expressive examples.

3.1   User Interaction

A typical example demonstrating the advantages of the combination of imperative and constraint-based programming is user interaction, as already seen by the introductory example. We want to consider here a further example which demonstrates besides the usage of the boolean solver.

We consider a user interface for configuring a product, say a computer. The choice of certain components (motherboards, cards, chips, etc.) may be compatible with particular others or may exclude them. We will express this by boolean constraints. For simplification we consider a small setting with only three components. Their choice can be (de)activated by means of buttons button[i], $i \in \{0, 1, 2\}$, while the following compatibility constraints must be ensured:

Constraint 1. At least one component must be chosen resp. its button activated.

Constraint 2. The choice of button[0] implies the choice of button[1].

Constraint 3. Activating button[2] excludes the second component, i.e. the choice of button[1].

Program 3.1 implements this setting. In lines 2-4 we require the three constraints given above. Line 5 initially activates button[0]. Within a while loop (lines 8-25) the following actions are performed: The output (line 10) of the current configuration by activated or deactivated buttons on the interface yields to an initial computation (resp. a recomputation in later passes) of values for the buttons consistent with the constraints 1, 2 and 3 and that of line 5. In line 11 we await a button click, which generates a value for the variable i: 1 for button[0], 2 for button[1], or 3 for button[2]. Then the constraint handle click_button is assigned a new constraint representing the last button click (line 17), where the variable button[i−1] stands for the clicked button. This variable is unfixed in line 18 and all other value assignments for constrainable variables linked with button[i−1] (this concerns button[i%3] and button[(i+1)%3]) are weakened setting their strength to weak (line 19) to hold them as stable as possible.

3.2   Puzzles

It is possible, of course, to withdraw to one paradigm and use pure imperative (by simply leaving out constrainable variables and constraints) or mostly declarative programs. A standard example for the latter are crypto-arithmetic puzzles, like the SEND-MORE-MONEY problem given in Program 3.2. The problem is described (and computed) by constraints (lines 2-8)[3] and imperative constructs only service for I/O (lines 9-11).

---

[3] Note that we apply the user-defined constraint dom from Program 2.6 here.

Program 3.1. Configuration of three components

```
1   constrained <bool> button [3];
2   require (button [0]  ||  button [1]  ||  button [2]); // constraint 1
3   require (button [0] -> button [1]);
    // constraint 2
4   require (button [2] -> !button [1]);
    // constraint 3
5   constraint_handle <bool> click_button=require(button [0] == true);
6   bool done = false;
7   int i;
8   while (!done)
9   {
10      ... // output button configuration here
11      ... // get button click on i here
12      switch (i)
13      {
14         case 1:
15         case 2:
16         case 3:
17            click_button = require (button [i-1]==!button [i-1]());
18            button [i-1]. unfix ();
19            button [i-1]. fix_all (weak);
20            break;
21         default:
22            done = true;
23            break;
24      }
25   }
```

With the help of dynamic expressions it is also possible to create such puzzles dynamically at run-time so that the user provides the participating words, like SEND, MORE and MONEY which are then composed into the puzzle. An example is given by the function example_dynamic_puzzle at [1].

3.3 Optimization

Optimization is one of the main uses of constraint programming. In TURTLE++ preferred values for given expressions allow optimization in a simple way without the need of special library functions. While this approach mainly works for small and simple optimization problems, for more sophisticated problems one may use constraint hierarchies as well provided by TURTLE++.

Our simple optimization pattern consists of four steps: Consider the rather primitive knapsack problem in Program 3.3.

In step one we declare a constrainable variable and assign to it an absolute minimum or maximum border as preferred value (line 6). In step two we define the constraints (lines 7-10) wrt. which the objective function (line 11) will be

Program 3.2. A crypto-arithmetic puzzle

```
1  constrained<int> s, e, n, d, m, o, r, y;
2  require (dom (s, 1, 9));
3  ...
4  require (dom (y, 0, 9));
5  require (alldifferent (s,e,n,d,m,o,r,y));
6  require (                 s*1000 + e*100 + n*10 + d
7                        + m*1000 + o*100 + r*10 + e
8            == m*10000 + o*1000 + n*100 + e*10 + y);
9  std::cout << "s:" << s();
10 std::cout << "e:" << e();
11 ...
```

Program 3.3. A knapsack problem: Implicit optimization by preferred values

```
1  void knapsack()
2  {
3     typedef constrained<double> double_c;
4     double capacity = 100.0;
5     double_c a, b, c;
6     double_c packed (capacity);
7     require (packed <= capacity);
8     require (a == 1.0 || a == 0.0);
9     require (b == 1.0 || b == 0.0);
10    require (c == 1.0 || c == 0.0);
11    require (a * 50.0 + b * 40.0 + c * 30.0 == packed);
12    std::cout << "used:" << packed() ;
13    std::cout << "a:" << a();
14    ...
15 }
```

optimized (step three). Finally (step four), by reading packed first (i.e. before all other constrainable variables in this sub-store) a value assignment closest to the given preferred value is calculated. The implicit fixing also immediately limits the other constrainable variables to values at the searched optimum.

The usage of preferred values for constrainable variables depends on the variables domain and the existence, form, and complexity of an optimization function of the concerning solver. Accordingly, a solver may also allow to optimize wrt. a certain optimization function or a number of variables.

4   Conclusion and Future Work

TURTLE++ arose from of the Turtle *language* [5] and was adapted and extended for its smooth integration as *library* into C++ to increase the acceptance of declarative concepts by users of an imperative language.

One main difference between TURTLE++ and Turtle is the time point for the computation of values for constrainable variables. While in Turtle this happens during the execution of the require statement, in TURTLE++ we use the more flexible but also more subtle approach of delayed bindings, implicit fixing and unfixing. This gives the user a more fine-grain control over the constraints and allows, in combination with the introduction of constraint handles, to redefine constraints or to readjust their strength during computation. Moreover TURTLE++ provides dynamic expressions to create constraints dynamically at run-time.

Other constraint libraries for imperative languages are e.g. ILOG [2] for C++ and firstcs[6] and Koalog[3] for Java. As opposed to TURTLE++ libraries like ILOG mostly do not utilize syntactic extension mechanisms present in the implementation language to the same extent, e.g. for constraint statements.

TURTLE++ attempts seamless integration of declarative concepts into an imperative language and thus clearly differs from the other libraries which explicitly separate the constraint-based parts from the imperative language constructs. This becomes most obvious when mixing declarative and imperative particles like in Program 3.1. We do not consider a declarative sub-procedure inside an imperative main program or explicitly invoke a solver. Instead, the declarative computation is integrated into the imperative one directly.

While firstcs and Koalog are FD-constraint libraries, TURTLE++ allows the handling of linear optimization problems and boolean constraints. Finite domain constraints are currently treated by user-defined constraints and the existing solvers only (e.g. see Program 3.2). Since TURTLE++ can be easily extended with new solvers, one interesting area of future research would be the integration of an FD-solver including search and the computation of sets of solutions (which is currently not supported because not compelling for linear optimization problems). The integration of search using backtracking relatives however, must be considered very carefully because they strongly interfere with the imperative approach of TURTLE++. One possibility (as mainly chosen by the other libraries) is again the separation of both paradigms by encapsulating the declarative parts. A tighter integration in the style of TURTLE++ is, thus, a challenging aim.

Furthermore, we intend to investigate the enhancement of TURTLE++ with new concepts like the extension of **if**-constructs with (user-defined) constraints. This would allow to also check relations between partially and non-instantiated constrainable variables but would require an entailment test on the condition. This way, in addition to the *a-priori* declaration of constraints using the require construct the user would be provided with an *a-posteriori* test of constraints.

References

1. TURTLE++. http://people.freenet.de/turtle++/. last visited 2006-08-14.
2. ILOG. ILOG Web Site. http://www.ilog.com. last visited 2006-08-14.
3. Koalog Constraint Solver (v3.0) Tutorial. http://www.koalog.com/resources/doc/jcs-tutorial.pdf , 2005. last visited 2006-08-14.

4. B.N. Freeman-Benson. *Constraint Imperative Programming*. PhD thesis, University of Washington, Department of Computer Science and Engenieering, 1991. Technical Report 91-07-02.
5. M. Grabmüller and P. Hofstedt. Turtle: A Constraint Imperative Programming Language. In *Twenty-third SGAI International Conference on Innovative Techniques and Applications of Artificial Intelligence*, number XX in Research and Development in Intelligent Systems. Springer, 2003.
6. Matthias Hoche, Henry Müller, Hans Schlenker, and Armin Wolf. firstcs - A Pure Java Constraint Programming Engine. In *International Workshop on Multiparadigm Constraint Programming Languages – MultiCPL*, Kinsale, Ireland, 2003.
7. Olaf Krzikalla. Constraint Imperative Programming with C++. In *International Workshop on Multiparadigm Constraint Programming Languages – MultiCPL*, Kinsale, Ireland, 2003.
8. G. Lopez. *The Design and Implementation of Kaleidoscope, a Constraint Imperative Programming Language*. PhD thesis, University of Washington, 1997.

Constraint Solving for Sequences in Software Validation and Verification

Nikolai Kosmatov

CASSIS, INRIA Lorraine
LIFC, University of Franche-Comté
16 route de Gray, 25030 Besançon France
kosmatov@lifc.univ-fcomte.fr

Abstract. Constraint programming techniques are successfully used in various areas of software engineering for industry, commerce, transport, finance etc. Constraint solvers for different data types are applied in validation and verification of programs containing data elements of these types. A general constraint solver for *sequences* is necessary to take into account this data type in the existing validation and verification tools. In this work, we present an original constraint solver for sequences implemented in CHR and based on T. Frühwirth's solver for lists with the propagation of two constraints: generalized concatenation and size. Experimental results show its better efficiency compared to the intuitive propagation algorithm based on subsequences. The applications of the solver (with the validation and verification tool BZTT) to different software engineering problems are illustrated by the example of a waiting room model.

Keywords: constraint solver, sequences, validation, verification.

1 Introduction

Research work of the last ten years has shown the effectiveness and fruitfulness of constraint logic programming in different areas of software engineering. *Representing of the system states by constraints* allows to group the states and to avoid their complete enumeration, impossible for a big or infinite system. *Before-After predicates* allow to represent each operation of the system in terms of constraints defining the system state before and after the operation execution. The constraint solvers are successfully used in *formal model validation based on the symbolic evaluation* to detect a too strong invariant, a too weak precondition or an inexecutable behavior. *Detecting of contradictions between the program and its formal specification* needs a constraint solver to compare the two constraint sets extracted from the program and from the specification. In *automatic test generating,* the solvers allow to generate tests satisfying the chosen test criterion, which usually can be stated in terms of constraints.

The development of constraint solvers for some data types has already permitted the symbolic evaluation of formal models containing data elements of these types. For example, the tool BZTT [5] uses the solver CLPS-B [4] and

M. Umeda et al. (Eds.): INAP 2005, LNAI 4369, pp. 25–37, 2006.

allows the animation and test generation for formal models containing integers, sets, functions and relations. BZTT was used to validate and verify software in different industrial projects for industry, transport, commerce and finance [4] (see also references in [4]), e.g. for PSA Peugeot Citroën, Schlumberger, Thales. The model evaluated by BZTT is written in a logic notation with sets like B [1] or Z [15]. Sequences are one of the data types used in these notations and representing finite lists of elements such as stacks, queues, communication channels, sequences of transitions or any other data with consecutive access to elements.

Nowadays there exists no validation and verification tool with an integrated constraint solver for sequences. The main motivation of this work is to develop such a solver, which is necessary to take into account sequences during the validation and verification of software. This solver must treat all different operations on sequences. It will be integrated into the existing constraint solvers for other data types such as CLPS-B [4] and used in validation and verification tools such as BZTT [5].

The problem of constraint solving for sequences is very close to that of words or lists. The fundamental result of Makanin [14] shows that the satisfiability of word equations (where the concatenation is the unique operation) is decidable. Kościelski and Pacholski [11] showed that for a given constant $c > 2$ the problem of the existence of a solution of length $\leq cd$ for an equation of length d is NP-complete. Therefore there does not exist any fast algorithm for word equations in the general case. The decidability of the existential theories of words is close to the borderline of decidability. Durnev [7] showed that the positive $\forall\exists^3$-theory of concatenation is unsolvable. The decidability of word equations with an additional equal-length predicate is still an open problem. We refer the reader to [2,10] for more detail on the word equations.

The general constraint solving problem for sequences is even more complicated than that for words, because sequences generalize words and are usually considered with more operations. Therefore it is impossible to provide a general and efficient constraint solver for sequences terminating for all constraint problems. Nevertheless, even a partial constraint solving technique of reasonable complexity would be extremely useful for applications. We know very few results in the general context. Prolog III [6] implements concatenation and size for lists. A representation of sequences by PQR trees is proposed in [3], but this approach is limited to bijective sequences (i.e. permutations of a given finite set E).

Our work aims to study the problem of constraint solving for sequences from the practical point of view. Since we cannot develop an efficient solver for any constraint problem with sequences, it is important to provide at least a partial constraint solving technique for the problems which appear in practice. This paper presents a constraint solving technique which implements 11 basic operations on sequences. It was developed in *Constraint Handling Rules* (CHR) [8] in SICStus Prolog. The CHR allow a very clear and easily modifiable implementation. The complete solver can be consulted and executed from the author's webpage [12], and the essential rules are given in the paper. We discuss the efficiency of our solver and compare it to another propagation technique based on subsequences. An application of the solver to model animation and validation shows that even this partial constraint solving technique can be successfully applied in practice.

The paper is organized as follows. In Section 2 we define sequences and operations on sequences appearing in the constraints. Section 3 describes our constraint solver for sequences. Section 4 shows some experimental results and compares the solver with another one. The applications of the solver to software validation and verification are illustrated by the specification of a waiting-room system in Section 5. We conclude and present the future work in Section 6.

2   Sequences and Constraints on Sequences

Definition. Let E be a set. *A sequence over E is a finite list of elements of E. The size (length) of a sequence S is the number of elements of S. The empty sequence (of size 0) is denoted by* $[\,]$.

Example. Let $E = \{1, 2, 3\}$, $S_1 = [\,]$, $S_2 = [3]$, $S_3 = [1, 2, 3]$, $S_4 = [2, 3, 1]$, $S_5 = [1, 1, 2, 1]$. Then the S_i are sequences over E.

Let us recall the usual operations on sequences which are used, for example, in the formal notations B [1] and Z [15]. We give in brackets an example with the notation commonly used in B. For the convenience of the reader, we prefer to use this logic notation (e.g. size $(S) = N$) rather than that of Prolog (e.g. S size N). Similarly, S size N, N #>= 5 may be abbreviated by size $(S) \geq 5$.

1. *the first element*   (first $[1, 2, 2, 2, 3] = 1$);
2. *the last element*   (last $[1, 2, 2, 2, 3] = 3$);
3. *the front, or deleting of the last element*   (front $[1, 2, 2, 2, 3] = [1, 2, 2, 2]$);
4. *the tail, or deleting of the first element*   (tail $[1, 2, 2, 2, 3] = [2, 2, 2, 3]$);
5. *prefix*   ($1 \rightarrow [2, 2, 2, 3] = [1, 2, 2, 2, 3]$);
6. *append*   ($[1, 2, 2, 2] \leftarrow 3 = [1, 2, 2, 2, 3]$);
7. *the size*   (size $[1, 2, 2, 2, 3] = 5$);
8. *take the first n elements*   ($[1, 2, 2, 2, 3] \uparrow 2 = [1, 2]$);
9. *remove the first n elements*   ($[1, 2, 2, 2, 3] \downarrow 2 = [2, 2, 3]$);
10. *the concatenation*   ($[1, 2, 2] \cap [2, 3] = [1, 2, 2, 2, 3]$).
11. *the reverse*   (rev $([1, 2, 3]) = [3, 2, 1]$).

In this paper, we focus our attention on the resolution of constraints for sequences with the operations 1–11, using an external numerical constraint solver such as CLP(FD) to solve the numerical constraints on the sequence size. The existing constraint solvers can be used for constraints of other data types.

Examples. Let E be a set and $1, 2 \in E$.
  1. $\{\, S' \leftarrow 1 = S,\ \text{first}\,(S) = 1,\ \text{tail}\,(S') = [2]\,\}$ has the solution $S = [1, 2, 1]$, $S' = [1, 2]$.
  2. $\{\, \text{front}\,(S) = [1, 1, 1],\ \text{size}\,(S) = 5\,\}$ is unsatisfiable, since the first constraint implies size $(S) = 3 + 1 = 4$.

3. The constraint $\text{front}(S) = [1]$ has the solutions $\{\, S = [1, x] \mid x \in E \,\}$. We have here infinitely many solutions iff E is infinite. A set of constraints on sequences can have infinitely many solutions not only for an infinite set E, but also if E is finite. Set $E = \{1, 2\}$. The constraint $[1] \cap S = S \cap [1]$ has infinitely many solutions: $[\,], [1], [1, 1], [1, 1, 1], \ldots$

3   Constraint Solver for Sequences

In this section we present a technique of constraint solving for sequences. It was implemented in the CHR language [8,9] in SICStus Prolog, and can be consulted and executed from [12]. The implementation in CHR has the advantage to be very clear and easy to experiment with. We describe the main part of the solver (after simple rewriting of some constraints in terms of others) directly by the corresponding CHR rules.

The algorithm is inspired by the generalized concatenation for lists [9] realized by Thom Frühwirth. *The generalized concatenation* $S = \text{conc}(S_1, S_2, \ldots, S_k)$ is equivalent to $(k - 1)$ simple concatenations of the sequences $S_1, S_2, \ldots, S_k$, that is, to $S = S_1 \cap S_2 \cap \ldots \cap S_k$. The first step of the algorithm is rewriting of the constraints 1–6, 8–10 in terms of conc and size according to the rules of Figure 1, where T and Y denote new variables standing for a sequence and an element respectively. This rewriting is executed at most once for each new constraint and leaves in the constraint store the constraints conc, size and rev only.

$$
\begin{aligned}
\text{first}(S) = X \quad &\Leftrightarrow \quad S = \text{conc}([X], T). \\
\text{last}(S) = X \quad &\Leftrightarrow \quad S = \text{conc}(T, [X]). \\
\text{front}(S) = S_1 \quad &\Leftrightarrow \quad S = \text{conc}(S_1, [Y]). \\
\text{tail}(S) = S_1 \quad &\Leftrightarrow \quad S = \text{conc}([Y], S_1). \\
X \to S_1 = S \quad &\Leftrightarrow \quad S = \text{conc}([X], S_1). \\
S_1 \leftarrow X = S \quad &\Leftrightarrow \quad S = \text{conc}(S_1, [X]). \\
S \uparrow N = S_1 \quad &\Leftrightarrow \quad S = \text{conc}(S_1, T),\ \text{size}(S_1) = N. \\
S \downarrow N = S_2 \quad &\Leftrightarrow \quad S = \text{conc}(T, S_2),\ \text{size}(T) = N. \\
S_1 \cap S_2 = S \quad &\Leftrightarrow \quad S = \text{conc}(S_1, S_2).
\end{aligned}
$$

Fig. 1. Rewriting rules

The second step of the algorithm treats these three constraints. The CHR rules for this part of the algorithm are given in Figure 2. Recall that a simplification rule `C1,...,Ci <=> D1,...,Dj` in CHR replaces the constraints `C1,...,Ci` in the constraint store by the list of constraints or Prolog goals `D1,...,Dj`. A guarded rule `C1,...,Ci <=> Guard | D1,...,Dj` is applied if in addition the Prolog goal `Guard` is true.

The rule `C1,...,Ci ==> D1,...,Dj` will add (or execute) the constraints (or Prolog goals) `D1,...,Dj` if the constraint store contains the constraints `C1,...,`, `Ci`, which are not deleted. We do not detail the passive constraint declaration `#Id ... pragma passive(Id)`, which is just an optimization and is not crucial. We refer the reader to [8] for more detail on the CHR language. The rule r01 aims

```
:- use_module(library(clpfd)).
:- use_module(library(chr)).

handler sequences.

constraints conc/2, size/2, rev/2, labeling/0.
operator(700,xfx,conc). % 'List conc Seq' means conc(List)=Seq
operator(700,xfx,size). % 'Seq size N' means size(Seq)=N

r01@ rev(R,S)                    <=>  reverse(R,S).
r02@ [] conc L                   <=>  L=[].
r03@ [R] conc L                  <=>  R=L.
r04@ [R|Rs] conc []              <=>  R=[], Rs conc [].
r05@ [[X|R]|Rs] conc L           <=>  L=[X|L1], [R|Rs] conc L1.
r06@ Rs conc L                   <=>  delete([],Rs,Rs1) | Rs1 conc L.
r07@ Rs conc L                   <=>  delete(L,Rs,Rs1) | Rs1 conc [].
r08@ R conc L                    ==>  lenPropagate(R,L).
r09@ [] size N                   <=>  N#=0.
r10@ [_|L] size N                <=>  N#=M+1, L size M.
r11@ L size N                    <=>  ground(N) | N1 is N, length(L,N1).
r12@ (X size N1)#Id \ X size N2  <=>  N1=N2 pragma passive(Id).
r13@ labeling, ([R|Rs] conc L)#Id <=> true |
    ( var(L) -> length(L,_) ; true),
    ( R=[], Rs conc L ; L=[X|L1], R=[X|R1], [R1|Rs] conc L1 ),
    labeling pragma passive(Id).

reverse([],[]).
reverse(R,L):- R size N, L size N, X size 1,
    [X,R1] conc R, [L1,X] conc L, reverse(R1,L1).

delete( X, [X|L],  L).
delete( Y, [X|Xs], [X|Xt]) :- delete( Y, Xs, Xt).

lenPropagate([], []).
lenPropagate([R|Rs],L) :- R size NR, L size NL, L1 size NL1,
    NL #= NR + NL1, lenPropagate(Rs,L1).
```

Fig. 2. The essential part of the solver in CHR

to propagate the constraint rev using an additional Prolog predicate **reverse**. The rules r02–r05 propagate the generalized concatenation Rs conc L until the first element of Rs is a non valuated variable. If it is the case, we can jump over this variable only by deleting empty sequences [] or the sequence L itself in Rs as shown in rules r06–r07.

If it is still not sufficient for a constraint conc $[R_1, R_2, ..., R_i] = L$, the rule r08 and **lenPropagate** establish the relation size $(R_1) + ... + \text{size}(R_i) = \text{size}(L)$ between the sizes of the sequences, which can help in propagation. The propagation for the constraint L size N (where N can be an arithmetic expression) is provided by the rules r08–r11.

To avoid repetitions, the rule r12 replaces the constraint X size N2 in presence of X size N1 by N1 #= N2. The rule r13 defines the labeling constraint, which is written at most once at the very end of the constraint list. It tries to find all possible solutions of the constraint problem and does not necessarily terminate.

4   Experimental Results

To evaluate the efficiency of our constraint solver (called in this section also Solver 1) we apply it to big constraint sets and compare the results to an intuitive propagation technique (called below Solver 2) based on subsequences in the beginning and the end of each sequence. The basic constraints of Solver 2 are size, $\uparrow$, $\downarrow$ and rev. The CHR implementation of both solvers are available at [12].

The constraint order being important for the resolution time, we define *constraint lists* rather than *constraint sets*, putting the constraints in a precise order.

Let $N \geq 1$, and let $C_{\text{tail}}(R, N)$ be the list of the following $2N + 1$ constraints on the sequence R:

$$\text{first}(R) = N, \ \text{tail}(R) = R_{N-1},$$
$$\text{first}(R_{N-1}) = N - 1, \ \text{tail}(R_{N-1}) = R_{N-2},$$
$$\cdots$$
$$\text{first}(R_1) = 1, \ \text{tail}(R_1) = R_0,$$
$$R_0 = [\,].$$

Let $C_{\text{tail}}^{inv}(R, N)$ be the list of the same constraints, where the lines are put in the inverse order:

$$R_0 = [\,],$$
$$\text{first}(R_1) = 1, \ \text{tail}(R_1) = R_0,$$
$$\cdots$$
$$\text{first}(R_{N-1}) = N - 1, \ \text{tail}(R_{N-1}) = R_{N-2},$$
$$\text{first}(R) = N, \ \text{tail}(R) = R_{N-1}.$$

Both $C_{\text{tail}}(R,N)$ and $C_{\text{tail}}^{inv}(R,N)$ have the unique solution $R = [N, N-1, \ldots, 2, 1]$.

Let $C_{\text{front}}(R, N)$ be the list of the $2N + 1$ constraints:

$$\text{last}(R) = N, \ \text{front}(R) = R_{N-1},$$
$$\text{last}(R_{N-1}) = N - 1, \ \text{front}(R_{N-1}) = R_{N-2},$$
$$\cdots$$
$$\text{last}(R_1) = 1, \ \text{front}(R_1) = R_0,$$
$$R_0 = [\,]$$

and let $C_{\text{front}}^{inv}(R, N)$ be the list of the same constraints with the inverse order of the lines. Their unique solution is $R = [1, 2, \ldots, N - 1, N]$.

To mix both types of constraints, we also consider the list $C_{alt}(R, N)$ alternating the lines of $C_{\text{tail}}(R, N)$ and of $C_{\text{front}}(R, N)$ and containing the first line

Time of resolution, sec.		
N	Solver 1	Solver 2
$C_{\text{tail}}(R,N)$ / $C_{\text{tail}}^{inv}(R,N)$		
10	0 / 0	0.08 / 0
20	0 / 0	1.2 / 0.03
50	0 / 0	42.78 / 0.34
100	0 / 0	1460 / 2.4
500	0.03 / 0.11	? / 305.5
$C_{\text{front}}(R,N)$ / $C_{\text{front}}^{inv}(R,N)$		
10	0.13 / 0.08	0.08 / 0.02
20	0.56 / 0.31	0.97 / 0.13
50	5.65 / 2.19	42.62 / 3.17
100	47.57 / 9.86	1367 / 50.78
500	? / 490.8	? / ?
$C_{alt}(R,N)$ / $C_{alt}^{inv}(R,N)$		
10	0.06 / 0.05	0.03 / 0.02
20	0.27 / 0.17	0.16 / 0.09
50	1.78 / 1.11	2.63 / 1.64
100	9.31 / 5	37.26 / 20.49
500	? / 242.9	? / ?

Fig. 3. Comparison of the resolution time

of $C_{\text{tail}}(R,N)$, the second line of $C_{\text{front}}(R,N)$, the third line of $C_{\text{tail}}(R,N)$, etc. As above, $C_{alt}^{inv}(R,N)$ puts the lines of $C_{alt}(R,N)$ in the inverse order. In both cases, $R = [N, N-2, \ldots, N-3, N-1]$ is the unique solution.

The choice of these constraint lists is motivated by constraint problems appearing in practice. Indeed, sequences often model data structures with consecutive access to elements, e.g. consecutive adding or removing of elements at the beginning or at the end of a sequence. In the context of software validation and verification, the constraint lists $C_{\text{tail}}/C_{\text{tail}}^{inv}$ come from consecutive adding or removing at the beginning of a sequence, $C_{\text{front}}/C_{\text{front}}^{inv}$ come from those at the end of a sequence, while C_{alt}/C_{alt}^{inv} mix both types of access. The reader will easily see that similar constraint problems may be obtained during the animation and validation of the model of Figure 4 introduced in Section 5.1 below.

Figure 3 shows the time of resolution (in seconds) for both constraint solvers applied to the constraint lists. The experimentations were realized on an Intel Pentium 4 computer with 2.40GHz, 376 Mb RAM. Unknown resolution time (greater than 30 minutes) is denoted by "?". The resolution time for the constraint lists with the direct and the inverse constraint order are separated by "/".

We see that our constraint solving algorithm (Solver 1) can be a little bit slower for small constraint sets while the resolution time is anyway less than 1 sec because of the rewriting step. But it becomes faster as soon as the resolution time becomes greater than 1-2 sec (for $N \geq 40$, i.e. for the number of constraints ≥ 80). For several hundreds of constraints ($N \geq 100$), Solver 2 becomes too slow or even goes out of memory, whereas our algorithm is much faster.

A very important characteristic for a solver is its *ordering factor*, i.e. to which extent the solver depends on the ordering of the constraints. Let us define *the ordering factor* (on constraint lists of length L) as the maximal ratio t/t_{inv}, where $t, t_{inv} > 0$ are the time of resolution for some constraint list (of length L) in the direct and in the inverse order of constraints respectively. The results of Figure 3 show that the ordering factor for Solver 1 on the tested constraint lists with $N = 100$ (i.e. of length $2N + 1 = 201$) is about $(47/9.8) \sim 5$, whereas that of Solver 2 can reach $(1460/2.4) \sim 600$. It shows that our constraint solving algorithm is less dependent on the constraint ordering, and therefore guarantees better efficiency in the worst case.

Note finally that Solver 1 has a more powerful propagation capacity than Solver 2 because it is not limited to the propagation at the beginning and the end of a sequence, but also takes into account the information in the middle of a sequence.

5   Applications to Software Validation and Verification

This section illustrates the applications of the constraint solver as part of a validation and verification tool such as BZTT to different problems in software validation and verification.

5.1   Waiting Room Example

Consider the example of a waiting room system specification given in Figure 4 (containing some errors which were introduced on purpose and will be detected and corrected below). This simple specification is written in B notation [1] and models the automatic client queue managing in a shop, travel agency etc. Suppose that each client goes first to one of several agents of the first type (say, sellers), than to one of several agents of the second type (say, cashiers). In this example, we consider two sellers A and B and one cashier C. In addition, seller B is the manager of the shop who takes clients only if the queue is rather long. The clients are represented by names which, for simplicity, are taken in the finite set $NAMES$. A system state is represented by the status *free* or *occupied* of each agent (variables *sellerA*, *sellerB*, *cashierC*), the name of the last client called by each agent (variables *clientA*, *clientB*, *clientC*), the queue of clients to sellers and the queue of clients to the cashier (variables *qSeller* and *qCashier* whose type is sequences over the set $NAMES$). Initially, all agents are *free*, the queues are empty sequences [ ] and the names of the latest called clients are arbitrary elements of $NAMES$. The invariant property must be verified in all system states. In this example, the invariant, denoted below by $\mathcal{I}nv$, defines the possible values of variables and the maximal queue length.

The evolution of the system is described by operations, which are defined by generalized substitutions and may have preconditions, input and output values. A new client *name* first registers himself in the system (or is registered by the receptionist not modelled here) who adds him at the end of *qSeller*, provided

MACHINE $WAITINGROOM$
SETS $STATES = \{free, occupied\}$;
    $NAMES = \{n1, n2, n3, n4, n5, n6, n7, n8, n9, n10, n11, n12, n13, n14, n15\}$
VARIABLES
    $sellerA$, $sellerB$, $cashierC$, $clientA$, $clientB$, $clientC$, $qSeller$, $qCashier$
INVARIANT
    $sellerA \in STATES \wedge sellerB \in STATES \wedge cashierC \in STATES \wedge$
    $clientA \in NAMES \wedge clientB \in NAMES \wedge clientC \in NAMES \wedge$
    $qSeller \in \text{seq}\,(NAMES) \wedge qCashier \in \text{seq}\,(NAMES) \wedge$
    $size(qSeller) \leq 10 \wedge size(qCashier) \leq 5$
INITIALISATION
    $sellerA := free \parallel sellerB := free \parallel cashierC := free \parallel$
    $clientA :\in NAMES \parallel clientB :\in NAMES \parallel clientC :\in NAMES \parallel$
    $qSeller := [\,] \parallel qCashier := [\,]$
OPERATIONS
$new\,(name) =$
    PRE $name \in NAMES \wedge size(qSeller) \leq 10$
    THEN $qSeller := qSeller \leftarrow name$
    END
$callA =$
    PRE $size(qSeller) > 0 \wedge sellerA = free$
    THEN $sellerA := occupied \parallel clientA := \text{first}\,(qSeller) \parallel qSeller := \text{tail}\,(qSeller)$
    END
$callB =$
    PRE $size(qSeller) > 12 \wedge sellerB = free$
    THEN $sellerB := occupied \parallel clientB := \text{first}\,(qSeller) \parallel qSeller := \text{tail}\,(qSeller)$
    END
$endA =$
    PRE $sellerA = occupied$
    THEN $sellerA := free \parallel qCashier := qCashier \leftarrow clientA$
    END
$endB =$
    PRE $sellerB = occupied$
    THEN $sellerB := free \parallel qCashier := qCashier \leftarrow clientB$
    END
$callC =$
    PRE $size(qCashier) > 0 \wedge cashierC = free$
    THEN $cashierC := occupied \parallel clientC := \text{first}\,(qCashier) \parallel$
      $qCashier := \text{tail}\,(qCashier)$
    END
$endC =$
    PRE $cashierC = occupied$
    THEN $cashierC := free$
    END
END

Fig. 4. Waiting room specification in B

that $name \in NAMES$ and the queue is not too long (operation new). The seller A can take the first client in the queue $qSeller$, provided that $sellerA$ is $free$ and $qSeller$ is not empty (operation $callA$). The seller B can take the first client in the queue $qSeller$, provided that $sellerB$ is $free$ and $qSeller$ is rather long (operation $callB$). An $occupied$ seller can finish serving his client by putting him at the end of $qCashier$ and changing the status to $free$ (operations $endA$, $endB$). The cashier C can take the first client from $qCashier$, provided that $cashierC$ is $free$ and $qCashier$ is not empty (operation $callC$). While being $occupied$, the cashier C can finish serving his client by changing the status to $free$ (operation $endC$).

$\mathcal{P}_{new} : \mathcal{I}nv \wedge name \in NAMES \wedge size(qSeller) \leq 10 \wedge qSeller' = qSeller \leftarrow name$

$\mathcal{P}_{callA} : \mathcal{I}nv \wedge size(qSeller) > 0 \wedge sellerA = free \wedge$
$\qquad sellerA' = occupied \wedge clientA' = \text{first}(qSeller) \wedge qSeller' = \text{tail}(qSeller)$

$\mathcal{P}_{callB} : \mathcal{I}nv \wedge size(qSeller) > 12 \wedge sellerB = free \wedge$
$\qquad sellerB' = occupied \wedge clientB' = \text{first}(qSeller) \wedge qSeller' = \text{tail}(qSeller)$

$\mathcal{P}_{endA} : \mathcal{I}nv \wedge sellerA = occupied \wedge sellerA' = free \wedge$
$\qquad\qquad\qquad\qquad\qquad\qquad qCashier' = qCashier \leftarrow clientA$

$\mathcal{P}_{endB} : \mathcal{I}nv \wedge sellerB = occupied \wedge sellerB' = free \wedge$
$\qquad\qquad\qquad\qquad\qquad\qquad qCashier' = qCashier \leftarrow clientB$

$\mathcal{P}_{callC} : \mathcal{I}nv \wedge size(qCashier) > 0 \wedge cashierC = free \wedge$
$\quad cashierC' = occupied \wedge clientC' = \text{first}(qCashier) \wedge qCashier' = \text{tail}(qCashier)$

$\mathcal{P}_{endC} : \mathcal{I}nv \wedge cashierC = occupied \wedge cashierC' = free$

Fig. 5. Before-After predicates

5.2   Applications

The following examples briefly illustrate the applications of the solver with the BZTT tool in different areas of software validation and verification.

1. *Representing of the system states and operations by constraints.* Figure 5 shows the *Before-After* predicates corresponding to the operations and describing all possible transitions of the system in terms of constraints. The *Before* part for each operation contains the invariant $\mathcal{I}nv$ and the precondition of the operation. The *After* part is the postcondition defining the state after the operation and containing only constraints of the form $X' = \ldots$, where X' denotes the new value of the variable X after the operation. For unchanged variables, we omit the trivial constraints $X' = X$ for short. This representation of the system states and operations in terms of constraints allows to group the states and to avoid their enumeration. Note that this enumeration is impossible even in this simplified example with small numbers ($\text{card}(NAMES) = 15$) because of the great number of sequences over $NAMES$.

2. *Model animation based on the symbolic evaluation.* Due to the constraint representation of the states and operations (*Before-After* predicates of Figure 5), the animation is not limited to the completely valuated states, but can be also applied to partially valuated ones.

3. *Formal model validation based on the symbolic evaluation: detecting of a too strong invariant, a too weak precondition or an inexecutable behavior.* The simple satisfiability verification of the *Before* part of each *Before-After* predicate allows to detect that the operation *callB* is inexecutable. Indeed, the solver detects that the *Before* predicate of *callB*

$$\ldots \wedge size(qSeller) \leq 10 \wedge \ldots \wedge size(qSeller) > 12 \wedge \ldots$$

is unsatisfiable. To correct this error, we can replace $size(qSeller) > 12$ by $size(qSeller) > 5$ in the precondition of the operation *callB*.

Another error in the specification is a too weak precondition $size(qSeller) \leq 10$ in $\mathcal{P}_{new}$ or a too strong invariant condition $size(qSeller) \leq 10$ in $\mathcal{I}nv$. Indeed, from a state with $size(qSeller) = 10$, the operation *new* can lead to a state with $size(qSeller') = 11$, which does not satisfy the invariant. To detect such errors, it is sufficient to verify if the invariant property is *always verified* after each operation. In other words, we should check whether the *Before-After* predicate of each operation is incompatible with $\neg\mathcal{I}nv'$, where $\mathcal{I}nv'$ is the invariant condition stated for the variables after the operation. For the operation *new*, the condition $\mathcal{P}_{new} \wedge \neg\mathcal{I}nv'$ rewritten in DNF form, contains the disjunct

$$\ldots \wedge size(qSeller) \leq 10 \wedge qSeller' = qSeller \leftarrow name \wedge size(qSeller') > 10,$$

so the solver easily detects that it is satisfiable for $size(qSeller) = 10$. To correct this error, we can, for example, replace $size(qSeller) \leq 10$ by $size(qSeller) < 10$ in the precondition of the operation *new*.

4. *Generating of tests satisfying a chosen criterion.* Various test coverage criteria are used to guide the (automatic) test generation or to evaluate a given set of tests. These criteria usually can be expressed in terms of constraints, so a constraint solver can be efficiently used for test generation. To detect domain errors, it is necessary to use boundary coverage criteria, which are useful for other error types as well. A new family of boundary coverage criteria for discrete domains and corresponding generation methods were proposed in [13]. They allow to find tests on the boundary of the domain of possible values of variables. Some of the criteria aim to reach the minimal and maximal values of each variable in the generated tests. These criteria can be easily adapted for sequences by minimizing and maximizing the length of each sequence. For example, the set with the following four tests for the operation *endA* will satisfy the **MD** (multi-dimensional) criterion [13] for sequence lengths (we omit here $sellerA = occupied$ and the values of other variables):

$$qSeller = [], \quad qCashier = [];$$
$$qSeller = [n1, n2, \ldots, n9, n10], \quad qCashier = [];$$
$$qSeller = [], \quad qCashier = [n1, n2, n3, n4, n5];$$
$$qSeller = [n1, n2, \ldots, n9, n10], \quad qCashier = [n11, n12, n13, n14, n15].$$

5. *Validation of the formal model by tests.* The execution of the generated tests followed by the invariant verification can be used to validate the model. For example, the execution of the operation $endA$ on the following test (which may be generated according to the **MD** criterion):

$$qSeller = [], \quad qCashier = [n1, n2, n3, n4, n5], \quad sellerA = occupied, \quad clientA = n6$$

will lead to the state with $qCashier' = [n1, n2, n3, n4, n5, n6]$, where the invariant condition $size(qCashier) \leq 5$ is not satisfied. This too strong invariant could be also detected as shown in **3** above. To correct this error we can delete the unjustified condition $size(qCashier) \leq 5$ from the invariant.

6. *Testing of an implementation of the formal model.* Due to the constraint representation of the states and operations of the system, in black-box testing the constraint solver allows to obtain *an oracle* predicting the correct state after executing of the tests on the implementation. In white-box testing, the constraint solver gives in addition the possibility *to detect the contradictions* between the model and the implementation by comparing the constraint sets extracted from the model (see Figure 5) and from the implementation.

Integration of the constraint solver for sequences into a validation and verification tool such as BZTT [5] will make these operations automatic or semi-automatic and will provide a convenient graphical interface. We refer the reader to [4] for more detail on the application of constraint solving to different problems of software engineering in the BZTT method.

6 Conclusion and Future Work

We presented the problem of constraint solving for sequences and proposed a constraint solving technique for the usual operations used in such notations as B and Z. Our experiments show that our method is rather efficient on big constraint sets and gives satisfactory results even on sets of several hundreds of constraints. It is due to the uniformity of the approach: although we express some simple constraints in terms of a more complicated and more general constraint $conc$, it minimizes the number of different constraints and the number of constraint handling rules and finally provides a much faster solver for big constraint sets. The example in Section 5 shows various applications of the solver to software engineering in a validation and verification tool such as BZTT. In this example, the solver was called by hand since it has not yet been completely integrated into BZTT. All the other steps (formal model parsing, generating of Before-After predicates, dealing with constraint sets etc.) are implemented and can be done automatically.

The future work will include the following:

- to integrate the solver into BZTT like it was already done for the existing solver CLPS-B [4];
- to apply the solver as part of the BZTT to validation and verification of real-sized software with sequences.

Acknowledgment. The author would like to thank Fabrice Ambert, François Fages, Thom Frühwirth, Arnaud Gotlieb and Bruno Legeard for profitable discussions and their interest to this project.

References

1. J.-R. Abrial. The B-Book: Assigning Programs to Meanings. Cambridge University Press, 1996. ISBN 0521496195.
2. M. Lothaire. Algebraic Combinatorics on Words. Cambridge University Press, 2002. ISBN 0521812208.
3. L. Berkaoui, B. Legeard. Représentation de séquences définies sur des ensembles non instanciés par arbre PQR partiel. In Actes de JFPLC'98, Nantes, France, 251–266, May 1998. Hermès.
4. F. Bouquet, B. Legeard, F. Peureux. CLPS-B – Constraint solver to animate a B specification. International Journal on Software Tools for Technology Transfer, 6 (2004), No. 2, 143–157.
5. The BZ-Testing-Tools web site, http://lifc.univ-fcomte.fr/~bztt, University of Franche-Comté, Besançon.
6. A. Colmerauer. An introduction to Prolog III. Communications of the ACM, 33(1990), No. 7, 69–90.
7. V. G. Durnev. Studying algorithmic problems for free semi-groups and groups. In: S. Adian, A. Nerode (Eds). Logical Foundations of Computer Science (LFCS 97). Lect. Notes Comp. Sci., 1234(1997), 88–101. Springer-Verlag. ISBN 3540630457.
8. T. Frühwirth. Theory and Practice of Constraint Handling Rules. In: P. Stuckey, K. Marriot (Eds.). Special Issue on Constraint Logic Programming. Journal of Logic Programming, 37(1998), No. 1–3, 95–138.
9. T. Frühwirth. The CHR web site. http://www.informatik.uni-ulm.de /pm/fileadmin/pm/home/fruehwirth/chr.html, Universität Ulm.
10. J. Karhumäki, F. Mignosi, W. Plandowski. The expressibility of languages and relations by word equations. Journal of the ACM, 47(2000), No. 3, 483–505.
11. A. Koscielski, L Pacholski. Complexity of Makanin's Algorithm. Journal of the ACM, 43(1996), No. 4, 670–684.
12. N. Kosmatov. Constraint solving for sequences web site. http://lifc.univ-fcomte.fr/ ~kosmatov/sequences, University of Franche-Comté, Besançon.
13. N. Kosmatov, B. Legeard, F. Peureux, M. Utting. Boundary Coverage Criteria for Test Generation from Formal Models. In Proc. of the 15th Int. Symp. on Software Reliability Engineering (ISSRE'04), Saint-Malo, France, 139–150, November 2004. IEEE Computer Society Press.
14. G. S. Makanin. The problem of solvability of equations in a free semigroup. Mat. Sbornik (N.S.), 103 (1977), No. 2, 147–236 (in Russian). English translation in: Math. URSS Sbornik, 32(1977), 129–198.
15. J. M. Spivey. The Z Notation: A Reference Manual. Prentice-Hall, 2nd edition, 1992. ISBN 0139785299.

Using a Logic Programming Language with Persistence and Contexts

Salvador Abreu and Vitor Nogueira

Universidade de Évora and CENTRIA FCT/UNL, Portugal
{spa, vbn}@di.uevora.pt

Abstract. This article merges two approaches: one dealing with persistence for logic programs, as provided by a relational database back-end and another which addresses the issues of logic program structuring, by way of the parametric context. We claim that these two can be effectively combined to obtain a language which offers significant gains in expressiveness over previous work. This claim is experimentally backed by the applications that have been developed using these tools.

1 Introduction

Contexts: The idea of Contextual Logic Programming (CxLP) was introduced in the late 1980s by Monteiro and Porto [7] and is related to similar efforts such as that by Miller described in [6]. The purpose of CxLP was initially to deal with Prolog's traditionally flat predicate namespace, which seriously hindered its usability in larger scale projects. The impact of these extensions has mostly failed to make it back into the mainstream language, as the most widely distributed implementations only provide a simple, SICStus-like module mechanism, if any.

A more recent proposal [3] rehabilitates the ideas of Contextual Logic Programming by viewing contexts not only as shorthands for a modular theory but also as the means of providing dynamic attributes which affect that theory: we are referring to unit arguments, as described in Abreu and Diaz's work. It is particularly relevant for our purposes to stress the *context-as-an-implicit-computation* aspect of CxLP, which views a context as a first-class Prolog entity – a term, behaving similarly to an object in OOP languages.

Persistence: having persistence in a Logic Programming language is a required feature if one is to use it to construct actual information systems; this could conceivably be provided by Prolog's internal database but is best accounted for by software designed to handle large quantities of factual information efficiently, as is the case in relational database management systems. The semantic proximity between relational database query languages and logic programming languages have made the former privileged candidates to provide Prolog with persistence, and this has long been recognized.

ISCO [2] is a proposal for Prolog persistence which includes support for multiple heterogeneous databases and which access to technology beyond relational databases, such as LDAP directory services or DNS. ISCO has been successfully

M. Umeda et al. (Eds.): INAP 2005, LNAI 4369, pp. 38–47, 2006.

used in a variety of real-world situations, ranging from the development of a university information system to text retrieval or business intelligence analysis tools.

ISCO's approach for interfacing to DBMSs involves providing Prolog declarations for the database relations, which are equivalent to defining a corresponding predicate, which is then used as if it were originally defined as a set of Prolog facts. While this approach is convenient, its main weakness resides in its present inability to relate distinct database goals, effectively performing joins at the Prolog level. While this may be perceived as a performance-impairing feature, in practice it's not the show-stopper it would seem to be because the instantiations made by the early database goals turn out as restrictions on subsequent goals, thereby avoiding the filter-over-cartesian-product syndrome.

Contexts and persistence: considering that it is useful to retain the regular Prolog notation for persistent relations which is an ISCO characteristic, we would like to explore the ways in which contexts can be taken advantage of, when layered on top of the persistence mechanisms provided by ISCO. In particular we shall be interested in the aspects of common database operations which would benefit from the increase in expressiveness that results from combining Prolog's declarativeness and the program-structuring mechanisms of Contextual Logic Programming.

We shall illustrate the usefulness of this approach to Contextual Logic Programming by providing examples taken from a large scale application, written in GNU Prolog/CX, our implementation of a Contextual Constraint Logic Programming language. More synthetic situations are presented where the constructs associated with a renewed specification of Contextual Logic Programming are brought forward to solve a variety of programming problems, namely those which address compatibility issues with other Prolog program-structuring approches, such as existing module systems. We also claim that the proposed language and implementation mechanisms can form the basis of a reasonably efficient development and production system.

The remainder of this article is structured as follows: section 2 recapitulates on ISCO, while section 3 presents our revised specification of Contextual Logic Programming, stressing the relevance of unit arguments. In section 4 we show some uses for a unified language, which uses both persistence and contexts. Finally, section 5 draws some conclusions and attempts to point at unsolved issues, for further research.

2 Persistence with ISCO

It is not the purpose of this article to introduce the ISCO language, but a short review of its main features is useful for the discussion ahead.

ISCO has been described in [2] and comes as an evolution of the Logic description language presented in [1]. It is a mediator language in that an ISCO program may transparently access data from several distinct sources in a uniform way: all behave as regular Prolog predicates. Some relevant advantages

ISCO holds over competing approaches are its ability to concurrently interface to several legacy systems, its high performance by virtue of being derived from GNU-Prolog and its simplicity.

Predicate declarations: predicates that are to be associated with an external representation must be declared. This is necessary because DBMSs need to have table fields *named* and *typed* and none of this information is derivable from a regular Prolog predicate.

Example 1 (ISCO class teacher)

```
class teacher.
    name:        text.
    department:  text.
    degree:      text.
```

A class `teacher` can be declared in ISCO as in example 1. This defines predicate `teacher/3`, which behaves as a database predicate but relies on an external system (e.g. an RDBMS) to provide the actual facts.

Class declarations in ISCO may reflect inheritance, although that isn't shown in the previous example. Several features of SQL have been mapped into ISCO: keys and indexes, foreign keys and sequences to name a few.

Operations: classes in ISCO stand for *persistent predicate declarations*. The way these may be used is similar to what is done in Prolog for "database" predicates:

- non-deterministic sequential access to all clauses,
- insertion of new facts (*la* `assertz/1`),
- removal of specific facts (*la* `retract/1`)

The use of relational database back-ends spurred the adoption of an "update-like" operation in ISCO, which has no traditional Prolog counterpart.

These operations may specify constraints on their arguments to limit the tuples they apply to. These may be actual CLP(FD) constraints or more specific syntactic constructs, designed to provide a minimal yet useful set of features to tap into the potential efficiency provided by the RDBMS: for example, there are notations to specify solution ordering or substring matching.

Outlook: ISCO-based logic programs access the RDBMS-resident relations one-at-a-time, i.e. each predicate maps directly to queries onto the corresponding table. This results in joins being performed at the Prolog level, which may impair efficiency in some cases. This cannot be easily dealt with, as calls to class predicates may be mixed with regular Prolog goals, so that it's hard to determine beforehand what compound SQL query could be generated to effect a proper database-side join. Using Draxler's Prolog-to-SQL compiler[4] could improve this situation somewhat, but it has yet to be done.

3   Overview of Contextual (Constraint) Logic Programming

Contextual Logic Programming (CxLP) [7] is a simple yet powerful language that extends logic programming with mechanisms for modularity. In CxLP a finite set of Horn clauses with a given name is designated by *unit*. In [3] we presented a new specification for CxLP, which emphasizes the OOP aspects by means of a stateful model, allowed by the introduction of unit arguments. Using the syntax of GNU Prolog/CX, consider a unit named `teacher` to represent some basic facts about the teaching at a University:

Example 2 (CxLP unit teacher)

```
:-unit(teacher).

name(N)        :- teacher(N, _, _).
department(D)  :- teacher(_, D, _).
degree(D)      :- teacher(_, _, D).

teacher(john, cs, phd).
teacher(bill, cs, msc).
```

The only difference between the code of example 2 and a regular logic program is the first line that declares the unit name. Consider also another unit to represent information about courses, in example 3:

Example 3 (CxLP unit course)

```
:-unit(course).

teacher(N) :- course(N, _).
course(C)  :- course(_, C).

course(john, ai).
course(bill, lp).
```

A set of units is designated as a *contextual logic program*. With the units above we can build a program P = {teacher, course}. If we consider that teacher and course designate sets of clauses, then the resulting program is given by the union of these sets.

For a given CxLP program, we can impose an order on its units, leading to the notion of *context*. Contexts are implemented as lists of unit designators and each computation has a notion of its *current context*. The program denoted by a particular context is the union of the predicates that are defined in each unit. We resort to the *override semantics* to deal with multiple occurrences of a given predicate: only the topmost definition is visible.

To construct contexts, we have the *context extension* operation given by the operator :> . The goal U :> G extends the *current context* with unit U and resolves goal G in the new context. For instance, to find out about the academic qualification of the person who taught the Logic Programming course (lp), we could ask:

> teacher :> course :> (course(N, lp), teacher(N, _, DEG))

In this goal, we start by extending the initially empty ([]) context with unit teacher, obtaining context [teacher]. This context is again extended with unit course, yielding the context [course, teacher], and it is in the latter context that goal course(N, lp), teacher(N, _, DEG) is derived.

3.1   Units with Arguments

In [3] we add *units arguments* as a significant part of the CxLP programming model: a unit argument can be interpreted as a "unit global" variable, i.e. one which is shared by all clauses defined in the unit. Unit arguments help avoid the annoying proliferation of predicate arguments, which occur whenever a global structure needs to be passed around. For instance, the teacher unit could be rewritten as in example 4:

Example 4 (CxLP unit teacher with arguments)

```
:- unit(teacher(NAME, DEPARTMENT, QUALIFICATIONS)).

name(NAME).
department(DEPARTMENT).
qualifications(QUALIFICATIONS).

teacher(john, cs, phd).
teacher(bill, cs,  msc).

item :- teacher(NAME, DEPARTMENT, QUALIFICATIONS).
```

In this modified version, we have three unit argument NAME, DEPARTMENT and QUALIFICATIONS, along with three unary predicates to *access* these arguments. There is a new predicate item/0 that instantiates all unit arguments using facts from the database.

To answer the same question as before, and considering a similar change was done to unit course we could say:

> course(N, lp) :> item, teacher(N, _, DEG) :> item.

The way in which this query works is substantially different, though, because we are now instantiating variables which occur in the units, not in the goals. In fact, the goals are now bare.

3.2   Contextual Constraint Logic Programming

It was a natural thing to try to combine contextual and constraint logic programming, yielding what we call *Contextual Constraint Logic Programming* or CCxLP. This paradigm subsumes CLP [5] and enriches CxLP, by allowing unit arguments and contexts to be constrained variables.

Considering again the GNU Prolog/CX implementation, where the CLP scheme is particularized to Finite Domains (CLP(FD)) and reified Booleans (CLP(B)), we can define the unit of example 5 to represent the 24–Hour timekeeping system:

Example 5 (CxLP unit time)

```
:- unit(time(HOUR, MINUTE, SECOND)).

args :- fd_domain(HOUR, 0, 23),
        fd_domain(MINUTE, 0, 59),
        fd_domain(SECOND, 0, 59).

hour(HOUR).
minute(MINUTE).
second(SECOND).
```

Using unit `time` to express the 9-to-5 working hours, we can simply do:
```
time(T) :> (args, hour(H), H #>= 9, H # =< 17).
```
which will result in variable T having variable subterms which are constrained variables which correspond to the time period in question. This sort of situation is explored in more depth in [8].

3.3   On the Implementation of Contexts

GNU Prolog implements the Prolog language with a flat namespace, leaving it up to the standard development environment tools, in particular the link editor, to resolve predicate name references. This approach is clearly inadequate in a dynamic setting such as that which is associated with contextual Logic Programs. To briefly recapitulate on [3], the target WAM variant used in GNU Prolog/CX has been extended with two new instructions which have to be sensitive to the current context; these are: `cxt_call(P/N,V)` and `cxt_execute(P/N,V)` where P/N is the predicate to call and V is a variable (i.e. a WAM register specifier) designating the context to use. Both instructions first look for a definition for P/N in the global predicate table (containing all built-in predicates and predicates not defined inside a unit). If no global definition is found, the current context is scanned until a definition is found. This process is summarized in figure 1.

There is no need to add further instructions to the WAM instruction set architecture, as all the remaining functionality may be carried out by accessing regular Prolog data structures using the available instruction set. For example, the K and CK registers which are specific to the Contextual LP extention to the WAM can simply be mapped to fixed WAM Xi registers, thereby benefiting from the save-restore management which is already being performed by the GNU Prolog compiler `pl2wam`. This particular option proved optimal in terms of the generated code quality, because the context registers are not backed up into the Yi registers unless they actually need to.

The present implementation of GNU Prolog/CX also includes dynamic unit loading under Linux and MacOS X. This feature overcomes the limitation that

trail value of K and CK if needed (testing their time-stamp)
K ← V
CK ← K
if there is a definition for P/N in the global table **then**
   goto this definition
while K is of the form [E|K'] **do**   // ie. K is not empty
   let T be the predicate table associated to <functor/arity> of E
   if there is a definition for P/N in T **then**
     goto this definition
   K ← K'
end
error P/N is an undefined predicate

Fig. 1. Context search procedure

was previously felt where programs would need to be linked with the entire set of units which would be used at runtime. Dynamic loading in GNU Prolog/CX was greatly simplified because contextual execution already requires a lookup step to be performed, at call-time: the predicate lookup table which is used in this process can also be dynamically loaded and associated with a unit identifier (a compound term.)

4 Contexts in ISCO

University of Evora's Integrated Information System, SIIUE, is implemented in GNU Prolog/CX [3] and ISCO [2]. It relies on a relational database management system – PostgreSQL in the occurrence – for which an efficient, although very low-level, interface has been provided. We selected this approach rather than, for instance, resorting to the Draxler Prolog-to-SQL query generator [4] because the database is totally generated from within Prolog, both schema and data.

One "selling point" on ISCO is that modeling and implementation of information systems and related applications should be performed directly at the Logic Programming level, so we also want to hide the fact that there is an underlying relational database at all: it's only being used as a persistence provider.

Following an "extreme-contextual" approach, it was decided by design that every predicate which represents a problem-domain relation would also have an associated unit, of the same name and arity according to the number of arguments in the relation. This would hold whether the predicate is implemented as a set of facts backed by the persistency mechanism, or as a regular predicacte with non-fact clauses, as would be the case for a computed relation.

Taking up the definition of example 1 (page 40), class **teacher** should now compile to code like that of example 6:

Example 6 (CxLP & ISCO unit teacher with arguments)

```
:- unit(teacher(NAME, DEPARTMENT, QUALIFICATIONS)).
```

```
name(NAME).
department(DEPARTMENT).
qualifications(QUALIFICATIONS).

item :- teacher(NAME, DEPARTMENT, QUALIFICATIONS).

teacher(A, B, C) :- <<SQL ACCESS CODE>>
```

The point is that all the code in this unit is generated by the ISCO compiler, which will include yet a few more predicates, in particular those required to deal with insertion, removal and tuple updates.

Following the CxLP approach, constrained queries to persistent relations are specified by constructing a *context* that constitutes a complete specification of the query: this context can be viewed as an implicict computation, in which the goal item will activate the intended query.

Example 7 (CxLP & ISCO constraing unit)

```
:- unit(where(CONDITION)).
item :- CONDITION, :^ item.
```

Example 7 shows how a context component – a unit – may be used to impact the meaning of the item goal: it retains the semantics provided by the remainder of the context, after being put in a conjunction with an arbitrary goal, specified as a unit argument to unit where/1. The :^ operator is analogous to the **super** keyword in OO languages. An example of using this approach:

```
teacher(N,D,Q) :> where(member(Q, [bsc, msc]))
                :> :< TAs,
TAs :< item
```

The first goal binds variable TAs to a context which will generate all teachers which don't hold a PhD. degree. This is achieved with the solutions for the item predicate.

The :< unary operator unifies its argument with the *current context* while the similarly named binary operator effects a *context switch*.

In spite of its simplicity, this example is representative of the way programs are coded in ISCO and GNU Prolog/CX, with contexts representing generators being built and saved in a variable in which the item goal is subsequently evaluated: this can be thought of as the creation and storage of an object, followed by sending of messages to that object.

An Application: a simple yet illustrative example is that of maintaining a browser session. A session is a sequence of related web pages, pertaining to a specific interaction, as identified by user input. Sessions are represented by server-side information which persists across individual pages and is referenced by a client-side (CGI) variable.

A system such as Universidade de Évora's SIIUE [1] requires sessions. In order to provide session support using ISCO and GNU Prolog/CX, we resorted to a thin PHP layer, which collects all variables, be they provided in the URL, in a POST, as cookies or as a server-side variable. These are then supplied to the GNU Prolog/CX program as a unit, cgi/1, which provides predicates to access and enumerate variables.

The sequence of web pages is represented and managed using a sequence of contexts, each representing what may be done at a particular stage. The way a particular link which advances the session is represented is quite simple, as it only requires that:

- the current context be available, as a session variable,
- the link specify the next context, possibly as an extension to the current one,
- every such context should behave uniformly, allowing for the same predicate to render the HTML code.

5   Conclusions and Directions for Future Work

ISCO and GNU Prolog/CX have proven to be a good match, as they both provide useful extensions to Prolog, in particular if what we have in mind is the construction of complex information systems. This is certainly the case for SIIUE, which – at the time of this writing – total about 38000 lines of GNU Prolog/CX code in over 400 units, the persistent database currntly sports over 8 million tuples in 200 relations, a couple of which having over 1 million tuples. SIIUE is daily operated on by several thousand users.

This system has already been applied in a variety of situations, beyond the one that spurred its development, SIIUE. The range of application domains is incessantly growing. There are very promising developments in the fields of business intelligence and information retrieval, for which prototype systems have already been implemented.

One aspect which remains challenging is the development of a particular application with ISCO and GNU Prolog/CX, from scratch. We are presently looking into ways of integrating Logic Programming-based tools, such as ISCO and CxLP, into Content-Management Systems such as Plone or Joomla. It is our belief that these CMS will benefit from having plug-ins with the expressiveness of Prolog.

At present, ISCO joins are always performed on the Prolog side, thereby throwing away good opportunities for query optimization on the DBMS server side. We are presently working on this issue, and will possibly resort to Christoph Draxler's [4] Prolog-to-SQL compiler, although the task is made more difficult because ISCO allows for CLP(FD,$\mathcal{B}$) constraints to apply to variables.

Another approach which we are presently exploring involves associating more than just GNU Prolog's native FD constraints to query variables, by making use of an attributed-variable extension to GNU Prolog.

References

1. Salvador Abreu. A Logic-based Information System. In Enrico Pontelli and Vitor Santos-Costa, editors, 2nd *International Workshop on Practical Aspects of Declarative Languages (PADL'2000)*, volume 1753 of *Lecture Notes in Computer Science*, pages 141–153, Boston, MA, USA, January 2000. Springer-Verlag.
2. Salvador Abreu. Isco: A practical language for heterogeneous information system construction. In *Proceedings of INAP'01*, Tokyo, Japan, October 2001. Prolog Association of Japan.
3. Salvador Abreu and Daniel Diaz. Objective: in Minimum Context. In Catuscia Palamidessi, editor, *Logic Programming, 19th International Conference, ICLP 2003, Mumbai, India, December 9-13, 2003, Proceedings*, volume 2916 of *Lecture Notes in Computer Science*, pages 128–147. Springer-Verlag, 2003. ISBN 3-540-20642-6.
4. Christoph Draxler. A Powerful Prolog to SQL Compiler. Technical Report 92–61, Centre for Information and Language Processing, LudwigsMaximillians-Universität München, 1992.
5. Joxan Jaffar and Michael Maher. Constraint Logic Programming: a Survey. *The Journal of Logic Programming*, 19/20, May/July 1994.
6. Dale Miller. A logical analysis of modules in logic programming. *The Journal of Logic Programming*, 6(1 and 2):79–108, January/March 1989.
7. L. Monteiro and A Porto. Contextual logic programming. In Giorgio Levi and Maurizio Martelli, editors, *Proceedings of the Sixth International Conference on Logic Programming*, pages 284–299, Lisbon, 1989. The MIT Press.
8. Vitor Nogueira, Salvador Abreu, and Gabriel David. Towards Temporal Reasoning in Constraint Contextual Logic Programming. In Petra Hofstedt et al., editor, *Proceedings of the 3rd International Workshop on Multiparadigm Constraint Programming Languages MultiCPL'04*, pages 119–131. TU Berlin, September 2004.

On a Rough Sets Based Data Mining Tool in Prolog: An Overview

Hiroshi Sakai

Department of Mathematics and Computer Aided Science
Faculty of Engineering, Kyushu Institute of Technology
Tobata, Kitakyushu 804, Japan
sakai@mns.kyutech.ac.jp

Abstract. *Rough Non-deterministic Information Analysis* (*RNIA*)
is a framework for handling rough sets based concepts, which are defined
in not only *DISs* (*Deterministic Information Systems*) but also *NISs*
(*Non-deterministic Information Systems*), on computers. *RNIA* is
also recognized as a framework of data mining from uncertain tables.
This paper focuses on programs in prolog, and briefly surveys a software
tool for *RNIA*.

1 Introduction

Rough set theory offers a new mathematical approach to vagueness and un-
certainty, and the rough sets based concepts have been recognized to be very
useful [1,2,3,4]. This theory usually handles tables with deterministic information, which we call *Deterministic Information Systems* (*DISs*). Many applications of this theory to information analysis, data mining, rule generation,
machine learning and knowledge discovery have been investigated [5,6,7,8,9].

Non-deterministic Information Systems (*NISs*) and *Incomplete Information Systems* have been proposed for handling information incompleteness in
DISs [10,11,12,13,14,15,16,17]. In [10,11,12], the necessity of non-deterministic
information is shown. In [13,14], Lipski showed a question-answering system
besides an axiomatization of logic. The relation between rough logic and incomplete information is clarified in [15], and relational algebra with null values is
also discussed in [17].

We have also proposed a framework *RNIA* depending upon not only *DISs*
but also *NISs*, and we have realized a software tool. For realizing this tool, we
developed several effective algorithms, and we employed prolog for implementation. Because, it is necessary to handle non-deterministic cases in *NISs*, it may
be difficult to apply a procedural language like C for realizing this tool. As far as
the author knows, very little work deals with *NISs* nor incomplete information
on computers. Throughout this paper, we show several examples, which clarify
the role of this software tool for *RNIA*.

M. Umeda et al. (Eds.): INAP 2005, LNAI 4369, pp. 48–65, 2006.

2   Basic Definitions and Information Analysis in Deterministic Information Systems

This section surveys basic definitions on rough sets and rough sets based information analysis according to [1,2,3,4].

2.1   Basic Definitions

A *Deterministic Information System* (*DIS*) is a quadruplet $(OB, AT, \{VAL_A | A \in AT\}, f)$, where OB is a finite set whose elements are called *objects*, AT is a finite set whose elements are called *attributes*, VAL_A is a finite set whose elements are called *attribute values* and f is such a mapping that $f : OB \times AT \rightarrow \cup_{A \in AT} VAL_A$ which is called a *classification function*.

For $ATR = \{A_1, \cdots, A_n\} \subset AT$, we call $(f(x, A_1), \cdots, f(x, A_n))$ a *tuple* (for ATR) of $x \in OB$. If $f(x, A) = f(y, A)$ holds for every $A \in ATR \subset AT$, we see there is a relation between x and y for ATR. This relation is an equivalence relation over OB. Let $[x]_{ATR}$ denote an equivalence class $\{y \in OB | f(y, A) = f(x, A)$ for every $A \in ATR\}$, and let $eq(ATR)$ denote the family of all equivalence classes for ATR. We identify an equivalence relation for ATR with $eq(ATR)$. A formula $[A, f(x, A)]$ implies that $f(x, A)$ is the value of the attribute A. This is called a *descriptor*.

Now, let us show some rough sets based concepts defined in $DISs$ [1,3].

(i) The Definability of a Set: If a set $X \subset OB$ is the union of some equivalence classes in $eq(ATR)$, we say X is *definable* (for ATR) in DIS. Otherwise, we say X is *rough* (for ATR) in DIS. For example, if $X = [x_1]_{\{A\}} \cup [x_2]_{\{A\}}$ holds, X is characterized by a formula $[A, f(x_1, A)] \vee [A, f(x_2, A)]$. If X is not definable for any ATR, it is impossible to characterize X by means of conditions on descriptors.

(ii) The Consistency of an Object: Let us consider two disjoint sets $CON \subset AT$ which we call *condition attributes* and $DEC \subset AT$ which we call *decision attributes*. An object $x \in OB$ is *consistent* (with any other object $y \in OB$ in the relation from CON to DEC), if $f(x, A) = f(y, A)$ holds for every $A \in CON$ implies $f(x, A) = f(y, A)$ holds for every $A \in DEC$.

(iii) Dependencies among Attributes: We call a ratio $deg(CON, DEC) = |\{x \in OB | x$ is consistent in the relation from CON to $DEC \}|/|OB|$ the *degree of dependency* from CON to DEC. Clearly, $deg(CON, DEC) = 1$ holds if and only if every object $x \in OB$ is consistent.

(iv) Rules and Criteria (Support, Accuracy and Coverage): For any object $x \in OB$, let $imp(x, CON, DEC)$ denote a formula called an *implication*: $\wedge_{A \in CON} [A, f(x, A)] \Rightarrow \wedge_{A \in DEC} [A, f(x, A)]$. In most of work on rule generation, a rule is defined by an implication $\tau : imp(x, CON, DEC)$ satisfying some constraints. A constraint, such that $deg(CON, DEC) = 1$, has been proposed in [1]. Another familiar constraint is defined by three values in the following:

$support(\tau) = |[x]_{CON} \cap [x]_{DEC}|/|OB|$,
$accuracy(\tau) = |[x]_{CON} \cap [x]_{DEC}|/|[x]_{CON}|$,
$coverage(\tau) = |[x]_{CON} \cap [x]_{DEC}|/|[x]_{DEC}|$.

(v) Reduction of Condition Attributes in Rules: Let us consider such an implication $imp(x, CON, DEC)$ that x is consistent in the relation from CON to DEC. An attribute $A \in CON$ is *dispensable* in CON, if x is consistent in the relation from $CON - \{A\}$ to DEC.

Rough set theory makes use of equivalence classes for ATR. Every definition from (i) to (v) is examined by means of applying equivalence classes. As for the definability of a set $X \subset OB$, X is definable (for ATR) in a DIS, if and only if $\cup_{x \in X} [x]_{ATR} = X$ holds.

Now, let us show the most important proposition, which connects two equivalence classes $[x]_{CON}$ and $[x]_{DEC}$ with the consistency of x.

Proposition 1 [1]. For every DIS, (1) and (2) in the following are equivalent.
(1) An object $x \in OB$ is consistent in the relation from CON to DEC.
(2) $[x]_{CON} \subset [x]_{DEC}$.

According to Proposition 1, the degree of dependency from CON to DEC is equal to $|\{x \in OB | [x]_{CON} \subset [x]_{DEC}\}| / |OB|$. As for criteria *support*, *accuracy* and *coverage*, they are defined by equivalence classes $[x]_{CON}$ and $[x]_{DEC}$. As for the reduction of attributes values in rules, let us consider such an implication $imp(x, CON, DEC)$ that x is consistent in the relation from CON to DEC. Then, an attribute $A \in CON$ is dispensable, if $[x]_{CON-\{A\}} \subset [x]_{DEC}$ holds.

In this way, definitions from (i) to (v) are uniformly computed by means of applying equivalence classes in $DISs$.

2.2 Rough Sets Based Information Analysis in Deterministic Information Systems

Let us see an outline of rough sets based information analysis according to Table 1, which shows a relation between attributes $Head(ache)$, $Temp(erature)$ and Flu over a set *Patient* of objects. This table may be too small, but it will be sufficient to know rough sets based concepts.

Table 1. A deterministic information system

Patient	Head(ache)	Temp(erature)	Flu
p1	no	very_high	yes
p2	yes	very_high	yes
p3	no	normal	no

We identify a tuple with a set of implications, for example,

    imp1: [Head,no] $\Rightarrow$ [Flu,yes],

    imp2: [Head,no] $\wedge$ [Temp,very_high] $\Rightarrow$ [Flu,yes]

are extracted from patient $p1$, and

    imp3: [Head,no] $\Rightarrow$ [Flu,no]

is extracted from $p3$. Implication $imp1$ contradicts $imp3$, because the same condition $[Head, no]$ concludes the different decisions $[Flu, yes]$ and $[Flu, no]$. However, $imp2$ is consistent with implications from any other tuple. Most of rough sets based rules are defined by means of this concept of *'consistency'* [1,2,3,4]. We usually define rules in a *DIS* by consistent implications.

Three measures, *support*, *accuracy* and *coverage* are also applied to defining rules in *DISs* [1,2,4,8]. Each value of every measure is between 0 and 1. Implication *imp*1 occurs once in Table 1, so *support(imp*1)=1/3. This means *imp*1 represents about 33% data in Table 1. A formula [*Head, no*] occurs twice and [*Flu, yes*] occurs once under the condition of [*Head, no*], so *accuracy(imp*1)=1/2. This ratio 1/2 means the degree of the consistency of *imp*1. Similarly, a formula [*Flu, yes*] occurs twice and [*Head, no*] occurs once under the condition of [*Flu, yes*], so *coverage(imp*1)=1/2.

Equivalence classes in *DISs* are usually employed to examine every concept [1,2,3,4,5,6,7]. In Table 1, both *p*1 and *p*3 satisfy [*Head, no*], so *p*1 and *p*3 belong to the same class. Patient *p*2 only satisfies [*Head, yes*], so *p*2 belongs to another class. In this way, we have equivalence classes *h*1={*p*1, *p*3} and *h*2={*p*2} on an attribute *Head*. We similarly have equivalence classes *t*1={*p*1, *p*2} and *t*2={*p*3} on *Temp*, and *f*1={*p*1, *p*2} and *f*2={*p*3} on *Flu*.

According to Proposition 1, the concept of the consistency is examined by the inclusion of equivalence classes. The relation $h1 \not\subset f1$ implies that $p1, p3 \in h1$ are inconsistent for attributes *Head* and *Flu*, and the relation $t1 \subset f1$ implies $p1, p2 \in t1$ are consistent for attributes *Temp* and *Flu*.

Data dependency between attributes is also examined by equivalence classes. For attributes *CON*={*Head, Temp*} and *DEC*={*Flu*}, we have two families of all equivalence classes. *eq(CON)*={{*p*1}, {*p*2}, {*p*3}} and *eq(DEC)*={{*p*1, *p*2}, {*p*3}}, respectively. For every $X \in eq(CON)$, there exists $Y \in eq(DEC)$ such that $X \subset Y$. Therefore, every object is consistent with other object. In this case, the degree of dependency from *CON* to *DEC* is 1.

3 Rough Non-deterministic Information Analysis

A *Non-deterministic Information System (NIS)* is also a quadruplet (*OB*, *AT*, {*VAL_A*|*A* ∈ *AT*}, *g*), where $g : OB \times AT \to P(\cup_{A \in AT} VAL_A)$ (a power set of $\cup_{A \in AT} VAL_A$). Every set $g(x, A)$ is interpreted as that there is a real value in this set but this value is not known. Especially if the real value is not known at all, $g(x, A)$ is equal to VAL_A.

NISs were proposed by Pawlak, Orłowska and Lipski in order to handle information incompleteness in *DISs* [10,11,12,13,14].

In Table 2, it is possible to obtain a *DIS* by replacing every set with a value in every set. There are 16 possible *DISs*, which we name *derived DISs*. Table 1

Table 2. A non-deterministic information system

Patient	Head(ache)	Temp(erature)	Flu
p1	{no}	{very_high}	{yes}
p2	{yes, no}	{high, very_high}	{yes}
p3	{no}	{normal, high}	{yes, no}

is a derived DIS from NIS in Table 2. According to the interpretation to $NISs$, there exists a derived DIS with real information in these 16 derived $DISs$. Two modalities *certainty* and *possibility*, which are defined by means of all derived $DISs$, are introduced into $NISs$.

(Certainty). If a formula α holds in every derived DIS from a NIS, α also holds in the unknown real DIS.

(Possibility). If a formula α holds in some derived $DISs$ from a NIS, there exists such a possibility that α holds in the unknown real DIS.

We have coped with several issues related to these two modalities, for example, the definability of a set in $NISs$ [18,19], the consistency of an object in $NISs$, data dependency in $NISs$ [20], rules in $NISs$ [21], reduction of attributes in $NISs$ [22], etc. An important problem is how to compute two modalities depending upon all derived $DISs$ from a NIS. A simple method, such that every definition is sequentially computed in all derived $DISs$ from a NIS, is not suitable, because the number of derived $DISs$ from a NIS increases in exponential order. We have solved this problem by means of applying either inf and sup information or *possible equivalence relations* [19,20,21].

4   An Overview of a Tool for RNIA

Now, we sequentially refer to a software tool handling $NISs$. This tool mainly consists of the following:

(1) *Programs for checking the definability of a set*
(2) *Programs for equivalence relations*
(3) *Programs for data dependency*
(4) *Programs for rule generation*

Programs are implemented in prolog and C, and they are realized on a workstation with 450 MHz UltraSparc CPU.

4.1   An Exemplary Non-deterministic Information System

Table 3 is an artificial database, which is automatically generated by using a random number generation program. The following is the real prolog data expressing Table 3. According to this syntax, it is possible to handle any $NISs$.

```
% more data.pl
object(10,8).
data(1,[3,[1,3,4],3,2,5,5,[2,4],3]).
data(2,[2,[3,4],[1,3,4],4,[1,2],[2,4,5],2,2]).
data(3,[[4,5],5,[1,5],5,2,5,[1,2,5],1]).
     :        :        :
data(9,[2,3,5,3,[1,3,5],4,2,3]).
data(10,[4,2,1,5,2,[4,5],3,1]).
```

In Table 3, there are $12(= 2^2 \times 3)$ derived $DISs$ for attributes $\{A, B\}$, and we see there exists a DIS, which contains real information, in 12 derived $DISs$.

Table 3. An exemplary NIS. Here, $OB=\{1,2,\cdots,10\}$ and $AT=\{A,B,\cdots,H\}$. For object 1 and attribute A, the attribute value is definite, and it is 3. For object 1 and attribute B, there exists a set {1,3,4}. We interpret that either 1, 3 or 4 is the real attribute value, but it is impossible to decide the real value due to the information incompleteness.

OB	A	B	C	D	E	F	G	H
1	{3}	{1,3,4}	{3}	{2}	{5}	{5}	{2,4}	{3}
2	{2}	{3,4}	{1,3,4}	{4}	{1,2}	{2,4,5}	{2}	{2}
3	{4,5}	{5}	{1,5}	{5}	{2}	{5}	{1,2,5}	{1}
4	{1}	{3}	{4}	{3}	{1,2,3}	{1}	{2,5}	{1,2}
5	{4}	{1}	{2,3,5}	{5}	{2,3,4}	{1,5}	{4}	{1}
6	{4}	{1}	{5}	{1}	{4}	{2,4,5}	{2}	{1,2,3}
7	{2}	{4}	{3}	{4}	{3}	{2,4,5}	{4}	{1,2,3}
8	{4}	{5}	{4}	{2,3,5}	{5}	{3}	{1,2,3}	{1,2,3}
9	{2}	{3}	{5}	{3}	{1,3,5}	{4}	{2}	{3}
10	{4}	{2}	{1}	{5}	{2}	{4,5}	{3}	{1}

For attributes $\{A,B,C,D,E,F,G,H\}$, there are (more than 7 billion) derived $DISs$. It will be hard to enumerate 7346640384 derived $DISs$ sequentially.

4.2 Definability of a Set in NISs

In Table 3, there are two derived $DISs$ for attribute A. If the attribute value is 4 in object 3, the equivalence relation (or the family of all equivalence classes) is $\{\{1\},\{2,7,9\},\{3,5,6,8,10\},\{4\}\}$. Otherwise, the equivalence relation is $\{\{1\},\{2,7,9\},\{3\},\{5,6,8,10\},\{4\}\}$. We name such equivalence relation a *possible equivalence relation* (*pe*-relation), and name every element in a *pe*-relation a *possible equivalence class* (*pe*-class). In a DIS, there exists an equivalence relation for $ATR \subset AT$, however there may exist some possible equivalence relations for ATR in a NIS.

In a NIS, the definability of a set depends upon every derived DIS, and two modalities are introduced into the definability of a set. In programs, we identify an attribute with the ordinal number of this attribute, for example, we identify attributes B and C with 2 and 3, respectively. As for descriptors, we identify $[B,2]$ and $[C,3]$ with $[2,2]$ and $[3,3]$, respectively. Let us show the real execution of programs.

```
% more attrib_atr.pl
atr([1,2,3]).
% prolog
?-consult(tool.pl).
yes
?-translate_atr. [Operation 1]
File Name for Read Open:'data.pl'.
Attribute Definition File:'attrib_atr.pl'.
```

```
EXEC_TIME=0.076(sec)
yes
?-class([6,7]). [Operation 2]
[1] (EQUIVALENCE)RELATION:[[6],[7]] for ATR=[1,2,3]
    POSITIVE SELECTION: CONDITION OF 6:[4,1,5], CONDITION OF 7:[2,4,3]
    NEGATIVE SELECTION: CONDITION OF 2:[2,4,3], CONDITION OF 5:[4,1,5]
Possibly definable !!
EXEC_TIME=0.002(sec)
yes
?-class([3,4]).
[1] (EQUIVALENCE)RELATION:[[3],[4]] for ATR=[1,2,3]
    POSITIVE SELECTION: CONDITION OF 3:[4,5,1], CONDITION OF 4:[1,3,4]
    NEGATIVE SELECTION: NO
[2] (EQUIVALENCE)RELATION:[[3],[4]] for ATR=[1,2,3]
     :        :        :
[4] (EQUIVALENCE)RELATION:[[3],[4]] for ATR=[1,2,3]
    POSITIVE SELECTION: CONDITION OF 3:[5,5,5], CONDITION OF 4:[1,3,4]
    NEGATIVE SELECTION: NO
Certainly definable !!
EXEC_TIME=0.006(sec)
yes
```

According to this execution, a set $\{6, 7\}$ is *possibly definable*, namely there exist some $DISs$ which make a set $\{6, 7\}$ definable. On the other hand, a set $\{3, 4\}$ is *certainly definable*, namely this set is definable in all derived $DISs$.

In Operation 1, *data.pl* is translated to inf and sup information according to the attribute definition file *attrib_atr.pl*. Intuitively, inf is a set of objects with certain information and sup is a set of objects with possible information, for example, $inf(6, \{A, B, C\}, (4, 1, 5)) = \{6\}$, $sup(6, \{A, B, C\}, (4, 1, 5)) = \{5, 6\}$, $inf(7, \{A, B, C\}, (2, 4, 3)) = \{7\}$ and $sup(7, \{A, B, C\}, (2, 4, 3)) = \{2, 7\}$. For such inf and sup, every equivalence class CL, which depends upon an object x, attributes ATR and its tuple, satisfies $inf(x, ATR, tuple) \subset CL \subset sup(x, ATR, tuple)$.

In Operation 2, the definability of a set $\{6, 7\}$ is examined. Three lists are initialized to $EQ = \{\}$(Equivalence Relation), $PLIST = \{\}$(Positive Selection List) and $NLIST = \{\}$(Negative Selection List). In $\{6, 7\}$, the first object 6 is picked up. Here, the applicable equivalence classes of object 6 are $\{6\} (= inf)$ and $\{5, 6\} (= sup)$. Since $\{5, 6\} \not\subset \{6, 7\}$, $\{6\}$ is selected, and lists are revised to $EQ = \{\{6\}\}$ and $PLIST = \{[6, (4, 1, 5)]\}$. At the same time, $\{5, 6\}$ is rejected, and object 5 must have the different tuple from (4,1,5). Since there exist other tuples except (4,1,5) in object 5, $[5, (4,1,5)]$ is added to the list of the negative selection, namely $NLIST = \{[5, (4, 1, 5)]\}$. The same procedure is repeated for a new set $\{7\} (= \{6, 7\} - \{6\})$. Similarly, just an equivalence class $\{7\} (= inf)$ is applicable to this new set. The tuple (2,4,3) does not violate the current selections, so $[7, (2,4,3)]$ is added to the list of the positive selection, and $[2, (2,4,3)]$ is added to the list of the negative selection. Namely, we have $EQ = \{\{6\}, \{7\}\}$,

$PLIST=\{[6,(4,1,5)],[7,(2,4,3)]\}$ and $NLIST=\{[5,(4,1,5)],[2,(2,4,3)]\}$. Since we have an empty set in the next step, we know a set $\{6,7\}$ is definable according to selections. The order of the translation program depends upon $|derived\ DISs|\times|OB|^2$, and the order of program $class(SET)$ depends upon the number of derived $DISs$, which make SET definable. We show program $class0$, which is the main part of program $class$.

```
class0(ATT,SET,EQ,EQ_Ans,PLIST,PLIST_Ans,NLIST,NLIST_Ans)
  :-SET==[],EQ_Ans=EQ,PLIST_Ans=PLIST,NLIST_Ans=NLIST.
class0(ATT,[X|X1],EQ,EQ_Ans,PLIST,PLIST_Ans,NLIST,NLIST_Ans)
  :-candidate(ATT,[X|X1],CAN,PLIST,PLIST1,NLIST,NLIST1),
    minus([X|X1],CAN,REST),
    class0(ATT,REST,[CAN|EQ],EQ_Ans,PLIST1,PLIST_Ans,NLIST1,NLIST_Ans).
ATT:Attributes, SET:A set of objects, EQ,PLIST,NLIST:Temporary lists,
EQ_Ans,PLIST_Ans,NLIST_Ans:Obtained lists for pe-classes, PLIST and NLIST,
CAN:A candidate of pe-class including object X, REST:REST=[X|X1]-CAN.
```

In program $class0$, `candidate(ATT,SET,CAN,PLIST,PLIST1,NLIST,NLIST1)` finds a pe-class CAN which satisfies the next two conditions.

(1) $CAN \subset SET$, and $inf \subset CAN \subset sup$.
(2) This CAN makes no contradiction for $PLIST$ and $NLIST$.

The details of this algorithm are in [18,19].

4.3 Possible Equivalence Relations in NISs

A set of all pe-classes is a kind of reduced information from databases, and these pe-classes contain enough information to calculate most of rough set concepts.

Let us consider methods to obtain all kinds of pe-relations for any set of attributes. The first method is as follows;

(Method 1). Because OB is definable in all derived $DISs$, we solve the definability of a set OB, and we pick up a pe-relation from the variable EQ.

However, Method 1 depends upon $|derived\ DISs|$, and the number of derived $DISs$ increases in exponential order. So, we propose the second method.

(Method 2). Let $peq(A)$ be a pe-relation for a set A of attributes and $peq(B)$ be a pe-relation for a set B of attributes. Then, $\{M \subset OB|M = CL_A \cap CL_B, CL_A \in peq(A), CL_B \in peq(B)\}$ be a pe-relation for a set $A \cup B$. According to this property, we first generate all pe-relations for each attribute, and we execute program $merge$ for obtaining all kinds of pe-relations.

For handling equivalence relations in C language, we introduced two arrays $head[]$ and $succ[]$. For example, we express a class $\{1,2,3\}$ by $head[1]=head[2]=head[3]=1$, $succ[1]=2$, $succ[2]=3$ and $succ[3]=0$. Program $merge$ generates new arrays $head_{A\cup B}[]$ and $succ_{A\cup B}[]$ from $head_A[]$, $succ_A[]$, $head_B[]$ and $succ_B[]$. The order of $merge$ is $o(|OB|)$ in the best case, and the order is $o(|OB|^2)$ in the worst case [20]. In Method 2, it also seems necessary to apply program $merge$

|*derived DISs*| times. However in reality, lots of *pe*-relations become the same *pe*-relation, and the cases of applying *merge* are drastically reduced.

Let us show the real execution according to Method 2.

```
?-translate.
File Name for Read Open:'data.pl'.
EXEC_TIME=0.242(sec)
yes
?-pe. [Operation 3]
<< Attribute 1 >>
   [1]  [[1],[2,7,9],[3,5,6,8,10],[4]]  1
   [2]  [[1],[2,7,9],[3],[4],[5,6,8,10]]  1
   POSSIBLE CASES 2
<< Attribute 2 >>
   [1]  [[1,5,6],[2,4,9],[3,8],[7],[10]]  1
   [2]  [[1,5,6],[2,7],[3,8],[4,9],[10]]  1
         :        :       :
<< Attribute 8 >>
   [1]  [[1,6,7,8,9],[2,4],[3,5,10]]  1
   [2]  [[1,6,7,8,9],[2],[3,4,5,10]]  1
         :        :       :
   [54]  [[1,9],[2],[3,4,5,6,7,8,10]]  1
   POSSIBLE CASES 54
EXEC_TIME=1.520(sec)
yes
```

In Operation 3, all *pe*-relations of each attribute are generated, and *pe*-relations are stored in files from 1.*pe* to 8.*pe*. For attribute 1 which means attribute A, there are two *pe*-relations $\{\{1\}, \{2, 7, 9\}, \{3, 5, 6, 8, 10\}, \{4\}\}$ and $\{\{1\}, \{2, 7, 9\}, \{3\}, \{4\}, \{5, 6, 8, 10\}\}$. There are 54 derived *DISs* and 54 kinds of *pe*-relations for attribute 8.

```
% more 1.rs [Operation 4]
object(10).
attrib(1).
cond(1,1,1,3).
pos(1,1,1).
cond(2,1,1,2).
pos(2,1,1).
cond(3,1,1,4).
      :      :      :
inf([1,1,1],[1,1,1],[[1],[1]]).
sup([1,1,1],[1,1,1],[[1],[1]]).
inf([2,1,1],[2,1,1],[[2,7,9],[1,1,1]]).
```

```
inf([7,1,1],[2,1,1],[[],[]]).
inf([9,1,1],[2,1,1],[[],[]]).
   :        :        :
inf([8,1,1],[5,1,1],[[],[]]).
inf([10,1,1],[5,1,1],[[],[]]).
% more 1.pe
10 1 2 2 1 0 2 7 9 0 3 5 6 8 10 0 0 4 0 -1 1 1 0 2 7 9 0 3 0
4 0 5 6 8 10 0 -1 1
% more merge.dat
123.pe
3
1.pe
2.pe
3.pe
% merge [Operation 5]
Merging
1.pe...
2.pe...
3.pe...
EXEC_TIME=0.010(sec)
% more 123.pe
10 3 216 4 1 0 2 0 3 0 4 0 5 0 6 0 7 0 8 0 9 0 10 0 -1 120
1 0 2 0 3 0 4 0 5 6 0 7 0 8 0 9 0 10 0 -1 60 1 0 2 7 0 3 0
4 0 5 0 6 0 8 0 9 0 10 0 -1 24 1 0 2 7 0 3 0 4 0 5 6 0 8 0
9 0 10 0 -1 12
```

In Operation 4, inf and sup information is displayed. The contents in the file
1.*pe* are also displayed. Every number 0 discriminates each *pe*-class. In Operation
5, all *pe*-relations for attributes $\{A, B, C\}$ are generated. Program *merge* generates new *pe*-relations based on a set of *pe*-relations, which are defined in a file
named *merge.dat*. In the generated file 123.*pe*, there are 216 derived $DISs$ and 4
kinds of *pe*-relations, i.e., 120 *pe*-relations of $\{\{1\}, \{2\}, \cdots, \{10\}\}$, 60 *pe*-relations
of $\{\{1\}, \{2\}, \cdots, \{5, 6\}, \cdots, \{10\}\}$, 24 *pe*-relations of $\{\{1\}, \{2, 7\}, \{3\}, \cdots, \{10\}\}$
and 12 *pe*-relations of $\{\{1\}, \{2, 7\}, \{3\}, \cdots, \{5, 6\}, \cdots, \{10\}\}$.

Let us show execution time for other $NISs$ in Table 4. In Table 5, $N1$ denotes
the number of derived $DISs$ for $ATR=\{A, B, C\}$, and $N2$ denotes the number
of distinct *pe*-relations.

4.4   Degrees of Dependency in NISs

In a DIS, the degree of dependency $deg(CON, DEC)$ from CON to DEC is
an important criterion for measuring the relation from CON to DEC. The
concept of the consistency can be characterized by the inclusion relation of
equivalence classes according to Proposition 1, i.e., object x is consistent if and
only if $[x]_{CON} \subset [x]_{DEC}$ for $[x]_{CON} \in eq(CON)$ and $[x]_{DEC} \in eq(DEC)$. Thus,
the numerator in the degree is $|\cup \{[x]_{CON} | [x]_{CON} \subset [x]_{DEC}\}|$, which is easily

Table 4. Definitions of $NISs$

NIS	$||OB||$	$||AT||$	$Derived\_DISs$
NIS_1	30	5	$7558272(= 2^7 \times 3^{10})$
NIS_2	50	5	$120932352(= 2^{11} \times 3^{10})$
NIS_3	100	5	$1451188224(= 2^{13} \times 3^{11})$

Table 5. Execution time (sec). M1 means Method 1 and M2 means Method 2. If there exist lots of *pe*-relations, Method 2 seems more effective than Method 1.

NIS	$translate(in\_prolog)$	$pe(in\_prolog)$	$merge(in\_C)$	$N1$	$N2$
NIS_1	$M1 : 0.134/M2 : 0.308$	$M1 : 13.351/M2 : 1.415$	$M1 : 0/M2 : 0.690$	5832	120
NIS_2	$M1 : 0.200/M2 : 0.548$	$M1 : 7.489/M2 : 8.157$	$M1 : 0/M2 : 0.110$	5184	2
NIS_3	$M1 : 0.483/M2 : 1.032$	$M1 : 56.300/M2 : 16.950$	$M1 : 0/M2 : 2.270$	20736	8

calculated by using $eq(CON)$ and $eq(DEC)$. The order of this calculation depends upon the size of object $|OB|$.

In a NIS, there exist some derived $DISs$, so there exist the minimum and the maximum degree of dependency. Predicate *depratio* means 'dependency with consistent ratio for every object'.

```
% depratio [Operation 6]
File Name for Condition:123.pe
File Name for Decision:8.pe
------ Dependency Check -------------------------
CRITERION 1(Num_of_Consistent_DISs/Num_of_All_DISs)
   Number of Derived DISs:11664
   Number of Derived Consistent DISs:8064
   Degree of Consistent DISs:0.691
CRITERION 2(Total_Min_and_Max_Degree)
   Minimum Degree of Dependency:0.600
   Maximum Degree of Dependency:1.000
------ Consistency Ratio for Every Object ---------
   Object 1:1.000(=11664/11664)
   Object 2:0.889(=10368/11664)
   Object 3:1.000(=11664/11664)
      :       :       :
   Object 9:1.000(=11664/11664)
   Object 10:1.000(=11664/11664)
EXEC_TIME=0.040(sec)
yes
```

In Operation 6, the degree of dependency from attributes $\{A, B, C\}$ to $\{H\}$ is examined. For a set of attributes $\{A, B, C, H\}$, there are 11664 derived $DISs$. Therefore, it is necessary to obtain each degree of dependency in 11664 derived $DISs$. For solving this problem, we apply *pe*-relations. In reality, there exist only

Table 6. Execution time(sec). $N3$ denotes the number of derived $DISs$ for $\{A, B, C, E\}$, and $N4$ denotes the number of combined pairs of pe-relations in $\{A, B, C\}$ and $\{E\}$.

NIS	$depratio$	$N3$	$N4$
NIS_1	0.080	104976	2160
NIS_2	0.060	279936	108
NIS_3	0.130	4478976	1728

4 pe-relations for a set of attributes $\{A, B, C\}$. and 54 pe-relations for $\{H\}$. It is possible to know all degree of dependency by means of checking the combinations of 4 and 54 pe-relations. The number of combinations is 216(=4×54).

According to these two criterion values, we define the data dependency from CON to DEC in $NISs$. In Operation 6, 69% of all derived $DISs$ are consistent, and the minimum degree of dependency is 0.6. We may agree the dependency from $\{A, B, C\}$ to $\{H\}$. In Table 6, let us show execution time of $depratio$ from $\{A, B, C\}$ to $\{E\}$ in other $NISs$.

4.5   Support, Accuracy and Coverage of Rules in NISs

Three measures *support*, *accuracy* and *coverage* in $DISs$ are extended to *minimum* and *maximum* of them, for example, *minacc* and *maxacc*.

Let us consider an implication $imp4$:[2,5]∧[5,2]⇒[8,1] from object 3 in Table 3. This implication $imp4$ appears in all 17946 derived $DISs$ for attributes $\{B, E, H\}$, so the minimum and the maximum values of three measures are definable for attributes $\{B, E, H\}$. The calculation of values depends upon all 17946 derived $DISs$, however it is possible to obtain these values due to the following results.

For a NIS, let us consider an implication τ:$[CON, \zeta] \Rightarrow [DEC, \eta]$. Let INA denote a set $[sup(x, CON, \zeta) - inf(x, CON, \zeta)] \cap sup(x, DEC, \eta)$, and let $OUTA$ denote a set $[sup(x, CON, \zeta) - inf(x, CON, \zeta)] - inf(x, DEC, \eta)$. Let INC denote a set $[sup(x, DEC, \eta) - inf(x, DEC, \eta)] \cap sup(x, CON, \zeta)$, and let $OUTC$ denote a set $[sup(x, DEC, \eta) - inf(x, DEC, \eta)] - inf(x, CON, \zeta)$. Then, the following holds [21]. Including the definitions of $inf(object, attributes, tuple)$ and $sup(object, attributes, tuple)$, some definitions are in [21].

(1) $minsup(\tau) = |inf(x, CON, \zeta) \cap inf(x, DEC, \eta)|/|OB|$.

(2) $maxsup(\tau) = |sup(x, CON, \zeta) \cap sup(x, DEC, \eta)|/|OB|$.

(3) $minacc(\tau) = \frac{(|inf(x, CON, \zeta) \cap inf(x, DEC, \eta)|)}{(|inf(x, CON, \zeta)| + |OUTA|)}$.

(4) $maxacc(\tau) = \frac{(|inf(x, CON, \zeta) \cap sup(x, DEC, \eta)| + |INA|)}{(|inf(x, CON, \zeta)| + |INA|)}$.

(5) $mincov(\tau) = \frac{(|inf(x, CON, \zeta) \cap inf(x, DEC, \eta)|)}{(|inf(x, DEC, \eta)| + |OUTC|)}$.

(6) $maxcov(\tau) = \frac{(|sup(x, CON, \zeta) \cap inf(x, DEC, \eta)| + |INC|)}{(|inf(x, DEC, \eta)| + |INC|)}$.

In this way, it is possible to obtain these values by using inf and sup information.

```
?-threevalues(3,[[2,5],[5,2]]).  [Operation 7]
[(0.1,0.1),(1.0,1.0),(0.142,0.333)]
EXEC_TIME=0.001(sec)
yes
```

In Operation 7, the minimum and the maximum values of support, accuracy and coverage for $imp4$ are sequentially (0.1,0.1), (1.0,1.0) and (0.142,0.333). Since the minimum value of *accuracy* is 1.0, $imp4$ is consistent in all derived $DISs$.

4.6   Certain and Possible Rules in NISs

In Table 3, let us consider $imp4$ in the previous subsection and $imp5$:[1,4]∧[2,5]⇒ [8,1] from object 3. Implication $imp4$ is definite, and $imp4$ is consistent in all derived $DISs$. In this case, we say $imp4$ is *globally consistent (GC)*. On the other hand $imp5$ is indefinite, since [1,4] is selected from [1,4]∨[1,5]. Implication $imp5$ is consistent in some derived $DISs$, and we say $imp5$ is *marginal (MA)*. According to this consideration, we define 6 classes of implications in Table 7.

Table 7. Six classes of implications in NISs

	GC(Globally_Consistent)	MA(Marginal)	GI(Globally_Inconsistent)
Definite	DGC	DMA	DGI
Indefinite	IGC	IMA	IGI

In $DISs$, there exist only two classes DGC and DGI. These two classes are extended to 6 classes in $NISs$. In Table 7, implications in DGC class are not influenced by the information incompleteness, therefore we name implications in DGC class *certain rules*. We also name implications in either IGC, DMA or IMA classes *possible rules*.

For an implication imp, we may sequentially examine the consistency of imp and we know the class which imp belongs to. However, this method depends upon all derived $DISs$. There exists another method, which depends upon inf and sup information, to examine the class [21].

For $imp4$, $sup(3,\{B,E\},(5,2))=sup(3,\{B\},(5)) \cap sup(3,\{E\},(2))=\{3,8\} \cap \{2,3,4,5,10\}=\{3\}$, and $inf(3,\{H\},(1))=\{3,5,10\}$ holds. In this case, the inclusion relation $sup(3,\{B,E\},(5,2)) \subset inf(3,\{H\},(1))$ also holds, and this implies $imp4$ is GC. Similarly for $imp5$, $sup(3,\{A,B\},(4,5))=\{3,8\}$ holds. In this case, the inclusion relation $sup(3,\{A,B\},(4,5)) \subset inf(3,\{H\},(1))$ does not hold, and this implies $imp5$ is not GC. However, $inf(3,\{A,B\},(4,5))=\{3,8\}$ and $sup(3,\{H\},(1))=\{3,4,5,6,7,8,10\}$ holds, and the inclusion relation $inf(3,\{A,B\},(4,5)) \subset sup(3,\{H\},(1))$ holds. This implies $imp5$ is MA.

4.7   Minimal Certain Rules in NISs

Let us consider two implications $imp6$:[2,2]⇒[8,1] and $imp7$: [2,2]∧[3,1]⇒[8,1] from object 10. Both implications are certain rules, and $imp6$ is simpler than

$imp7$, because $[3,1]$ is added to the condition part of $imp6$. A *minimal* certain rule is a certain rule whose condition part is simpler than any other certain rules.

Now, we focus on minimal certain rule generation. Implication $imp7$ from object 10 belongs to DGC class, so it is possible to generate minimal certain rules from object 10. In this case, we employ a *discernibility function* $DF_{DGC}(10)$ of object 10. We have extended a discernibility function in $DISs$ [23] to a discernibility function in $NISs$. For the decision attribute $\{H\}$, we employ $inf(10, \{H\}, (1)) = \{3, 5, 10\}$. In DGC class, it is necessary to discriminate each object in $\{1, 2, 4, 6, 7, 8, 9\} = \{1, \cdots, 10\} - inf(10, \{H\}, (1))$ from $inf(10, \{H\}, (1))$. Since $sup(10, \{A\}, (4)) = \{3, 5, 6, 8, 10\}$ and $1 \notin sup(10, \{A\}, (4))$, the condition $[A,4]$ can discriminate object 1 from object 10. Similarly, each condition $[B,2]$, $[C,1]$, $[D,5]$, $[E,2]$ and $[G,3]$ can discriminate object 1 from object 10. In this way, a disjunction $([A,4] \vee [B,2] \vee [C,1] \vee [D,5] \vee [E,2] \vee [G,3])$ becomes a condition, which discriminate object 1 from object 10. Let $DISC(10,1)$ denote this disjunction. A *discernibility function* $DF_{DGC}(10)$ is $\wedge_{i=1,2,4,6,7,8,9} DISC(10,i)$.

Theorem 2. [22] Let us suppose that an implication $[CON, \zeta] \Rightarrow [DEC, \eta]$ from object x belongs to DGC class. For a minimal solution SOL of $DF_{DGC}(x)$, $\wedge_{[A, \zeta_A] \in SOL} [A, \zeta_A] \Rightarrow [DEC, \eta]$ is a minimal certain rule from x.

4.8 Minimal Certain Rule Generation in NISs

We have proposed some algorithms to obtain a minimal solution of $DF_{DGC}(x)$. The details are in [22]. Let us show real execution.

```
% more attrib_rule.pl
decision([8]).
decval([1]).
condition([1,2,3,4,5,6,7]).
```

File *attrib_rule.pl* defines the implication: *condition* $\Rightarrow [8,1]$.

```
?-translate_rule. [Operation 8]
File Name for Read Open:'data.pl'.
Attribute Definition File:'attrib_rule.pl'.
EXEC_TIME=0.076(sec)
yes
?-init.
DECLIST:<inf=[3,5,10]>
Certain Rules come from [3,5,10]
EXEC_TIME=0.003(sec)
yes
```

In Operation 8, inf and sup information is created. Then, program $init$ examines objects, which a certain rule can be generated from. In this case, we know that certain rules are generated from objects 3, 5 and 10.

```
?-minimal. [Operation 9]
<<Minimal Certain Rules from object 3>>
  DF:[[1,[2,5],[4,5],[5,2]], ···,[9,[2,5],[4,5],[5,2],[6,5]]]
<<Minimal Certain Rules from object 5>>
  DF:[[1,[1,4],[4,5]], ···,[8,[2,1],[7,4]],[9,[1,4],[2,1],[4,5],[7,4]]]
<<Minimal Certain Rules from object 10>>
  [2,2]=>[8,1][324/324(=6/6,54/54),DGC:Common]
  Rule covers objects [10], [(0.1,0.1),(1.0,1.0),(0.142,0.333)]
EXEC_TIME=0.015(sec)
yes
```

In Operation 9, program *minimal* tries to generate minimal certain rules, whose condition part consists of only core or common descriptors. As for objects 3 and 5, there is no such minimal certain rule, and every discernibility function in each object is displayed. For object 10, there exists such a minimal certain rule, which is *imp6*. For objects 3 and 5, we apply interactive method.

```
?-solall(5). [Operation 10]
Input Descriptors to Start Exhaustive Search:5.
Exhaustive Search for less than 32 Cases !!
<<Minimal Certain Rules from object 5>>
   Core Descriptors:[]
   DF without Core:[[1,[1,4],[4,5]],[2,[1,4],[2,1],[4,5],[7,4]],
   [4,[1,4],[2,1],[4,5],[7,4]],[6,[4,5],[7,4]],[7,[1,4],[2,1],[4,5]],
   [8,[2,1],[7,4]],[9,[1,4],[2,1],[4,5],[7,4]]]
   Currently Selected Descriptors:[]
   [Loop:1]
     Descriptors in DF:[[1,4],[2,1],[4,5],[7,4]]
     Exhaustive Search for [[1,4],[2,1],[4,5],[7,4]]
     Finally Selected Descriptors:[]
     [4,5]&[7,4]=>[8,1][5832/5832(=108/108,54/54),DGC]
         This rule covers objects [5],Coverage=0.333
         [(0.1,0.1),(1.0,1.0),(0.142),(0.333)]
     [2,1]&[4,5]=>[8,1][972/972(=18/18,54/54),DGC]
         This rule covers objects [5],Coverage=0.333
         [(0.1,0.1),(1.0,1.0),(0.142),(0.333)]
     [1,4]&[7,4]=>[8,1][3888/3888(=72/72,54/54),DGC]
         This rule covers objects [5],Coverage=0.333
         [(0.1,0.1),(1.0,1.0),(0.142,0.333)]
EXEC_TIME(for Exhaustive Search)=0.014(sec)
yes
```

In Operation 10, minimal certain rules from object 5 are handled. Predicate *solall*(x) means 'Solve all solutions from object x'. In Loop 1, there are four descriptors in this discernibility function, and this value is less than 5. Therefore, exhaustive search begins for all subsets of four descriptors. Three minimal certain

Table 8. Definitions of NISs

NIS	$|OB|$	$|AT|$	$|VAL_A|$	$derived\_DISs$
NIS_4	50	10	10	1.57×10^{18}
NIS_5	100	10	10	7.01×10^{35}
NIS_6	300	10	10	6.74×10^{86}

Table 9. Execution time(sec) of programs. The *object* column implies the number of objects, in which some minimal certain rules are generated. The execution time of *minimal* depends upon the number of objects.

NIS	$translate\_rule$	$minimal$	$object$	$solall$
NIS_4	0.896	0.723	7	0.764
NIS_5	6.503	3.589	16	1.370
NIS_6	49.892	35.345	21	2.943

rules are generated, and these rules are all minimal certain rules from object 5. If the condition of the threshold value is not satisfied, we select another descriptor and the absorption law is applied to reducing the discernibility function. Then, the next loop is invoked.

Let us show execution time for other $NISs$ in Table 8. In Table 9, the *object* column implies the number of objects, in which some minimal certain rules are generated. The execution time of *minimal* depends upon the number of objects. Program *solall* are also applied to an object in each NIS. In this execution, the threshold value was fixed to 10. Since $|AT|=10$, this program began to enumerate $1024(= 2^{10})$ subsets without specifying any descriptors, and generated all minimal certain rules. According to Table 9, we may employ a threshold value 10 for $NISs$, which consists of more than 10 attributes.

5 Concluding Remarks

An overview of a tool in prolog and a framework of Rough Non-deterministic Information Analysis ($RNIA$) are surveyed according to [19,20,21,22]. We follow rough sets based concepts in $DISs$ and propose a framework of $RNIA$. $NISs$, which were proposed by Pawlak, Orłowska and Lipski, have been recognized to be one of the most important framework for handling incomplete information. Therefore, $RNIA$ will also be an important framework for rough sets based information analysis under incomplete information.

Acknowledgment

The author gratefully acknowledges the helpful comments and suggestions of the reviewers. This work is partly supported by the Grant-in-Aid for Scientific

Research (C) (No.16500176, No.18500214) from Japanese Society for the Promotion of Science.

References

1. Z.Pawlak: *Rough Sets: Theoretical Aspects of Reasoning about Data*, Kluwer Academic Publishers, Dordrecht, 1991.
2. Z.Pawlak: Some Issues on Rough Sets, *Transactions on Rough Sets*, Int'l. Rough Set Society, vol.1, pp.1-58, 2004.
3. J.Komorowski, Z.Pawlak, L.Polkowski and A.Skowron: Rough Sets: a tutorial, *Rough Fuzzy Hybridization*, Springer, pp.3-98, 1999.
4. A.Nakamura, S.Tsumoto, H.Tanaka and S.Kobayashi: Rough Set Theory and Its Applications, *Journal of Japanese Society for AI*, vol.11, no.2, pp.209-215, 1996.
5. L.Polkowski and A.Skowron (eds.): *Rough Sets in Knowledge Discovery 1, Studies in Fuzziness and Soft Computing*, vol.18, Physica-Verlag, 1998.
6. L.Polkowski and A.Skowron (eds.): *Rough Sets in Knowledge Discovery 2, Studies in Fuzziness and Soft Computing*, vol.19, Physica-Verlag, 1998.
7. J.Grzymala-Busse: A New Version of the Rule Induction System LERS, *Fundamenta Informaticae*, vol.31, pp.27-39, 1997.
8. S.Tsumoto: Knowledge Discovery in Clinical Databases and Evaluation of Discovered Knowledge in Outpatient Clinic, *Information Sciences*, vol.124, pp.125-137, 2000.
9. Rough Set Software, *Bulletin of Int'l. Rough Set Society*, vol.2, pp.15–46, 1998.
10. E.Orłowska and Z.Pawlak: Representation of Nondeterministic Information, *Theoretical Computer Science*, vol.29, pp.27-39, 1984.
11. E.Orłowska (Ed.): *Incomplete Information: Rough Set Analysis*, Physica-Verlag, 1998.
12. S.Demri and E.Orłowska: *Incomplete Information: Structure, Inference, Complexity, Monographs in Theoretical Computer Science*, Springer, 2002.
13. W.Lipski: On Semantic Issues Connected with Incomplete Information Data Base, *ACM Trans. DBS*, vol.4, pp.269-296, 1979.
14. W.Lipski: On Databases with Incomplete Information, *Journal of the ACM*, vol.28, pp.41-70, 1981.
15. A.Nakamura: A Rough Logic based on Incomplete Information and Its Application, *Int'l. Journal of Approximate Reasoning*, vol.15, pp.367-378, 1996.
16. M.Kryszkiewicz: Rules in Incomplete Information Systems, *Information Sciences*, vol.113, pp.271-292, 1999.
17. M.Nakata and S.Miyamoto: Databases with Non-deterministic Information, *Bulletin of Int'l. Rough Set Society*, vol.7, pp.15-21, 2003.
18. H.Sakai and A.Okuma: An Algorithm for Finding Equivalence Relations from Tables with Non-deterministic Information, *Lecture Notes in AI*, Springer-Verlag, vol.1711, pp.64–72, 1999.
19. H.Sakai: Effective Procedures for Handling Possible Equivalence Relations in Non-deterministic Information Systems, *Fundamenta Informaticae*, vol.48, pp.343-362, 2001.
20. H.Sakai: Effective Procedures for Data Dependencies in Information Systems, *Rough Set Theory and Granular Computing, Studies in Fuzziness and Soft Computing*, Springer, vol.125, pp.167–176, 2003.

21. H.Sakai and A.Okuma: Basic Algorithms and Tools for Rough Non-deterministic Information Analysis, *Transactions on Rough Sets*, Int'l. Rough Set Society, vol.1, pp.209-231, 2004.
22. H.Sakai and M.Nakata: Discernibility Functions and Minimal Rules in Non-deterministic Information Systems, *Lecture Notes in Artificial Intelligence*, Springer-Verlag, Vol.3641, pp.254-264, 2005.
23. A.Skowron and C.Rauszer: The Discernibility Matrices and Functions in Information Systems, *Intelligent Decision Support - Handbook of Advances and Applications of the Rough Set Theory*, Kluwer Academic Publishers, pp. 331-362, 1992.

Not-First and Not-Last Detection for Cumulative Scheduling in $\mathcal{O}(n^3 \log n)^{\star}$

Andreas Schutt, Armin Wolf, and Gunnar Schrader

Fraunhofer FIRST, Kekuléstr. 7, D-12489, Germany
{Andreas.Schutt|Armin.Wolf|Gunnar.Schrader}@first.fraunhofer.de

Abstract. Not-first/not-last detection is the pendant of edge-finding in constraint-based disjunctive and cumulative scheduling. Both methods provide strong pruning algorithms in constraint programming. This paper shows that the not-first/not-last detection algorithm presented by Nuijten that runs in time $\mathcal{O}(n^3 k)$ is incorrect and incomplete, where n is the number of tasks and k is the number of different capacity requirements of these tasks. A new correct and complete detection algorithm for cumulative scheduling is then presented which runs in $\mathcal{O}(n^3 \log n)$.

1 Introduction

The allocation of activities or tasks on cumulative resources is a practical problem of strong relevance. It arises in resource constraint project scheduling as well as in production planning if resources like water, electric power, consumables or even human skills have to be considered. Furthermore, its underlying energetic reasoning is also valid for other constraint-based allocation problems, e.g. alternative disjunctive resources scheduling or non-overlapping placement of rectangles in a restricted two-dimensional area. Thus, this problem seems to be well-considered in constraint-based scheduling (e.g. in [3,4,5,9]).

Generalised pruning rules exist that are adapted from disjunctive resource scheduling as well as algorithms performing these generalised rules — *overload checking, (extended) edge-finding*, and *not-first/not-last detection*. However, a detailed examination of some of these algorithms presented in [3,9] showed that they are incomplete, i.e. pruning, which is possible regarding their rules, is not performed by the corresponding algorithms, resulting in weak search space reductions. Mercier and van Hentenryck [8] and ourselves independently recognised the incompleteness of (extended) edge-finding and, in parallel, worked out complete algorithms that have the same runtime complexity (not presented here).

To our knowledge, this paper shows some new and not yet published results: the incorrectness and the incompleteness of the *not-first/not-last detection* algorithms presented in [9]. While a correction of these algorithms is rather simple, the definition of *efficient and complete* algorithms is sophisticated: a new $\mathcal{O}(n^3 \log n)$ not-first/not-last detection algorithm is presented where n is the number of the

---

* The work presented in this paper is partly funded by the European Union (EFRE) and the state Berlin within the research project "inubit MRP", grant no. 10023515.

M. Umeda et al. (Eds.): INAP 2005, LNAI 4369, pp. 66–80, 2006.

considered activities. This algorithm uses balanced binary trees similar to the recent algorithms for disjunctive resource scheduling presented in [10,11].

The paper is organised as follows. The next section formally defines the considered cumulative resource scheduling problem. Not-last detection is then presented and a more general pruning rule is derived which is based on some observations reported in the appendix. It follows an examination of Nuijten's algorithm for not-first detection showing its incorrectness and incompleteness by examples. Following this, a new complete not-last detection algorithm is presented and its correctness and completeness is formally proven. For efficiency, this algorithm uses balanced binary trees. The paper concludes with a summary of the performed work and future activities.

2   The Cumulative Resource Scheduling Problem

The *(non-preemptive) cumulative resource scheduling problem* (CRSP) represents the fact that some activities or *tasks* $i, j, t, \ldots$ requiring capacities $c_i, c_j, c_t, \ldots$ have to be scheduled on a common resource offering a constant capacity C such that the tasks are processed without interruption and without exceeding the capacity of the resource at any time. It should be noted that the CRSP is more general than the non-overlapping placement problem for some rectangles of heights $c_i, cj, c_t, \ldots$. There, the rectangles are indivisible in any direction; however, in cumulative scheduling the tasks are decomposable with respect to their capacity requirements (cf. Figure 1).

Formally, the cumulative resource scheduling problem is defined as follows:

Definition 1 (adopted from [8]). *A* cumulative resource scheduling problem *(CRSP) is specified by a cumulative resource of capacity C and a finite task set T. Each task $t \in T$ is specified by its* release date r_t, *its* due date *or* deadline d_t, *its* processing time p_t, *and its* capacity requirement c_t, *all being natural numbers.*

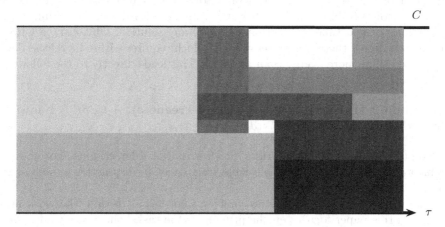

Fig. 1. A solution of a sample cumulative resource scheduling problem

The problem *is to find a* schedule, *i.e. a* solution *that assigns a* start time s_t *to each task so that its start time and its* end time, $s_t + p_t$, *are* feasible

$$\forall t \in T : r_t \leq s_t \leq s_t + p_t \leq d_t$$

and the cumulative constraint

$$\forall \tau : \sum_{t \in T, s_t \leq \tau < s_t + p_t} c_t \leq C$$

is satisfied for all time units τ. *The CRSP is* solvable *if such a schedule exists. Otherwise it is* unsolvable. *Finally,* n *denotes* $|T|$, *and* $e_t := c_t \cdot p_t$ *denotes the* energy *of a task* t.

In the following, we assume an underlying CRSP with its resource and tasks as specified in Definition 1, unless otherwise stated.

We also generalise the notions of release dates, due dates or deadlines, and energies for task sets, i.e.

$$r_\Omega := \min_{j \in \Omega} r_j, \qquad d_\Omega := \max_{j \in \Omega} d_j, \qquad \text{and} \qquad e_\Omega := \sum_{j \in \Omega} e_j$$

where Ω is any task set, especially the empty set. In this special case let

$$r_\emptyset := \infty, \quad d_\emptyset := -\infty, \quad \text{and} \quad e_\emptyset := 0 .$$

In general, CRSPs are NP-complete. Here, we refer to the argumentation of Baptiste et al. in [2] that CRSPs are generalisations of decision variants of two NP-complete problems (see [6]): the One-Machine Problems ($C = 1$, $c_i = 1$) and the m-Machine Problems ($C = m$, $c_i = 1$). Therefore CRSPs are NP-complete in the strong sense [6]. Thus, constraint solvers for CRSPs check a necessary condition for solvability and further use pruning rules to get rid of infeasible start times or end times that are not part of any solution. Obviously, a CRSP has no schedule if there is a subset of tasks which requires within its release date and its deadline more energy than available. This leads directly to the following definition:

Definition 2 (E-Feasibility or Overload Freeness). *A CRSP is* E-feasible *or* overload free *if* $\forall \Omega \subseteq T : C \cdot (d_\Omega - r_\Omega) \geq e_\Omega$.

In addition to the edge-finding rules, not-first/not-last detection is another fundamental technique to reduce infeasible start times in disjunctive as well as in cumulative scheduling.

Due to the symmetry of the not-first and not-last detection, the work presented in this paper focuses on the pruning of the tasks' end times while using the not-last detection rule. The adaptation of the results for the not-first detection is straight forward.

3   The Not-Last Detection Rule

The not-last detection rule is a pendant to one of the two instances of the edge-finding rules. One instance of edge-finding detects an "edge", i.e. a task that ends after some other tasks end — the "edge" is the latest task. Not-last detection finds a task that must end before at least one of some other tasks starts, i.e. the detected task is not the latest. In other words, there is no feasible schedule of the underlying CRSP such that the end time of the detected task is greater than the *latest start times* of the other tasks.

Definition 3 (Latest Start Times). *The* latest start time *of a task t is defined as* $lst_t := d_t - p_t$. *The* latest start time *of a task set Ω is defined as* $lstmax_\Omega := \max\{lst_t \mid t \in \Omega\}$.

With these notions, the core of the not-last detection rule is formally given by the following proposition:

Proposition 1 (adopted from [3,9]). *Let a CRSP be specified by a task set T and the capacity C. Then, for each $\Omega \subset T$ and each task $i \in T \setminus \Omega$ it holds: If*

$$lstmax_\Omega < d_i \le d_\Omega \ and \ e_\Omega + c_i(d_\Omega - \max(lst_i, r_\Omega)) > C(d_\Omega - r_\Omega),$$

is satisfied then all end times later than $lstmax_\Omega$ are inconsistent, i.e. for all schedules of the CRSP the condition $s_i + p_i \le lstmax_\Omega$ holds.

Proof. The proof is shown in [3,9].   □

Within this proof of correctness the restriction $d_i \le d_\Omega$ is not used and thus omittable. A formal proof of this observation is given in Proposition 2 in Appendix A. This results in a simplified formulation of the detection rule:

Definition 4 (The Not-Last Detection Rule). *Let a CRSP be specified by a task set T and the capacity C. It thus holds $\forall \Omega \subset T \, \forall i \in T \setminus \Omega$:*

$$lstmax_\Omega < d_i \land e_\Omega + c_i(d_\Omega - \max(lst_i, r_\Omega)) > C(d_\Omega - r_\Omega)$$
$$\Rightarrow s_i + p_i \le lstmax_\Omega \ .$$

It should be noted that the resulting, more general rule potentially prunes more end times. Consider the following instance of a CRSP where the resource has a capacity $C = 2$ and the task set is $T = \{a, b, c\}$ with

task	r	d	c	p	e	lst
a	5	9	1	3	3	6
b	5	10	1	4	4	6
c	1	11	1	5	5	6

Obviously, after Proposition 1 no pruning for task c is made, but for the more general rule the due date of task c is pruned by 6. More precisely, it holds

$lstmax_{\{a,b\}} = 6 < d_c, e_{\{a,b\}} = 7, r_{\{a,b\}} = 5, d_{\{a,b\}} = 10$ and $\max(lst_c, r_{\{a,b\}}) = 6$. Immediately, it follows: $7 + (10 - 6) = 11 > 2(10 - 5) = 10$, i.e. $d_c \leq 6$ holds.

From the not-last detection rule it is derived that

$$\min_{\Omega \subseteq T|\alpha} lstmax_\Omega \quad \text{with}$$

$$\alpha :\Leftrightarrow i \notin \Omega \wedge lstmax_\Omega < d_i \wedge e_\Omega + c_i(d_\Omega - \max(lst_i, r_\Omega)) > C(d_\Omega - r_\Omega)$$

is the least upper bound on the due date of task i with respect to this rule.

A greedy algorithm in time $\mathcal{O}(n^4)$ is derivable from this rule and outlined briefly: for each task (overall n) all *task intervals* (cf. [5]) (overall $\mathcal{O}(n^2)$) are considered, in which all maximal task sets (overall $\mathcal{O}(n)$) confer possibly latest start times are calculated for pruning the task's due date by the least upper bound.

4   Examination of Nuijten's Algorithm

Algorithm 1 shows CALCLB and its adaptations for the calculation of the lower bounds $LB2$ of the tasks' start times with respect to the not-first detection rule (see Section 4.4.4 in [9]). For compatibility, some notations are adapted to the notions used in this paper. We especially use E (for energy) instead of A (for area) and EET/eet (earliest end time) instead of ECT/ect (earliest completion time), where the *earliest end time* of a task t is $eet_t := r_t + p_t$ and $mineet_\Omega := \min_{j \in \Omega} eet_j$ of a task set Ω. Furthermore, all calculations which are solely used for edge-finding are shadowed, i.e. are in grey. Consequently, the calculations for "pure" not-first detection in CALCLB have cubic runtime complexity.

Nuijten claims that this algorithm calculates for each task $i \in T$ of a given CRSP

$$LB2[i] \quad = \quad \max_{\Omega \subset T|\beta} mineet_\Omega \quad \text{where}$$

$$\beta :\Leftrightarrow i \notin \Omega \wedge r_\Omega \leq r_i < mineet_\Omega \wedge$$
$$e_\Omega + c_i(\min(eet_i, d_\Omega) - r_\Omega) > C(d_\Omega - r_\Omega).$$

However, this is incorrect: consider the following instance of a CRSP where the resource has a capacity $C = 2$ and the task set is $T = \{a, b\}$ with

task	r	d	c	p	e	eet
a	7	13	1	5	5	12
b	10	14	1	4	4	14

Obviously, there are exactly two feasible schedules for this CRSP: $s_a = 7, s_b = 10$ and $s_a = 8, s_b = 10$.

Initially, $X[1] = Y[1] = a$ and $X[2] = Y[2] = b$ hold in CALCLB (cf. Algorithm 1). During the first iteration over y the value of $EET[1]$ in line 8 is undefined because $EET[1]$ is not initialised. This can be fixed by replacing line 4 by

4   **for** $j := 1$ **to** $n + 1$ **do** $EET[j] := \infty$;

Algorithm 1. CALCLB extended for Not-First Detection

Data: X is an array of tasks sorted by increasing release dates
Data: Y is an array of tasks sorted by increasing due dates
1 **for** $y := 1$ **to** n **do**
2   **if** $y = n \vee d_{Y[y]} \neq d_{Y[y+1]}$ **then**
3          $E := 0;\ l := -\infty;\ $ **for** $c \in Sc$ **do** $g_c := -\infty;$
4          $EET[n] := \infty;$
5   **for** $i := n$ **downto** 1 **do**
6   **if** $d_{X[i]} \leq d_{Y[y]}$ **then**
7                  $E := E + e_{X[i]};$
8                  $EET[i] := \min(EET[i], eet_{X[i]});$
9   **if** $d_{X[i]} > l$ **then** $l := d_{X[i]};$
10   **forall** $c \in Sc$ **do**
11                     $rest := E - (l - r_{X[i]})(C - c);$
12   **if** $rest/c > 0$ **then** $g_c := \max(g_c, r_{X[i]} + \lceil rest/c \rceil);$
13   **forall** $c \in Sc$ **do** $G[i][c] := g_c;$
14         $H := -\infty;$
15   **for** $x := 1$ **to** n **do**
16   **if** $d_{X[x]} > d_{Y[y]}$ **then**
17   **if** $E + e_{X[x]} > C(d_{Y[y]} - r_{X[x]})$ **then**
18                     $LB[x] := \max(LB[x], G[x][c_{X[x]}]);$
19   **if** $H + (e_{X[x]}/C) > d_{Y[y]}$ **then**
20                     $LB[x] := \max(LB[x], G[1][c_{X[x]}]);$
21   **else**
22                 $H := \max(H, r_{X[x]} + E/C);$
23                 $E := E - e_{X[x]};$
24             $E' := E;$
25   **for** $w := x - 1$ **downto** 0 **do**
26   **if** $d_{X[w]} \leq d_{Y[y]}$ **then**
27   **if** $EET[w] \leq r_{X[x]}$ **then** break;
28                     $E' := E' + e_{X[w]};$
29   **if** $E' + \min(eet_{X[x]}, d_{Y[y]}) > C(d_{Y[y]} - r_{X[w]})$ **then**
30                         $LB2[X[x]] := \max(LB2[X[x]], EET[w]);$

Further calculation fails at line 26 because $d_{X[0]}$ is not defined, which can be fixed by changing 0 to 1 in line 25:

   25   **for** $w := x - 1$ **downto** 1 **do** ...

Then calculation fails again in line 30 because $LB2[b]$ is not initialised; which is fixable by adding a proper initialisation:

   Data: $LB2$ is a array of the new release dates of tasks i initialised by its current release date r_i

Thus, the first iteration results in $LB2[b] = 12$, which is obviously incorrect. The reason is the wrong condition in line 29, which has to be replaced according to condition β:

29   **if** $E' + c_{X[x]}(\min(eet_{X[x]}, d_{Y[y]}) - r_{X[w]}) > C(d_{Y[y]} - r_{X[w]})$ **then** ...

Furthermore, the loop (lines 25 to 30) verifies whether the not-first detection rule holds for a set $\Omega_u := \{v \in T \mid r_u \leq r_v \wedge d_u \leq d_{Y[y]}\}$ and the task $X[x]$. This is an substantial error, because the sets $\Omega_u \setminus \{v \in \Omega_u \mid eet_v \leq r_{X[x]}\}$ have to verified.

The following instance of a CRSP, where the resource has a capacity $C = 2$ and the task set is $T = \{a, b, c, i\}$, shows by example, that under consideration of the previous corrections the algorithm does not detect the satisfaction of the rule for the task i and the set $\{a, c\}$:

task	r	d	c	p	e	eet
a	1	6	1	5	5	6
b	2	3	1	1	1	3
i	3	8	1	3	3	6
c	4	5	1	1	1	5

If $y = 3$ and $x = 3$ in the loop (lines 15 to 30), then $E' = 1$ and $EET[1] = EET[2] = 3$ before the loop in line 25. In the first iteration of this loop ($w = 2$) the conditions in lines 26 and 27 apply, so the loop (lines 25 to 30) is abandoned and no new lower bound for $X[x] = i$ is calculated. If the if-statement in line 27, which causes the break, will be removed, then the corrected condition in line 30 holds for $w = 1$. Due to the order of the array X (task b is before a) $LB2[i]$ are set to 3, which is no new lower bound for i. The following four corrections are made to fix this error:

1. In line 24 the new variable EET' is introduced, which is initialised with $EET[x + 1]$.
2. The condition $r_{X[x]} < eet_{X[w]}$ is connected with the condition in line 26 by conjunction.
3. The condition of the if-statement in line 27 is replaced by $EET' = \min(EET', eet_{X[w]})$.
4. The term $EET[w]$ in line 30 is replaced by EET'.

Algorithm 2 reflects these and further corrections. The additional corrections (underlined) are necessary for the correct computation of the minimal *eets* of the considered sets.

To show incompleteness, consider this corrected Algorithm 2 and another instance of a CRSP, where the resource has a capacity $C = 2$ and the task set is $T = \{a, b, c\}$ with

tasks	r	d	c	p	e	eet
a	7	9	1	1	2	9
b	5	12	1	5	5	10
c	6	14	2	4	8	10

This CRSP has exactly one solution: $s_b = 5, s_a = 7, s_i = 10$.

Now if we consider the task set $\Omega = \{b\}$ then $\min_{j \in \Omega} eet_j = 10$ holds, and the other values of Ω are $r_\Omega = 5, d_\Omega = 12$, and $e_\Omega = 5$. An evaluation of β shows

Algorithm 2. CALCLB extended for Not-First Detection (corrected)
Data: X is an array of tasks sorted by increasing release dates
Data: Y is an array of tasks sorted by increasing due dates
Data: $LB2$ is an array of the new release dates of tasks i initialised by its current release date r_i

```
1   for y := 1 to n do
2       if y = n ∨ dY[y] ≠ dY[y+1] then
3           E := 0;  for j := 1 to n+1 do EET[j] := ∞;
4           for i := n downto 1 do
5               if dX[i] ≤ dY[y] then
6                   E := E + eX[i];
7                   EET[i] := min(EET[i+1], eetX[i]);
8               else EET[i] := EET[i+1];
9           for x := 1 to n do
10              if dX[x] ≤ dY[y] then E := E − eX[x];
11              E' := E;  EET' := EET[x+1];
12              for w := x − 1 downto 1 do
13                  if dX[w] ≤ dY[y] and rX[x] < eetX[w] then
14                      EET' = min(EET', eetX[w]);
15                  E' := E' + eX[w];
16                  if E' + cX[x](min(eetX[x], dY[y]) − rX[w]) > C(dY[y] − rX[w])
                    then  LB2[X[x]] := max(LB2[X[x]], EET');
```

that this condition is satisfied for $i = c$, i.e. $c \notin \Omega$, $5 \leq r_c = 8 < 9$ and $5 + 2(\min(10,12) - 5) = 15 > 2(12 - 5) = 14$. It follows that $LB2[c]$ is at least greater than or equal to eet_b, i.e. $LB2[c] \geq 10$. However, Algorithm 2 computes $LB2[c] = 9$. The reason is that during the calculation of the EETs in the loop from line 4 to 8, $eet_a = 9$ is considered before $eet_b = 10$ because $X[3] = a$, $X[2] = c$, and $X[1] = b$ hold, which results always in $EET[w] = 9$ and $EET' = 9$ (before the loop in line 25) during the computation of $LB2[c] := \max(LB2[c], EET')$ in line 16.

The same problem arises if r_c, than eet_a is considered before eet_b by calculation of EET' in the loop (lines 25 to 30).

Consequently, CALCLB — corrected or not — is incomplete: only *some* lower bounds but in general *not the greatest* lower bounds of start times are computed. Thus, any pruning of the start times of tasks which are "not-first" with respect to some other tasks is suboptimal with respect to the not-first detection rule.

In [3] a private communication of Nuijten is mentioned where a possibly other, not-first/not-last detection algorithm with cubic complexity is merely mentioned. Nonetheless, to our knowledge, such an algorithm has not yet been published.

5   A Complete Not-Last Detection Algorithm

This section presents a correct and complete algorithm with a time complexity of $\mathcal{O}(n^3 \log n)$ and linear space complexity which implements the not-last rule as defined in Definition 4.

The concept of Algorithm 3 is to iterate over all necessary task intervals $[p, q] := \{t \in T \mid r_p \leq r_t \wedge d_t \leq d_p\}$ and to find for every task i (and interval) the subset $\Omega^* \subseteq [p, q]$ with the smallest $lstmax_{\Omega^* \setminus \{i\}}$ for which the not-last rule holds. In order to find Ω^*, we need only check $\mathcal{O}(n)$ subsets because we know that if an Ω satisfies the not-last rule then these maximal task sets $\{j \in [p, q] \mid lst_j \leq k = lstmax_\Omega\}$ (i.e. the set with maximal number of tasks with respect to one latest start time) will satisfy the not-last rule, too. Thus, it is sufficient to check the maximal set for all $k \in \{lst_j \mid j \in [p, q]\}$. Obviously, the checks can be done in linear time (e.g. when lists are used). In our case, however, we use a balanced binary tree similar to an idea of Vilím in [10,11], in order to reduce the complexity. Therefore, all checks are done in $\mathcal{O}(\log n)$. The concept will be explained in the following.

Algorithm 3. Not-Last Detection in $\mathcal{O}(n^3 \log n)$

Input : LST is an array of tasks sorted by increasing latest start times
Private: Θ is a balanced binary tree of tasks Ω balanced by $C(d_y - r_x) - e_\Omega$
Result: UB' is an array of the new upper bound of due dates of all tasks

1 **foreach** $i \in T$ **do** $UB'[i] := d_i$;
2 **foreach** $x \in T$ **do**
3   **foreach** $y \in T$ **do**
4   **if** $r_x > r_y$ **or** $d_x > d_y$ **then continue**;
5          $\Theta := \emptyset$, $E := C(d_y - r_x)$;
6   **for** $z := 1$ **to** n **do**
7              $i := LST[z]$, $emin(i) := c_i(d_y - \max(lst_i, r_x))$;
8   **if** $lst_i \geq d_y$ **then break**;
9   **if** $r_x \leq r_i$ **and** $d_i \leq d_y$ **then**
10   **if** $emin(i) \leq E$ **then** $emin(i) := c_i(d_y - d_i)$;
11                 $E := E - e_i$;
12   **if** $E < 0$ **then** no feasible schedule exists, **exit**;
13   insert i in the Θ-tree by $E(i) := E$;
14   **for** $z := 1$ **to** n **do**
15             $i := LST[z]$;
16   **if** $lst_i \geq d_y$ **then break**;
17   search j in the Θ-tree such that:
                 $E(j) = \max\{E(j') \mid j' \in \Theta : emin(i) > E(j')\}$;
18   **if** *such j exists* **then** $UB'[i] := \min(UB'[i], lst_j)$;

In Algorithm 3 the necessary task intervals are determined by the two outer loops. The balanced binary tree is created in the first innermost loop and traversed in the second loop in order to find a maximal pruning of the due date of one task. The first innermost loop iterates over an array of tasks sorted by increasing latest start times. Thus, the maximal task sets are built step-by-step beginning with the task with the smallest latest start time.

Every node of the binary tree will represent one of these task sets or — more precisely — the energy $E(\Omega)$ not needed by a particular task set Ω in the task interval under consideration. We will call this not needed energy the *free energy*, and the tree is balanced according to this free energy. For two maximal tasks $\Omega_1 \subseteq \Omega_2 \subseteq T$ apply not only $lstmax_{\Omega_1} \leq lstmax_{\Omega_2}$ but also $E(\Omega_1) \geq E(\Omega_2)$. Thus, it is possible to find a task set $\Omega^* \subseteq T$ within $\mathcal{O}(n)$ task sets with not more than $\mathcal{O}(\log n)$ steps. This found task set, namely the *maximising task set*, will maximise the right side of

$$0 > C(d_q - r_p) - c_i(d_p - \max(lst_i, r_p)) - e_{\Omega^* \setminus \{i\}} \ ,$$

which is the difference of the free energy and the minimal needed energy of the task i. In this case, we are looking to prune the due date of task i. The found set satisfies the following condition:

$$lstmax_{\Omega^* \setminus \{i\}} = \min_{\Omega \subseteq T \setminus \{i\} | \alpha} lstmax_{\Omega} \quad \text{with}$$
$$\alpha :\Leftrightarrow \Omega \subseteq [p, q] \wedge lstmax_{\Omega} \leq d_i \wedge e_{\Omega} - c_i(d_q - \max(lst_i, r_p)) > C(d_q - r_p) \ .$$

The task sets considered by Algorithm 3 are determined exactly by one task (which is the last task added to the task set in an execution of the algorithm). Because of this, the nodes not only represent task sets but also its task determined them. Following Vilím in [10,11] we will call the represented task set Θ and the balanced binary tree a Θ-tree, and we will also not differentiate between a task and the node representing this task. Any kind of balancing with respect to an order would do it for our purpose (as long as it allows the insertion and deletion of a node within $\mathcal{O}(\log n)$ and the access to the root within $\mathcal{O}(1)$ time).

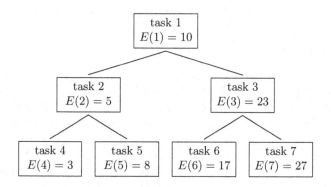

Fig. 2. Example of a Θ-tree

Figure 2 shows an example of a Θ-tree for the task interval $[p, q]$. A node contains a task j (respectively, the task set determined by that task) and the free energy $E(j) := C(d_q - r_p) - e_{\Omega_j}$ in the interval, where j represents the task set Ω_j. In other words, the free energy $E(j)$ is the energy which is not needed by the task set Ω_j (with respect to the capacity of the resource). To give an idea how the Θ-tree is used, we assume a task i. Obviously, the minimal energy occupied by this task in the task interval $emin(i)$ can be computed by $emin(i) = c_i(d_q - \max(lst_i, r_p))$. If task $i \in [p, q]$, it has to be inserted into the tree in order to represent the corresponding task set. Before insertion we have to differentiate two cases. First,

$emin(i)$ can be greater than the free energy E. In this case the not-last rule already holds with the previously inserted nodes, and it suffices to search for the maximising set Ω^* within these already created nodes. Hence, $emin(i)$ does not have to be changed. In the second case, when $emin(i)$ is less than the free energy E, the maximising set Ω^* can only be found in the nodes inserted after task i was inserted (if at all). Thus, the minimal needed energy of task i reduced the free energy of all these subsequently inserted nodes. It follows that in the search for the maximising set Ω^* the energy $emin(i)$ has to be reduced by the needed energy of task i. In order to find the maximising task set Ω^* the tree has to be traversed (in $\mathcal{O}(\log n)$ steps) as follows.

The search starts at the root. At every visited node j the condition $0 > E(j) - emin(i)$ is checked. If it is satisfied, the node j is noted and the search goes on with the right child. In the other case the search continues with the left child (without noting node j). In case node j is a leave the last recently noted node (after also checking the condition for the node j, of course) indicates the task set searched for, namely the maximising task set.

Suppose we have a task with $emin(i) = 19$ and a Θ-tree as shown in Figure 2, then the maximising set would be Ω_6. But for a task with $emin(i) = 2$ such a maximising task set would not exist.

Theorem 1. *Algorithm 3 is correct, complete, and runs in $\mathcal{O}(n^3 \log n)$. After its computation it holds: $UB'[i] = UB[i] := \min(d_i, \min_{\Omega \subseteq T \setminus \{i\} | \alpha} lstmax_\Omega)$ with $\alpha :\Leftrightarrow lstmax_\Omega < d_i \wedge e_\Omega + c_i(d_\Omega - \max(lst_i, r_\Omega)) > C(d_\Omega - r_\Omega)$.*

A formal proof of this theorem is given in Appendix A.

6   Conclusion

This paper revised not-first and not-last detection for cumulative scheduling. The detection is the pendant of edge-finding in constraint-based disjunctive and cumulative scheduling. Both methods provide strong pruning algorithms for constraint programming systems. The detection algorithms update the release and due dates of tasks that must be scheduled at least after or before a task of a set of other tasks. Three contributions are made in the paper. First, it is pointed out that Nuijten's detection algorithm is incorrect and incomplete because the algorithm only finds some update, but in general not the best. Second, a more general not-last detection rule is proposed which omits an unnecessary condition without loss of the correctness of this rule. Because of this, more release and due dates can be pruned. Finally, a novel not-last detection algorithm is presented, which is correct, complete and runs in time $\mathcal{O}(n^3 \log n)$, where n is the number of tasks. The key design is to iterate over all task intervals and search the best update for a task and a interval via balanced binary trees.

Future work focuses on an efficient implementation of the presented algorithm in our constraint solving system firstcs [7]. This implementation will be tested on some CRSP benchmarks examined in [1]. It will then be used, among other things, as an implicit constraint for alternative resources allocations and non-overlapping placements of rectangles in a two-dimensional area.

References

1. Philippe Baptiste and Claude Le Pape. Constraint propagation and decomposition techniques for highly disjunctive and highly cumulative project scheduling problems. *Constraints*, 5(1-2):119–139, 2000.
2. Philippe Baptiste, Claude Le Pape, and Wim Nuijten. Satisfiability tests and time-bound adjustments for cumulative scheduling problems, 1997.
3. Philippe Baptiste, Claude le Pape, and Wim Nuijten. *Constraint-Based Scheduling*. Number 39 in International Series in Operations Research & Management Science. Kluwer Academic Publishers, 2001.
4. Nicolas Beldiceanu and Evelyne Contjean. Introducing global constraints in CHIP. *Mathematical and Computer Modelling*, 12:97–123, 1994.
5. Yves Caseau and François Laburthe. Cumulative scheduling with task intervals. In Michael J. Maher, editor, *Proceedings of the 13th Joint International Conference and Syposium on Logic Programming - JICSLP 1996*, pages 363–377. MIT Press, 1996.
6. Michael R. Garey and David S. Johnson. *Computers and Intractability: A Guide to the Theory of NP-Completeness*. W. H. Freeman & Co., New York, NY, USA, 1979.
7. Matthias Hoche, Henry Müller, Hans Schlenker, and Armin Wolf. firstcs - A Pure Java Constraint Programming Engine. In Michael Hanus, Petra Hofstedt, and Armin Wolf, editors, *2nd International Workshop on Multiparadigm Constraint Programming Languages – MultiCPL'03*, 29th September 2003. Online available at uebb.cs.tu-berlin.de/MultiCPL03/Proceedings.MultiCPL03.RCoRP03.pdf.
8. Luc Mercier and Pascal Van Hentenryck. Edge finding for cumulative scheduling. http://www.cs.brown.edu/people/pvh/ef2.pdf, 6th July 2005.
9. Wilhelmus Petronella Maria Nuijten. *Time and Resource Constrained Scheduling*. PhD thesis, Eindhoven University of Technology, 1994.
10. Petr Vilím. $O(n \log n)$ filtering algorithms for unary resource constraint. In *Proceedings of the International Conference on Integration of AI and OR Techniques in Constraint Programming for Combinatorical Optimisation Problems – CP-AI-OR'04*, volume 3011 of *Lecture Notes in Computer Science*, pages 335–347. Springer Verlag, 2004.
11. Petr Vilím, Roman Barták, and Ondřej Čepek. Unary resource constraint with optional activities. In Marc Wallace, editor, *Principles and Practice of Constraint Programming – CP 2004, 10th International Conference*, volume 3258 of *Lecture Notes in Computer Science*, pages 62–76. Springer Verlag, 2004.

A   Theoretical Results

In the following it is shown that not-last detection without the restriction $d_i \leq d_\Omega$ for the considered task i and task set $\Omega \subseteq T \setminus \{i\}$ is still correct:

Proposition 2. *Let an E-feasible CRSP determined by a task set T and an overall capacity C of its cumulative resource be given. Further, let $\Omega \subset T$ and let $i \notin \Omega$ be another task in T. If it holds*

$$lstmax_\Omega < d_i \wedge e_\Omega + c_i(d_\Omega - \max(lst_i, r_\Omega)) > C(d_\Omega - r_\Omega)$$

then there is no feasible schedule of this CRSP where $s_i + p_i > lstmax_\Omega$ holds.

Proof. It is assumed that there is a feasible schedule of the considered CRSP satisfying $s_i + p_i > lstmax_\Omega$. Obviously, it holds $e_\Omega \leq C(d_\Omega - r_\Omega)$ because the CRSP is E-feasible. Thus, $c_i(d_\Omega - \max(lst_i, r_\Omega))$ must be positive, i.e. $d_\Omega > \max(lst_i, r_\Omega)$ and thus $d_\Omega > lst_i \geq s_i$.

Assuming the task i finishes at $s_i + p_i < d_\Omega$. Further, all tasks in Ω will start before i finishes, i.e. $lstmax_\Omega < d_i$. Thus the energy $c_i(d_\Omega - s_i - p_i)$ cannot be occupied by any task in $\Omega \cup \{i\}$ in the time window $[r_\Omega, d_\Omega)$, however, the energy $c_i(s_i + p_i - \max(s_i, r_\Omega))$ is occupied by the task i , i.e.

$$e_\Omega + c_i(d_\Omega - s_i - p_i) + c_i(s_i + p_i - \max(s_i, r_\Omega))$$
$$= e_\Omega + c_i(d_\Omega - \max(s_i, r_\Omega))$$
$$\geq e_\Omega + c_i(d_\Omega - \max(lst_i, r_\Omega))$$

holds.

Let us assume that the task i finishes at $s_i + p_i \geq d_\Omega$. Further all tasks in Ω will start before i finishes (i.e. $lstmax_\Omega < d_i$). Thus the energy $c_i(d_\Omega - \max(s_i, r_\Omega))$ is occupied by the task i in the time window $[r_\Omega, d_\Omega)$, i.e.

$$e_\Omega + c_i(d_\Omega - \max(s_i, r_\Omega)) \geq e_\Omega + c_i(d_\Omega - \max(lst_i, r_\Omega))$$

holds, too.

In conclusion, $e_\Omega + c_i(d_\Omega - \max(lst_i, r_\Omega)) \leq C(d_\Omega - r_\Omega)$ must hold in both cases if the schedule is feasible. However, it does not hold, i.e. the schedule is infeasible. □

Obviously, this generalisation is transformable to the symmetric not-first-detection.

In the following, we show that Theorem 1 holds, i.e. that Algorithm 3 is correct, complete, and has a complexity of $\mathcal{O}(n^3 \log n)$, and we restrict our attention to E-feasible CRSPs only. In order to do that, first we have to prove a property of the nodes in the balanced tree. Let $p, q \in T$ be tasks with $r_p \leq r_q$ and $d_p \leq d_q$, and let LST be an array of tasks sorted by increasing latest start times. Furthermore, let $\Omega_z := \Omega_{(z,p,q)} = \{j \in [p, q] \mid j = LST[z'] \wedge z' \leq z\}$ with $z \in [1, n]$ and $\Omega_0 := \emptyset$. It follows that $lstmax_{\Omega_z} \leq lst_{LST[z]}$. If $LST[z] \in [p, q]$ then it equals.

Proposition 3. *If $x = p$, $y = q$ in Algorithm 3 and if it is before line 3 then it holds before the zth iteration of the loop (lines 3–3):*

$$\Omega_{z-1} = \Theta \wedge E = C(d_q - r_p) - e_{\Omega_{z-1}} \text{ and} \quad (1)$$
$$\forall j \in \Theta : E(j) = C(d_q - r_p) - e_{\Omega_k} \text{ where } j =: LST[k] \quad (k \leq z - 1) . \quad (2)$$

Proof. Induction over the sorted array LST.

Basis $z = 1$: For $x = p$ and $y = q$ the first innermost loop was not iterated at all. From this it follows that $\Theta = \emptyset$ and $E = C(d_q - r_p)$ (see line 3). Because $\Omega_{1-1} = \Omega_0 = \emptyset$ the basis holds.

Inductive step $z \rightarrow z + 1$: Let $u = LST[z]$. The induction hypothesis is, that for all $z' < z + 1$ before the z'th loop iteration the conditions (1) and (2) hold.

Because the tasks in the array LST are sorted by increasing latest start times, it holds that $\Omega_{z-1} = \Omega_z \setminus \{LST[z]\}$. In order to show the induction step two cases have to be considered, namely $u \in \Omega_z$ and $u \notin \Omega_z$.

First we consider the case $u \in \Omega_z$. In this case the condition in line 3 is true for the zth loop iteration. According to the induction hypothesis E was updated with $C(d_q - r_p) - e_{\Omega_{z-1}} - e_u = C(d_q - r_p) - e_{\Omega_z}$ (line 3), and u was inserted into the tree Ω_{z-1} with this energy E. Thus, the conditions (1) and (2) hold.

The second case is $u \notin \Omega_z$, and the condition in line 3 during the zth loop iteration is not true. Because of this, E remains the same and u is not added to the tree. Because $\Omega_z = \Omega_{z-1}$ and by the induction hypothesis the proposition holds.   □

Proof (Theorem 1). First, the correctness and completeness of Algorithm 3 is shown, followed by the proof for its runtime.

The algorithm is correct and complete if the following holds for every task $i \in T$:

$$UB'[i] = UB[i] := \min(d_i, \min_{\Omega \subseteq T \setminus \{i\} | \alpha} lstmax_{\Omega})$$

with $\alpha :\Leftrightarrow lstmax_{\Omega} < d_i \wedge e_{\Omega} + c_i(d_{\Omega} - \max(lst_i, r_{\Omega})) > C(d_{\Omega} - r_{\Omega})$.

Let $i \in T$ be any task. First $UB'[i] \le UB[i]$ is shown. If $UB[i] = d_i$, then it holds that $UB'[i] \le d_i$ because of line 3 and 3. Without loss of generality, let $UB[i] < d_i$. Then a task set exists $\Omega \subseteq T \setminus \{i\}$ for which the following holds:

$$UB[i] = lstmax_{\Omega} \wedge e_{\Omega} + c_i(d_{\Omega} - \max(lst_i, r_{\Omega})) > C(d_{\Omega} - r_{\Omega}). \qquad (3)$$

Let $p, q \in \Omega$ be the tasks with $r_p = r_{\Omega}$ and $d_q = d_{\Omega}$, and let $u := LST[z_u] \in T$ be the last task in the array LST with $lst_u = UB[i]$ and $u \in [p, q]$. Hence, $\Omega \subseteq \Omega_{z_u}$, thus, the condition (3) also holds for the set Ω_{z_u}. Furthermore, let z be the number with $i = LST[z]$. According to Proposition 3 it follows that before the second innermost loop the tree Θ corresponds to the set Ω_n and for all tasks $j \in \Theta : E(j) = C(d_q - r_p) - e_{\Omega_v}$ with $j = LST[v]$. Now we have to differentiate between the cases $z_u < z$ and $z_u \ge z$.

Assume $z_u < z$ applies. Then $u \in \Theta$ before the zth iteration of the loop (lines 3–3) and the condition $emin(i) \le E$ in line 3 is not satisfied due to:

$$c_i(d_q - \max(lst_i, r_p)) > C(d_q - r_p) - e_{\Omega_{z_u}} \ge C(d_q - r_p) - e_{\Omega_{z-1}} = E.$$

For this reason $emin(i) = c_i(d_q - \max(lst_i, r_p))$ after the loop. So the algorithm finds in the zth iteration of the second innermost loop an j with:

$$E(j) = \max\{E(j') \mid j' \in \Theta : emin(i) > E(j')\} \ge E(u).$$

Thus, the condition in line 3 holds, and the value $UB'[i]$ is updated to $\min(UB'[i], lst_j)$. As a result of $E(j) \ge E(u)$ and Proposition 3 it follows that $\Omega_{z_j} \subseteq \Omega_{z_u} \setminus \{i\}$ with $j = LST[z_j]$. So $UB'[i] \le lst_j \le lst_u = UB[i]$ holds for $z_u < z$.

Assume $z_u \geq z$ applies. If $i \notin [p,q]$ or $c_i(d_q - \max(lst_i, r_p)) > E$ in the zth iteration of the loop (lines 3–3) then $emin(i) = c_i(d_q - \max(lst_i, r_p))$ after the loop and the same consequences as in case $z_u < z$ applies for the zth iteration of the loop (lines 3–3). If $i \in [p,q]$ and $c_i(d_q - \max(lst_i, r_p)) \leq E$ then $emin(i) = c_i(d_q - d_i)$ after the loop and for all $z_{j'} < z$ applies:

$$c_i(d_q - d_i) \leq c_i(d_q - d_i) + e_i = c_i(d_q - \max(lst_i, r_p)) \leq E \leq E(j').$$

So the algorithm finds in the zth iteration of the second innermost loop an $j \in \Theta$ with $E(j) \geq E(u)$, thus, $\Omega_z \subseteq \Omega_{z_j} \subseteq \Omega_{z_u}$ holds. Remark: $c_i(d_q - d_i) > E(u)$ applies because of $i \in \Omega_{z_u}$. And $UB'[i]$ is updated by $\min(UB'[i], lst_j) \leq lst_u$. Consequently, $UB'[i] \leq UB[i]$ holds.

Now $UB'[i] \geq UB[i]$ is shown by antithesis. If $UB'[i] < UB[i]$ then tasks $p, q, u \in T \setminus \{i\}$ exist, and the following holds for $x = p$ and $y = q$ in the zth loop iteration (lines 3–3):

$$lst_u = UB'[i] < d_i \wedge u \in \Theta \wedge E(u) = \max\{E(j') \mid j' \in \Theta : emin(i) > E(j')\}.$$

But with Proposition 3 it follows that (independent of $z_u < z$ or $z_u \geq z$):

$$e_{\Omega_{z_u} \setminus \{i\}} + c_i(d_q - \max(lst_i, r_p)) > C(d_q - r_p) \geq C(d_{\Omega_{z_u} \setminus \{i\}} - r_{\Omega_{z_u} \setminus \{i\}})$$

with $u = LST[z_u]$. Thus, the not-last rule would be true for the task i and the set $\Omega_{z_u} \setminus \{i\}$. This leads to the contradiction:

$$UB[i] \leq lst_u = UB'[i] < UB[i].$$

Thus, it holds that $UB'[i] = UB[i]$. In other words, the Algorithm 3 ist correct and complete.

It remains to show that the runtime is $\mathcal{O}(n^3 \log n)$. The runtime has to be derived from the four nested for loops, respectively, from the operations in the innermost loops. The lines 3–3 will be repeated at most n^3 times. As we mentioned before, the insertion of a new node in the Θ-tree (line 3) as well as the search for a node j (line 3) will take $\mathcal{O}(\log n)$ time. Thus, it follows that the total runtime is $\mathcal{O}(n^3 \log n)$.   □

Calc/Cream: OpenOffice Spreadsheet Front-End for Constraint Programming

Naoyuki Tamura

Information Science and Technology Center, Kobe University,
1-1 Rokkodai, Nada, Kobe 657-8501, Japan
tamura@kobe-u.ac.jp

Abstract. Calc/Cream is a constraint programming system with a spreadsheet front-end implemented on OpenOffice.org Calc and Java language. Constraint problems are described by users as cell expressions on a spreadsheet, and solutions are searched by the constraint solver and shown as cell values by the system. It is also possible to use Basic macros to customize the system.

1 Introduction

Constraint programming is widely used to develop various applications including constraint satisfaction problems and optimization problems, such as production planning and scheduling, etc.

Constraint programming is originally studied as an extension of logic programming languages. However, after 1990's, several constraint programming extensions of OOL (C++ and Java) are proposed including ILOG Solver[1], ILOG JSolver[2,3], Koalog[4], JACK[5], JCL[6], and Cream[7,8].

However, developing constraint programming applications is still a difficult task. It is important to provide a programming environment which is easy to use for constraint application developers.

In this paper, we describe a constraint programming system with a spreadsheet front-end implemented on OpenOffice.org Calc[9] and Java language. In this Calc/Cream system[1] developed as a port of HECS system[10,11][2], users can write their constraint problems as cell expressions on a spreadsheet.

There are several works on constraint spreadsheet systems, such as Chew and David[12], Hyvönen[13], Intellisheet[14], and Knowledgesheet[15].

Compared with these systems, Calc/Cream is more flexible because it is developed as a simple add-in of OpenOffice.org Calc which is an open-source software and the functionality of the original spreadsheet system is not modified.

---

[1] http://bach.istc.kobe-u.ac.jp/cream/calc.html
[2] http://kaminari.istc.kobe-u.ac.jp/hecs/

M. Umeda et al. (Eds.): INAP 2005, LNAI 4369, pp. 81–87, 2006.
© Springer-Verlag Berlin Heidelberg 2006

2 Cream: Class Library for Constraint Programming in Java

2.1 Features of Cream

Cream[7,8] is a class library helping Java programmers to develop intelligent programs requiring constraint satisfaction or optimization on finite domains.

The followings are features of Cream.

- 100% Pure Java: Whole programs are written in Java.
- Open source: Cream is distributed as a free software with source code [3].
- Natural description of constraints: Various constraints can be naturally described within Java syntax.
- Easy enhancements: Programmers can easily enhance/extend constraint descriptions and satisfaction algorithms.
- Various optimization algorithms: In addition to complete search algorithms, various local search algorithms are available, such as Simulated Annealing and Taboo Search, etc.
- Cooperative local search: Several local search solvers can be executed in parallel for cooperative local search.

2.2 Example Program of Cream

Fig. 1 shows an example program of Cream.

```java
import jp.ac.kobe_u.cs.cream.*;

public class FirstStep {
  public static void main(String args[]) {
    // Create a constraint network
    Network net = new Network();
    // Declare variables
    IntVariable x = new IntVariable(net);
    IntVariable y = new IntVariable(net);
    // x >= 0
    x.ge(0);
    // y >= 0
    y.ge(0);
    // x + y == 7
    x.add(y).equals(7);
    // 2x + 4y == 20
    x.multiply(2).add(y.multiply(4)).equals(20);
    // Solve the problem
    Solver solver = new DefaultSolver(net);
    Solution solution = solver.findFirst();
    int xv = solution.getIntValue(x);
    int yv = solution.getIntValue(y);
    System.out.println("x = "+xv+", y = "+ yv);
  }
}
```

Fig. 1. Example program of Cream

---

[3] http://bach.istc.kobe-u.ac.jp/cream/

- `Network` is a class for constraint network consisting of constraint variables and constraint conditions. New constraint network is created by the constructor invocation `new Network()`.
- New constraint variable in the network `net` is created by the constructor `new IntVariable(net)`.
- New constraint $x \geq 0$ is added by executing a method `x.ge(0)`. Similarly, constraints $y \geq 0$, $x + y = 7$, $2x + 4y = 20$ are added to the network.
- After adding all variables and constraints to the network, a constraint solver (using constraint propagation and backtrack) is created by the constructor `new DefaultSolver(net)`.
- First solution is searched by `solver.findFirst()`.
- The value of the variable `x` is extracted from the solution by using a method call `solution.getIntValue(x)`.

2.3   Other Features of Cream

The followings are other unique features of Cream.

- Serialized Constraint: `Serialized` constraint can be used to describe a condition in which given intervals are not overlapped each other (useful for scheduling problems).
- Optimization: A `setObjective` method can be used to specify an objective variable for optimization problems.
- Local Search Algorithms: Local search algorithms including Simulated Annealing (`SASearch`) and Taboo Search (`TabooSearch`) can be used for some optimization problems.
- Cooperative local search: A `ParallelSolver` can be used for cooperative local search in which several local search solvers can be executed in parallel.

2.4   Java Classes of Cream

As shown in the previous example program, Cream consists of following classes.

- `Network` class implements constraint networks. A constraint network consists of variables, constraints, and an objective variable (optional).
- `Variable` class implements variables. A variable is a component of a constraint network. A variable is constructed with an initial domain which specifies the set of elements over which the variable ranges.
- `IntVariable` class is a subclass of the `Variable` class, and implements integer variables.
- `Domain` is an abstract class for domains.
- `IntDomain` class implements integer domains.
- `Constraint` is an abstract class for constraints. The subclass should implement `satisfy` method which makes the constraint to be arc-consistent.
- `IntComparison`, `IntArith`, and `IntFunc` classes implements constrains on integer variables.
- `Serialized` class implements a constraint where given integer intervals are not overlapped each other.

- `Solver` is an abstract class for constraint solvers.
- `DefaultSolver` is a branch-and-bound solver.
- `LocalSearch` is a random-walk solver for problems including `Serialized` constraints.
- `SASearch` is a subclass of `LocalSearch`, and implements Simulated Annealing search.
- `TabooSearch` is a subclass of `LocalSearch`, and implements Taboo search.
- `ParallelSolver` is a subclass of `Solver`, and executes several solvers in parallel.

For more details of Cream implementation, please refer to to the Cream web page[7].

3   Calc/Cream: Constraint Spreadsheet

3.1   Features of Calc/Cream

Calc/Cream is a constraint programming system with a spreadsheet front-end implemented on OpenOffice.org Calc and Java language.

In Calc/Cream, constraint problems are described by users as cell expressions on a spreadsheet, therefore users do not need to study the use of programming languages.

Calc/Cream is developed as a simple add-in of OpenOffice.org Calc and the functionality of the original spreadsheet system is not modified.

3.2   Example of Calc/Cream

Fig. 2 shows an example of Calc/Cream solving an old Japanese elementary school problem:

> There are some cranes and tortoises. They are 7 in total, and their legs are 20 in total. How many cranes and tortoises are there?

The number of cranes is assigned to the cell B2, the number of tortoises is assigned to the cell B3, and a solution satisfying B2+B3=7 and 2*B2+4*B3=20 will be searched by the solver.

The left hand side of the Fig. 2 shows cell expressions described by a user. By pressing a START button (not shown in the figure), a solution satisfying

	A	B	C
1		Number	Legs
2	Crane	0	=B2*2
3	Tortoise	0	=B3*4
4	Total	7	20
5	Condition	=B2+B3=B4	=C2+C3=C4
6		=CVARIABLES(B2:B3;0;100)	=CONSTRAINTS(B2:C5)

	A	B	C
1		Number	Legs
2	Crane	4	8
3	Tortoise	3	12
4	Total	7	20
5	Condition	TRUE	TRUE
6		...	...

Fig. 2. Example of Calc/Cream (Cranes and Tortoises)

cell expressions specified by `CONSTRAINTS` is searched by changing cell values specified by `CVARIABLES`.

In this example, a solution satisfying the following conditions is searched.

- The cell value of C2 is equal to B2*2.
- The cell value of C3 is equal to B3*4.
- The cell value of B2+B3=B4 is true.
- The cell value of C2+C3=C4 is true.
- The cell values of B2 and B3 are within the interval $[0, 100]$.

The right hand side of the Fig. 2 shows the search result.

Fig. 3 shows an example finding a solution of a semi magic square problem which assigns different numbers of 1–9 to cells B2–D4 so that the summations of each rows and columns are equal to 15.

	A	B	C	D
1	=CNOTEQUALS(B2:D4)	=SUM(B2:B4)=15	=SUM(C2:C4)=15	=SUM(D2:D4)=15
2	=SUM(B2:D2)=15	0	0	0
3	=SUM(B3:D3)=15	0	0	0
4	=SUM(B4:D4)=15	0	0	0
5	=CVARIABLES(B2:D4;1;9)			
6	=CONSTRAINTS(A1:D4)			

Fig. 3. Example of Calc/Cream (Semi Magic Square)

`CVARIABLES(B2:D4;1;9)` means each cell value of B2–D4 is an integer from 1 to 9, and `CNOTEQUALS(B2:D4)` means these have different values each other. Expressions such as `SUM(B2:D2)=15` means the summation of each row or column is equal to 15.

3.3   How Calc/Cream Works

The following shows how Calc/Cream works after pressing the "Start" button.

- The spreadsheet is scanned, and cells containing variables and constraints are parsed to tree structures, and they are added to constraint network of Cream.
- Cream solver is invoked to start solving.
- Values of the obtained solution is written back to the spreadsheet.

The following StarBasic macro performs the above procedure.

```
Const JAVA_SERVICE = "com.sun.star.loader.Java2"
Const CREAM_SERVICE = "jp.ac.kobe_u.cs.cream.uno.CreamAddins"

Dim object_cream As Object
```

```
Sub CStartButton
    # Create UNO service to use Cream
    CreateUnoService(JAVA_SERVICE)
    object_cream = CreateUnoService(CREAM_SERVICE)

    # Scan spreadsheet and add constraints
    Dim sheetIndex(0) As Object
    sheetIndex() = Array(0, 1, 2)
    object_cream.CScanDocument(ThisComponent, sheetIndex())

    # Start Cream solver
    If Not object_cream.CStart() Then
        MsgBox "No Solutions !!"
    EndIf
End Sub
```

The following macro implements the Next button.

```
Sub CNextButton
    CreateUnoService(JAVA_SERVICE)
    object_cream = CreateUnoService(CREAM_SERVICE)

    If Not object_cream.CNext() Then
        MsgBox "No More Solutions !!"
    End If
End Sub
```

4   Summary

This paper presents Cream class library for constraint programming in Java, and Calc/Cream constraint spreadsheet system which is developed as an add-in of OpenOffice.org Calc.

Both systems are still under development, and further enhancements are planned in near future.

Acknowledgments

We would like to give special thanks to Takashi Shinozaki, Hideaki Okamoto, and Mutsunori Banbara for helping to develop Calc/Cream system.

Calc/Cream was developed as a part of HECS (HEterogeneous Constraint Solver) system[10,11] which was supported in part by METI and IPA (The Information-technology Promotion Agency) under grant of 2003 Exploratory Software Project. Some improvement ideas of Calc/Cream are obtained through the discussion with Mr. Kino, a project manager of IPA Exploratory Software Project.

References

1. Puget, J.F.: A C++ Implementation of CLP. (ILOG) http://www.ilog.com/.
2. ILOG: (ILOG JSolver) http://www.ilog.com/.
3. Chun, A.H.W.: Constraint programming in Java with JSolver. In: Proceedings of the First International Conference on the Practical Application of Constraint Technologies and Logic Programming (PACLP99). (1999)
4. Koalog: (An Overview of Koalog Constraint Solver) http://www.koalog.com/.
5. Abddennadher, S., Krämer, E., Saft, M., Schumauss, M.: JACK: A Java constraint kit. In: Proceedings of the International Workshop on Functional and (Constraint) Logic Programming (WFLP 2001). (2001)
6. Artificial Intelligence Laboratory of EPFL Switzerland: (JCL: Java Constraint Library) http://liawww.epfl.ch/JCL/.
7. Tamura, N.: (Cream Programmers Guide) http://bach.istc.kobe-u.ac.jp/cream/.
8. Ohnishi, S., Tasaka, H., Tamura, N.: Efficient representation of discrete sets for constraint programming. In: Proceedings of the International Conference on Constraint Programming (CP-2003). (2003) 920–924
9. OpenOffice.org: (OpenOffice.org) http://www.openoffice.org/.
10. Banbara, M., Tamura, N., Inoue, K., Kawamura, T.: Java implementation of a heterogeneous constraint solving system. (final report of IPA Exploratory Software Project 2002) (2003)
11. Banbara, M., Tamura, N., Inoue, K., Kawamura, T., Hamaki, H.: Java implementation of a distributed constraint solving system. (final report of IPA Exploratory Software Project 2003) (2004)
12. Chew, T., David, J.M.: A constraint-based spreadsheet for cooperative production planning. In: Proceedings of the AAAI Sigman Workshop in Knowledge-Based Production Planning, Scheduling and Control. (1992)
13. Hyvönen, E., Pascale, S.D.: A new basis for spreadsheet computing: Interval solver for Microsoft Excel. In: Proceedings of the Sixteenth National Conference on Artificial Intelligence and Eleventh Conference on Innovative Applications of Artificial Intelligence (AAAI/IAAI 1999). (1999) 799–806
14. Adachi, Y.: Intellisheet: A spreadsheet system expanded by including constraint solvers. In: Proceedings of the IEEE Symposia on Human-Centric Computing Languages and Environments (HCC'01). (2001) 173–179
15. Gupta, G., Akhter, S.F.: Knowledgesheet: A graphical spreadsheet interface for interactively developing a class of constraint programs. (In: Proceedings of the Second International Workshop on Practical Aspects of Declarative Languages (PADL 2000)) 308–323

$\mathcal{O}(n \log n)$ Overload Checking for the Cumulative Constraint and Its Application[*]

Armin Wolf and Gunnar Schrader

Fraunhofer FIRST, Kekuléstr. 7, D-12489 Berlin, Germany
{Armin.Wolf|Gunnar.Schrader}@first.fraunhofer.de

Abstract. Overload checking is an important method for *unary* as well as for *cumulative* resource constraints in constraint-based scheduling, as it tests for a sufficient inconsistency property. While an algorithm with time complexity $\mathcal{O}(n \log n)$ exists that is known for unary resource constraints, to our knowledge no such algorithms have been established to date for overload checking in cumulative constraints on n tasks. In this paper, an $\mathcal{O}(n \log n)$ overload checking algorithm is presented as well as its application to a more specific problem domain: the non-overlapping placement of n rectangles in a two-dimensional area. There, the runtime complexity of overload checking is $\mathcal{O}(n^3 \log n)$.

1 Introduction

The allocation of activities or tasks on cumulative resources is a practical problem of strong relevance. It arises in resource constraint project scheduling as well as in production planning if continuous or non-attributable resources like water, electric power, or even human skills are to be taken into account. Thus, this problem is well-considered in constraint-based scheduling (e.g. in [1,3,5]). Generalised pruning rules exist that are adopted from the rules for unary resource which may only be allocated or used exclusively. These generalised rules are *overload checking, (extended) edge-finding* and *not-first/not-last detection*. To our knowledge, only algorithms are known that have quadratic or cubic runtime complexity with respect to the number of the considered tasks.

This paper presents a new $\mathcal{O}(n \log n)$ overload checking algorithm which proves the absence of an *overload*, i.e. the required workload for some tasks is never greater than the available capacity. Here, n is the number of considered tasks.

The paper is organised as follows. The next section formally defines the considered cumulative resource scheduling problem. Further, the term *overload* is defined and the corresponding checking rule is formulated in a general sense, i.e. for all non-empty subsets of the considered set of tasks. It is shown that only n specific subsets of tasks need be taken into account. In Section 3 efficient

---

[*] The work presented in this paper is funded by the European Union (EFRE) and the state of Berlin within the framework of the research project "inubit MRP", grant no. 10023515.

implementation issues are considered. Specifically, it is shown that structuring the tasks in balanced binary trees allows for an efficient $\mathcal{O}(n \log n)$ calculation of these maximal values adopting some recent approaches for the unary resource constraint problem [7,8]. Section 4 applies the presented overload checking developed for cumulative scheduling problems to a more specific problem domain: the non-overlapping placement of rectangles in a two-dimensional area. Finally, Section 5 concludes the work presented in this paper, summarises ongoing work and shows the directions of future work.

2   The Cumulative Resource Scheduling Problem

The *(non-preemptive) cumulative resource scheduling problem* represents the fact that some activities or *tasks* $t_1, \ldots, t_n$ requiring capacities $c(t_1), \ldots, c(t_n)$ have to be scheduled on a common resource offering a constant capacity C, such that the tasks are processed without interruption and without exceeding the capacity of the resource at any time. More formally, the problem is defined as follows:

Definition 1 (adopted from [3]). *A task t is a non-interruptible activity having a non-empty set of potential start times S_t, i.e. a finite integer set which is the domain of its variable start time. Furthermore, a task t has a fixed duration $d(t)$ and a fixed required capacity $c(t)$, both of which are positive integer values.*[1]

Given a non-empty set of tasks $T = \{t_1, \ldots, t_n\}$ ($n \geq 1$) and a common resource offering a capacity C, i.e. a positive integer value, the problem is to find a schedule, i.e. some start times $s(t_1) \in S_{t_1}, \ldots, s(t_n) \in S_{t_n}$ such that the cumulative constraint

$$\forall \tau : \sum_{t \in T, s(t) \leq \tau < s(t) + d(t)} c(t) \leq C$$

is satisfied, i.e. for each point in time τ the sum of the tasks' capacity requirements is not greater than the resource's capacity.

The cumulative resource scheduling problem is solvable *if such a schedule exists. Otherwise it is* unsolvable.

Finally, a cumulative resource scheduling problem is determined by this set of tasks T and the capacity C of the resource where they have to be scheduled.

In the following, we assume that such a set of tasks T and such a resource with capacity C is given, unless otherwise stated.

For each task $t \in T$ its *earliest start time* is $\mathsf{est}(t)$ and its *latest completion time* is $\mathsf{lct}(t)$. Given the actual set of potential start times S_t of a task $t \in T$ it holds $\mathsf{est}(t) := \min(S_t)$ and $\mathsf{lct}(t) := \max(S_t) + d(t)$. In extension, we define for each non-empty subset of tasks M of T ($M \neq \emptyset, M \subseteq T$):

$$\mathsf{est}(M) := \min_{t \in M}\{\mathsf{est}(t)\} \quad \text{and} \quad \mathsf{lct}(M) := \max_{t \in M}\{\mathsf{lct}(t)\} .$$

---

[1] A generalisation where only the *workload* $c(t) \cdot d(t)$ of the task t is fixed is possible, too.

Further, the *workload* of M is defined as

$$W(M) := \sum_{m \in M} c(m) \cdot d(m) \ .$$

2.1 Overload Checking

A necessary condition for the existence of a schedule for a cumulative resource scheduling problem determined by a set of tasks T and the capacity C is that each non-empty subset of tasks $M \neq \emptyset, M \subseteq T$ is not overloaded, i.e. the workload of the tasks in M is not greater than the available energy:

$$W(M) \leq C \cdot (\mathsf{lct}(M) - \mathsf{est}(M)) \ .$$

Here, the available energy is the product of the resource's capacity and the available time beginning at the earliest start time of the considered tasks and finishing at their latest completion time.

Proposition 1. *No schedule exists for the cumulative resource scheduling problem determined by a set of tasks T and the capacity C, if there is a non-empty subset of tasks $M \neq \emptyset, M \subseteq T$ such that there is an* overload, *i.e.*

$$W(M) > C \cdot (\mathsf{lct}(M) - \mathsf{est}(M))$$

holds.

Proof. We assume that there is a schedule for this problem, meaning that especially for $M := \{t_{i_1}, \dots, t_{i_k}\}$ there are start times $s(t_{i_1}) \in S_{t_{i_1}}, \dots, s(t_{i_k}) \in S_{t_{i_k}}$ such that the *cumulative constraint*

$$\forall \tau : \sum_{t \in M, s(t) \leq \tau < s(t)+d(t)} c(t) \leq C$$

is a fortiori satisfied. Thus, if we accumulate the workload of all tasks in M, it immediately follows that

$$\sum_{\mathsf{est}(M) \leq \tau < \mathsf{lct}(M)} \left(\sum_{t \in M, s(t) \leq \tau < s(t)+d(t)} c(t) \right) = W(M)$$

$$\leq C \cdot (\mathsf{lct}(M) - \mathsf{est}(M)) \ ,$$

i.e. there is no overload, which contradicts $W(M) > C \cdot (\mathsf{lct}(M) - \mathsf{est}(M))$. Thus, there is no schedule for the considered problem.   □

A naive overload checking of all $2^n - 1$ non-empty subsets of T is not necessary. As in the unary case, the consideration of at most n^2 *task intervals* [4,5,9] is sufficient. Recent advances [7,8] consider only n task intervals satisfying some optimality criterion. We show that in the cumulative case it is sufficient (and necessary) to consider n task intervals satisfying some adapted optimality criterion.

If for each $i = 1, \ldots, n$ a non-empty subset of tasks

$$P_i \subseteq \{t \mid t \in T \wedge \mathsf{lct}(t) \leq \mathsf{lct}(t_i)\}$$

is known such that $C \cdot \mathsf{est}(P_i) + W(P_i)$ is *maximal*, i.e.

$$C \cdot \mathsf{est}(P_i) + W(P_i)$$
$$= \max(\{C \cdot \mathsf{est}(N) + W(N) \mid N \neq \emptyset \wedge N \subseteq \{t \mid t \in T \wedge \mathsf{lct}(t) \leq \mathsf{lct}(t_i)\}\}) \;,$$

then these n sets of tasks have to be checked for an overload:

Proposition 2. *Let a cumulative resource scheduling problem be determined by a set of tasks T and a capacity C.*

Then, there is a set of tasks $M \neq \emptyset, M \subseteq T$ such that $W(M) > C \cdot (\mathsf{lct}(M) - \mathsf{est}(M))$ holds if and only if $C \cdot \mathsf{est}(P_i) + W(P_i) > C \cdot \mathsf{lct}(t_i)$ holds for an $i \in \{1, \ldots, n\}$ and a set of tasks $P_i \subseteq \{t \mid t \in T \wedge \mathsf{lct}(t) \leq lct(t_i)\}$, with $C \cdot \mathsf{est}(P_i) + W(P_i) = \max(\{C \cdot \mathsf{est}(Q) + W(Q) \mid Q \neq \emptyset \wedge Q \subseteq \{t \mid t \in T \wedge \mathsf{lct}(t) \leq \mathsf{lct}(t_i)\}\})$.

Proof. We assume that there is a set of tasks $M \neq \emptyset, M \subseteq T$ such that $W(M) > C \cdot (\mathsf{lct}(M) - \mathsf{est}(M))$ and thus $C \cdot \mathsf{est}(M) + W(M) > C \cdot \mathsf{lct}(M)$ holds. Then, let t_i be the task in M $(t \in M)$ such that $\mathsf{lct}(t_i) = \mathsf{lct}(M)$ holds. Obviously, $M \subseteq \{t \mid t \in T \wedge \mathsf{lct}(t) \leq \mathsf{lct}(t_i)\}$ holds and by the definition of P_i it follows that $C \cdot \mathsf{est}(P_i) + W(P_i) \geq C \cdot \mathsf{est}(M) + W(M) > C \cdot \mathsf{lct}(M)$ and thus $C \cdot \mathsf{est}(P_i) + W(P_i) > C \cdot \mathsf{lct}(t_i)$.

Now, if we assume that $C \cdot \mathsf{est}(P_i) + W(P_i) > C \cdot \mathsf{lct}(t_i)$ holds for an $i \in \{1, \ldots, n\}$ and a non-empty set of tasks $P_i \subseteq \{t \mid t \in T \wedge \mathsf{lct}(t) \leq lct(t_i)\}$, where $C \cdot \mathsf{est}(P_i) + W(P_i)$ is maximal. Obviously, for $M := P_i$ it holds that $C \cdot \mathsf{est}(M) + W(M) > C \cdot \mathsf{lct}(t_i) \geq C \cdot \mathsf{lct}(M)$ and thus $W(M) > C \cdot (\mathsf{lct}(M) - \mathsf{est}(M))$. $\quad\square$

The following interesting property of some sets of tasks which is especially valid for the sets P_i shows that these sets are task intervals:

Lemma 1. *Let a cumulative resource scheduling problem be determined by a non-empty set of tasks T and the capacity C and let a set of tasks $M \neq \emptyset, M \subseteq T$ be given. Further, let $P \neq \emptyset, P \subseteq M$ be a subset of tasks such that $C \cdot \mathsf{est}(P) + W(P)$ is maximal with respect to all non-empty subsets of M, i.e.*

$$C \cdot \mathsf{est}(P) + W(P) = \max_{N \neq \emptyset, N \subseteq M} \{C \cdot \mathsf{est}(N) + W(N)\} \;.$$

Then, for each task $t \in M$ with $\mathsf{est}(P) \leq \mathsf{est}(t)$ it holds that $t \in P$, i.e.

$$P = \{t \mid t \in M \wedge \mathsf{est}(t) \geq \mathsf{est}(P)\} \;.$$

Proof. Let us assume that there is a task $t \in M \setminus P$ with $\mathsf{est}(P) \leq \mathsf{est}(t)$. Then, $\mathsf{est}(P \cup \{t\}) = \mathsf{est}(P)$ and $W(P \cup \{t\}) = W(P) + c(t) \cdot d(t) > W(P)$ hold. Thus, $C \cdot \mathsf{est}(P \cup \{t\}) + W(P \cup \{t\}) > C \cdot \mathsf{est}(P) + W(P)$ holds, i.e. $C \cdot \mathsf{est}(P) + W(P)$ is *not* maximal with respect to all non-empty subsets of M. This means that for each task $t \in M$ with $\mathsf{est}(P) \leq \mathsf{est}(t)$ it holds that $t \in P$. $\quad\square$

Thus, $P_i = \{t \mid t \in T, \mathsf{est}(P_i) \leq \mathsf{est}(t), \mathsf{lct}(t) \leq \mathsf{lct}(t_i)\}$ holds for $i = 1, \ldots, n$.

3 Implementation Issues

Let a cumulative resource scheduling problem be given which is determined by a set of tasks $T = \{t_1, \ldots, t_n\}$ with $n \geq 1$ and a capacity C. We now assume that the tasks $t_1, \ldots, t_n$ are sorted in not-descending order with respect to their earliest start times, i.e. it holds that $\mathsf{est}(t_1) \leq \cdots \leq \mathsf{est}(t_n)$.

Furthermore, it is assumed that for each non-empty subset of tasks M of T ($M \neq \emptyset, M \subseteq T$) there is a corresponding *balanced binary tree* such that the following holds:

$$\forall t_i \in M \; \forall t_j \in \mathsf{Left}(t_i) : est(t_j) \leq est(t_i) \;,$$
$$\forall t_i \in M \; \forall t_j \in \mathsf{Right}(t_i) : est(t_j) \geq est(t_i) \;,$$

$$\forall t_i \in M : \mathsf{Left}(t_i) \cap \mathsf{Right}(t_i) = \emptyset$$
$$\forall t_i \in M : t_i \notin \mathsf{Left}(t_i) \cup \mathsf{Right}(t_i)$$
$$\exists t_r \in M : \mathsf{Left}(t_r) \cup \{t_r\} \cup \mathsf{Right}(t_r) = M \;.$$

Each node in the balanced tree named by the corresponding task $t_i \in M$ is annotated with:

- the *accumulated work* $W(t_i)$ to be performed in the subset of tasks in the subtree rooted by the task node t_i;
- the *maximal energy level* $E(t_i)$ of all non-empty subsets of tasks in the subtree rooted by the task node t_i.

To be precise, $W(t_i)$ and $E(t_i)$ are abbreviations:

$$W(t_i) := W(\{t_i\} \cup \mathsf{Left}(t_i) \cup \mathsf{Right}(t_i)) \;,$$
$$E(t_i) := E(\{t_i\} \cup \mathsf{Left}(t_i) \cup \mathsf{Right}(t_i)) \;.$$

While $W(M)$ is the sum of required work $c(t) \cdot d(t)$ of all tasks t in M, $E(M)$ is the maximum of the "base energy level" $C \cdot \mathsf{est}(N)$ plus the accumulated work $W(N)$ of all non-empty subsets N of the tasks in M (cf. Proposition 3).

To be complete and well-defined, we use the following conventions:

$$\max(\emptyset) := -\infty \;,$$
$$W(\emptyset) := 0 \;,$$
$$E(\emptyset) := -\infty \;.$$

Within the tree representing the non-empty subset of tasks M we define:

$$W(t_i) := W(\mathsf{Left}(t_i)) + c(t_i) \cdot d(t_i) + W(\mathsf{Right}(t_i)) \;,$$
$$E(t_i) := \max(\{E(\mathsf{Left}(t_i)) + c(t_i) \cdot d(t_i) + W(\mathsf{Right}(t_i)) \;,$$
$$C \cdot \mathsf{est}(t_i) + c(t_i) \cdot d(t_i) + W(\mathsf{Right}(t_i)),$$
$$E(\mathsf{Right}(t_i))\}) \;.$$

The following example shows how these values are computed in a concrete balanced binary tree:

Example 1. If there are tasks $T = \{t_1, \ldots, t_5\}$ with earliest start times (est) $2, 3, 4, 5, 6$ and workloads $(c \cdot d)$ $21, 15, 8, 9, 18$, and the overall capacity of the cumulative resource is $C = 5$, then the values W and E are computed from the leaves to the root within the corresponding balanced binary tree presented in Figure 1.

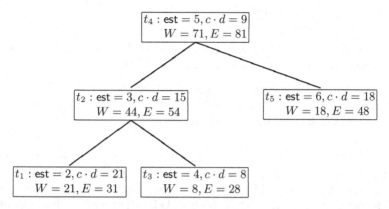

Fig. 1. A balanced binary tree of tasks and their corresponding workloads and energies

The next proposition shows that the intended values are actually computed as follows:

Proposition 3. *Let* $M := \{t_i\} \cup \mathsf{Left}(t_i) \cup \mathsf{Right}(t_i)$ *be a non-empty set of tasks in the subtree rooted by the task node* t_i. *Then, it holds that*

$$W(t_i) := W(M) = \sum_{s \in M} c(s) \cdot d(s) \ ,$$

$$E(t_i) := E(M) = \max(\{C \cdot \mathsf{est}(N) + W(N) \mid N \subseteq M \wedge N \neq \emptyset\}) \ .$$

Proof. By induction over the size of M.

Let $|M| = 1$, i.e. $M := \{t_i\}$ is a non-empty set of tasks in the subtree consisting of the task node t_i. By definition and conventions it holds that

$$W(t_i) := W(M) = 0 + c(t_i) \cdot d(t_i) + 0$$
$$= \sum_{s \in M} c(s) \cdot d(s) \ ,$$

$$E(t_i) := E(M) = \max(\{-\infty, C \cdot \mathsf{est}(t_i) + c(t_i) \cdot d(t_i) + 0, -\infty\})$$
$$= C \cdot \mathsf{est}(t_i) + W(t_i)$$
$$= \max(\{C \cdot \mathsf{est}(N) + W(N) \mid N \subseteq M \wedge N \neq \emptyset\})$$

because, there is only one such N, namely $\{t_i\}$.

Now, let $|M| = n + 1$ and t_i be the root in the binary tree which corresponds to M. Then, by induction hypothesis

$$W(M) := W(\mathsf{Left}(t_i)) + c(t_i) \cdot d(t_i) + W(\mathsf{Right}(t_i))$$

$$= \sum_{t \in \mathsf{Left}(t_i)} c(t) \cdot d(t) + (c(t_i) \cdot d(t_i)) + \sum_{t \in \mathsf{Right}(t_i)} c(t) \cdot d(t)$$

$$= \sum_{t \in \mathsf{Left}(t_i) \cup \{t_i\} \cup \mathsf{Right}(t_i)} c(t) \cdot d(t)$$

$$= \sum_{t \in M} c(t) \cdot d(t) \ .$$

Further, let $P \neq \emptyset, P \subseteq M$ be a subset of tasks such that $C \cdot \mathsf{est}(P) + W(P)$ is maximal with respect to all non-empty subsets of M, i.e.

$$C \cdot \mathsf{est}(P) + W(P) = \max_{N \neq \emptyset, N \subseteq M} \{C \cdot \mathsf{est}(N) + W(N)\} \ .$$

Now, we distinguish three different cases:

1. $\mathsf{est}(P) = \mathsf{est}(t_j)$ and $t_j \in \mathsf{Left}(t_i)$:
   Thus, by Lemma 1, it holds that $C \cdot \mathsf{est}(P) + W(P) = C \cdot \mathsf{est}(P) + W(\{t \in \mathsf{Left}(t_i) \mid \mathsf{est}(t) \geq \mathsf{est}(P)\}) + c(t_i) \cdot d(t_i) + W(\mathsf{Right}(t_i))$ because of the order in the tree. Further, $\mathsf{est}(P) + W(\{t \in \mathsf{Left}(t_i) \mid \mathsf{est}(t) \geq \mathsf{est}(P)\})$ is maximal with respect to all non-empty subsets of $\mathsf{Left}(t_i)$; otherwise there would be a non-empty $L \subseteq \mathsf{Left}(t_i)$ with $\mathsf{est}(L) \neq \mathsf{est}(P)$ such that $C \cdot \mathsf{est}(L) + W(L) > \mathsf{est}(P) + W(\{t \in \mathsf{Left}(t_i) \mid \mathsf{est}(t) \geq \mathsf{est}(P)\})$ would hold, i.e. $C \cdot \mathsf{est}(P) + W(P)$ would not be maximal with respect to all non-empty subsets of M. Thus, by induction hypothesis it holds that $E(\mathsf{Left}(t_i)) = C \cdot \mathsf{est}(P) + W(\{t \in \mathsf{Left}(t_i) \mid \mathsf{est}(t) \geq \mathsf{est}(P)\})$, i.e. the proposition about $E(M)$ holds.
2. $\mathsf{est}(P) = \mathsf{est}(t_i)$:
   Thus, by Lemma 1 it holds that $C \cdot \mathsf{est}(P) + W(P) = C \cdot \mathsf{est}(t_i) + c(t_i) \cdot d(t_i) + W(\mathsf{Right}(t_i))$ because of the order in the tree, i.e. the proposition about $E(M)$ holds.
3. $\mathsf{est}(P) = \mathsf{est}(t_j)$ and $t_j \in \mathsf{Right}(t_i)$:
   Thus, by Lemma 1 it holds that $C \cdot \mathsf{est}(P) + W(P) = C \cdot \mathsf{est}(P) + W(\{t \in \mathsf{Right}(t_i) \mid \mathsf{est}(t) \geq \mathsf{est}(P)\})$. Analogously to the first case, it holds that $\mathsf{est}(P) + W(\{t \in \mathsf{Right}(t_i) \mid \mathsf{est}(t) \geq \mathsf{est}(P)\})$ is maximal with respect to all non-empty subsets of $\mathsf{Right}(t_i)$. Thus, by induction hypothesis it holds that $E(\mathsf{Right}(t_i)) = C \cdot \mathsf{est}(P) + W(\{t \in \mathsf{Right}(t_i) \mid \mathsf{est}(t) \geq \mathsf{est}(P)\})$, i.e. the proposition about $E(M)$ holds. □

This means that based on the balanced binary trees for all subsets of tasks we are able to compute for each $i = 1, \ldots, n$ the value $C \cdot \mathsf{est}(P_i) + W(P_i)$ very efficiently:

Corollary 1. *Let a cumulative resource scheduling problem be determined by a set of tasks T and the capacity C. Consequently, the following holds for each $i = 1, \ldots, n$:*

$$E(\{t \mid t \in t \wedge \mathsf{lct}(t) \leq \mathsf{lct}(t_i)\})$$
$$= \max(\{C \cdot \mathsf{est}(Q) + W(Q) \mid Q \neq \emptyset \wedge Q \subseteq \{t \mid t \in T \wedge \mathsf{lct}(t) \leq \mathsf{lct}(t_i)\}\})$$
$$=: C \cdot \mathsf{est}(P_i) + W(P_i)$$

for the non-empty subset P_i.

Additionally, if we order the tasks in T such that $\mathsf{lct}(t_1) \leq \cdots \leq \mathsf{lct}(t_n)$ holds, then the computation of $E(\{t_1, \ldots, t_j, t_{j+1}\})$ based on the calculations for $E(\{t_1, \ldots, t_j\})$ has a complexity of $\mathcal{O}(\log n)$ for $j = 1, \ldots, n$. Thus, for all j the total complexity is $\mathcal{O}(n \log n)$.

Algorithm 1. An $\mathcal{O}(n \log n)$ overload checking algorithm for cumulative scheduling problems.

Input : An ordered sequence of tasks $T = \{t_1, \ldots, t_n\}$ such that
$\mathsf{lct}(t_1) \leq \cdots \leq \mathsf{lct}(t_n)$ holds
and the capacity C of the cumulative resource.
Private: A balanced binary tree M of tasks ordered with respect to their ests
and a maximal energy level E of all non-empty subsets of tasks
within this balanced binary tree M.

1 **begin**
2     $M \leftarrow \emptyset$;
3   **for** $i = 1, \ldots, n$ **do**
4        $M \leftarrow M \cup \{t_i\}$;
5   compute $E \leftarrow E(M)$;
       // overload check:
6   **if** $E > C \cdot \mathsf{lct}(t_i)$ **then**
7   exit with failure;
          // because of the detected overload

8 **end**

Proposition 4. *Let a cumulative resource scheduling problem be determined by a set of tasks T and the capacity C. Then, Algorithm 1 performs overload checking with a runtime complexity of $\mathcal{O}(n \log n)$.*

Proof. The correctness of the algorithm and its $\mathcal{O}(n \log n)$ runtime complexity follows immediately from Proposition 2, using Corollary 1. $\square$

Example 2. Considering the tasks T in Example 1. If for their latest completion time $\mathsf{lct}(T) \leq 16$ holds, then there is an overload because

$$E(T) = 81 > 80 \geq C \cdot \mathsf{lct}(T)$$

holds, too.

4   Overload Checking for Non-overlapping Rectangles

Overload checking for cumulative scheduling is also applicable to non-overlapping rectangle placement problems in a two-dimensional area. These problems are defined as follows:

Definition 2 (adopted from [2]).
A rectangle r has a non-empty set of X-values X_r, i.e. a finite integer set which is the domain of its variable x-coordinate as well as a non-empty set of Y-values Y_r, i.e. a finite integer set which is the domain of its variable y-coordinate. Furthermore, a rectangle r has a fixed width $w(t)$ and a fixed height $h(t)$, both of which are positive integer values.

Given a non-empty set of rectangles $R = \{r_1, \ldots, r_n\}$ ($n > 1$) the problem is to find a non-overlapping placement *of these rectangles, i.e. some x- and y-coordinates $x(r_1) \in X_{r_1}, y(r_1) \in Y_{r_1}, \ldots, x(r_n) \in X_{r_n}, y(r_n) \in Y_{r_n}$ such that the condition*

$$\bigwedge_{1 \leq i < j \leq n} (x(r_i) \leq x(r_j) < x(r_i) + w(r_i) \vee x(r_j) \leq x(r_i) < x(r_j) + w(r_j))$$
$$\longrightarrow \quad (y(r_i) + h(r_i) \leq y(r_j) \vee y(r_j) + h(r_j) \leq y(r_i))$$
$$\wedge \quad (y(r_i) \leq y(r_j) < y(r_i) + h(r_i) \vee y(r_j) \leq y(r_i) < y(r_j) + h(r_j))$$
$$\longrightarrow \quad (x(r_i) + w(r_i) \leq x(r_j) \vee x(r_j) + w(r_j) \leq x(r_i))$$

is satisfied, i.e. if any two different rectangles might overlap on the x-axis then one must be above or below the other and if they might overlap in the y-axis then one must be left or right from the other.

The non-overlapping placement problem for rectangles is solvable *if such a placement exists. Otherwise it is* unsolvable. *Finally, such a non-overlapping placement problem is* determined *by the given set of rectangles R.*

One necessary condition for an overlap-free placement of some rectangles in a two-dimensional area is the availability of enough space in each horizontal (vertical) stripe bounded by the minimum and maximum y-coordinates (x-coordinates) of each non-empty subset containing those rectangles having y-coordinates (x-coordinates) between these boundaries. — Due to symmetry, only horizontal stripes are considered in the following; the "vertical case" behaves similar.

For a formal proposition, we define for any non-empty subset of rectangles $P \neq \emptyset, P \subseteq R$ the values

$$X_{\min}(P) := \min(\bigcup_{p \in P} X_p) \quad \text{and} \quad X_{\max}(P) := \max(\{\max(X_p) + h(p) \mid p \in P\}) \ ,$$

$$Y_{\min}(P) := \min(\bigcup_{p \in P} Y_p) \quad \text{and} \quad Y_{\max}(P) := \max(\{\max(Y_p) + h(p) \mid p \in P\}) \ .$$

Proposition 5. *No placement exists for a non-overlapping placement problem determined by a set of rectangles R, if there is a non-empty subset of rectangles $P \neq \emptyset, P \subseteq R$ such that there is an* overload, *i.e.*

$$\sum_{p \in P} w(p) \cdot h(p) > (X_{\max}(P) - X_{\min}(P)) \cdot (Y_{\max}(P) - Y_{\min}(P))$$

holds.

Proof. We assume that there is a placement for this problem, meaning that especially for $P := \{r_{i_1}, \ldots, r_{i_k}\} =: \{p_1, \ldots, p_k\}$ there are coordinates $x(p_1) \in X_{p_1}, y(p_1) \in Y_{p_1}, \ldots, x(p_k) \in X_{p_k}, y(p_k) \in Y_{p_k}$ such that the condition

$$\bigwedge_{1 \leq i < j \leq k} (x(p_i) \leq x(p_j) < x(p_i) + w(p_i) \vee x(p_j) \leq x(p_i) < x(p_j) + w(p_j))$$
$$\longrightarrow \quad (y(p_i) + h(p_i) \leq y(p_j) \vee y(p_j) + h(p_j) \leq y(p_i))$$
$$\wedge \quad (y(p_i) \leq y(p_j) < y(p_i) + h(p_i) \vee y(p_j) \leq y(p_i) < y(p_j) + h(p_j))$$
$$\longrightarrow \quad (x(p_i) + w(p_i) \leq x(p_j) \vee x(p_j) + w(p_j) \leq x(p_i))$$

is satisfied, i.e. the rectangles in P are placed overlap-free in the 2-dimensional area $[X_{\min}(P), X_{\max}(P)] \times [Y_{\min}(P), Y_{\max}(P)]$. Thus, as deduced from geometry, it immediately follows that the occupied area fits in the available area:

$$\sum_{p \in P} w(p) \cdot h(p) \leq (X_{\max}(P) - X_{\min}(P)) \cdot (Y_{\max}(P) - Y_{\min}(P)) \ ,$$

i.e. there is no overload. This contradiction disproves our assumption, thus there is no placement for the considered problem.   □

Example 3. The non-overlapping placement of the rectangles $R := \{A, B, C\}$ in Figure 2 requires that

- each rectangle r has enough space in the stripe reaching from $\min(Y_r)$ to $\max(Y_r) + h(r)$ — which is obviously satisfied per definition,
- A and B have enough space in the stripe reaching from $Y_{\min} = 0$ to $Y_{\max} = 5$,
- B and C have enough space in the stripe reaching from $Y_{\min} = 2$ to $Y_{\max} = 7$,
- A and C have enough space in the widest stripe from $Y_{\min} = 0$ to $Y_{\max} = 7$ — which is obviously covered by the next condition,
- all rectangles have enough space in the stripe reaching from $Y_{\min}(R) = \min(\bigcup_{r \in R} Y_r) = 0$ to $Y_{\max}(R) = \max(\{\max(Y_r) + h(r) \mid r \in R\}) = 7$,

which is satisfied for this problem instance.

Now, considering any such subset of rectangles $P \neq \emptyset, P \subseteq R$ and the boundaries of the horizontal stripe reaching from $Y_{\min} = \min(\bigcup_{r \in P} Y_r)$ to $Y_{\max} = \max(\{\max(Y_r) + h(r) \mid r \in P\})$ the cumulative scheduling problem determined by the set of tasks

$$T_P = \{t_r \mid r \in P \wedge S_{t_r} = X_r \wedge d(t_r) = w(r) \wedge c(t_r) = h(r)\}$$

and the capacity $C_P = Y_{\max}(P) - Y_{\min}(P)$ must be solvable, otherwise the non-overlapping placement problem defined by R is unsolvable. — We call the cumulative scheduling problem determined by T_P and C_P the *cumulative problem of P*.

Proposition 6. *Let a non-overlapping placement problem be determined by a set of rectangles R. If this problem is solvable, then for any non-empty subset of rectangles $P \neq \emptyset, P \subseteq R$ the cumulative problem of P is solvable, too.*

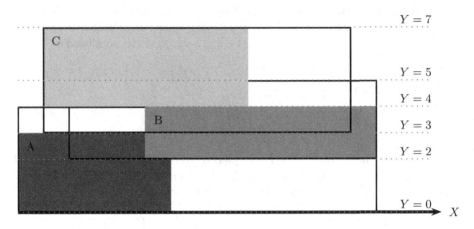

Fig. 2. A non-overlapping placement problem for some rectangles A, B, and C

Proof. We assume that there is a non-overlapping placement of the rectangles in $R = \{r_1, \ldots, r_n\}$, i.e. some valid x- and y-coordinates $x(r_1) \in X_{r_1}, y(r_1) \in Y_{r_1}, \ldots, x(r_n) \in X_{r_n}, y(r_n) \in Y_{r_n}$. We now consider any non-empty subset $P := \{p_1, \ldots, p_m\} \subseteq R$. Further, for any fixed x-coordinate x let $P_x := \{p \in P \mid x(p) \leq x < x(p) + w(p)\} =: \{p_{x_1}, \ldots, p_{x_k}\}$. We assume that the rectangles in P_x are ordered such that

$$y(p_{x_1}) < y(p_{x_1}) + h(p_{x_1}) \leq y(p_{x_2}) < \ldots \leq y(p_{x_{k-1}}) < y(p_{x_k}) + h(p_{x_k})$$

holds. Such an order exists because the rectangles are placed overlap-free.

Defining $Y_{min}(P) := \min(\bigcup_{p \in P} Y_p)$ and $Y_{max}(P) := \max(\{\max(Y_p) + h(p) \mid p \in P\})$ it follows immediately that

$$\sum_{j=1}^{k} h(p_{x_j}) \leq Y_{max}(P) - Y_{min}(P)$$

holds, especially if P_x is empty; then the sum's value is zero. Consequently,

$$\forall x : \sum_{p \in P, x(p) \leq x < x(p) + w(p)} h(p) \leq C_P$$

is satisfied for $C_P := Y_{max}(P) - Y_{min}(P)$, i.e. the cumulative problem of P is solvable, too. $\square$

Obviously, only at most n^2 cumulative problems have to be checked for solvability: for any two rectangles p and q with $\min(Y_p) \leq \max(Y_q) + h(q)$ and where the subset of rectangles[2]

$$I_{p,q} := \{r \in R \mid \min(Y_p) \leq \min(Y_r) \wedge \max(Y_r) + h(r) \leq max(Y_q) + h(q)\}$$

---

[2] The definition of this subset is adopted from the definition of *task intervals* [4,5,9].

is non-empty the problem $C_{I_{p,q}}$ has to be considered. Thus, for an overload checking concering non-overlapping placement of n rectangles we have to perform these checks for at most $n(n-1)/2$ cumulative scheduling problems over at most n tasks which has in total a runtime complexity of $\mathcal{O}(n^3 \log n)$ if the necessary subsets of rectangles are determined. However, their determination might be performed while *sweeping* (cf. [2,9]) over the boundaries of the stripes:

For a given set of rectangles $R = \{r_1, \ldots, r_n\}$ to be placed overlap-free, each minimal and each different maximal y-coordinate plus height is considered as an *event*. We assume that these $m \leq 2n$ events are sorted such that $e_u \leq e_v$ holds for $1 \leq u \leq v \leq m$ and $u < v$ holds if $\min(Y_{r_i})_u = (\max(Y_{r_j}) + h(r_j))_v$ holds for $1 \leq i, j \leq n$. Then we iterate from 1 to m over these events. An event which represents a minimal y-coordinate appends the corresponding rectangle to a list of rectangles which is initially empty. An event which represents a

---

Algorithm 2. An $\mathcal{O}(n^3 \log n)$ overload checking algorithm for non-overlapping placement problems.

Input : A set of rectangles $R = \{r_1, \ldots, r_n\}$ and an ordered sequence of events $E = e_1, \ldots, e_m (m \leq 2n)$ containing each minimal y-coordinate (possible more than once) and each different maximal y-coordinate plus height (only once), such that it holds
  – $e_u \leq e_v$ for $1 \leq u \leq v \leq m$ and
  – $u < v$ if $\min(Y_{r_i})_u = (\max(Y_{r_j}) + h(r_j))_v$ is valid for $1 \leq i, j \leq n$.
Output: false, if an overload is detected; true otherwise.
Private: A list of rectangles L, a subset of rectangles P, and a y-coordinate c;

```
1  begin
2  │  L ← λ;
   │  // the list of rectangles is initially empty
3  │  for u = 1, . . . , m do
4  │  │  if e_u = min(Y_{r_i}) then
5  │  │  │  L ← L ∘ r_i;
6  │  │  else if e_u = max(Y_{r_j}) + h(r_j) then
7  │  │  │  P ← ∅;
8  │  │  │  c ← ∞;
9  │  │  │  let L = r_{i_1} ∘ · · · ∘ r_{i_k};
10 │  │  │  for v = k, . . . , 1 do
11 │  │  │  │  if max(Y_{r_v}) + h(r_v) ≤ e_u then
12 │  │  │  │  │  if min(Y_{r_v}) < c then
13 │  │  │  │  │  │  if |P| > 1 then
14 │  │  │  │  │  │  │  check the cumulative problem of P for an overload;
   │  │  │  │  │  │  │  // here C_P = e_u − c
15 │  │  │  │  │  │  │  if there is an overload return false;
16 │  │  │  │  │  │  c ← min(Y_{r_v});
17 │  │  │  │  │  P ← P ∪ {r_v};
18 │  return true;
19 end
```

maximal y-coordinate performs a backward iteration over this list maintaining a set of rectangles which is initially empty. During this inner iteration, it is checked whether the maximal y-coordinate is less than or equal to the current event's value. If so, the maintained set — if containing more than one rectangle — defines a new cumulative scheduling problem within the stripe reaching from the minimal y-coordinate of the last recently considered rectangle in the list to the value of the currently considered event. The current value is then noted as the new final one to be most recently considered and added to the maintained set. — All these processing steps are summarised in Algorithm 2.

This algorithm assumes the generation and sorting of the events which have a runtime complexity of $\mathcal{O}(n \log n)$ for n rectangles. Additionally the generation of the sets of rectangles for each stripe has quadratic runtime complexity. Thus, in total, the runtime complexity for overload checking concerning n rectangles to be placed overlap-free is $O(n^3 \log n)$. A fortiori, this also holds for the special case where all rectangles have unary heights, i.e. all capacity requirements are one. Thus, for the *alternative resources constraint* [10] the presented runtime complexity of $\mathcal{O}(n^4)$ has now been improved to be $\mathcal{O}(n^3 \log n)$ for n tasks.

5   Conclusion, Ongoing and Future Work

In this paper we formulated the rule for *overload checking* in cumulative scheduling. This formulation is based on some subsets of tasks maximising some values, which are used for deciding and performing pruning. Based on this theoretical work, we showed and formally proved that the structuring of the tasks in balanced binary trees allows for the efficient $\mathcal{O}(n \log n)$ calculation of the maximised values, and thus the $\mathcal{O}(n \log n)$ runtime performance of the formulated and proved overload checking rule. Further, we applied overload checking for cumulative problems to non-overlapping placement problems of rectangles resulting in an overload checking algorithm for these problems having $\mathcal{O}(n^3 \log n)$ runtime complexity. Future work focuses on the improvement of this algorithm. We will examine whether there are sets of rectangles satisfying some maximality criterion that allows again the usage of balanced binary trees reducing the runtime complexity hopefully to $\mathcal{O}((n \log n)^2)$.

To date, we have realised and used a first implementation of the presented overload checking algorithm within our `firstcs` (FIRST's Constraint Solver) Java library [6]. Our main focus hereby was first of all a practical proof of concept of the theoretical results described above. We tested the implementation against a first real-world resource allocation problem, where episodes of several TV programmes (several hundreds) must be distributed to a given number of video recorders (around five) for recording. There we used the alternative resource constraint and a redundant cumulative constraint for energetic reasoning. Especially, the efficient overload checking of the cumulative constraint was used to decide whether the number of available video recorders is sufficient instead of the $\mathcal{O}((n^4)$ algorithm presented in [10]. This results in a faster detection of inconsistencies.

In the medical domain we can now more efficiently compute the minimum amount of resources like dialysers or CT apparatus in order to achieve maximal daily throughputs of patients. In a similar vein, a calculation can be made to match the number of available beds with the amount of operations to be performed. The necessary hospital staff can easily be factored into this equation.

References

1. Philippe Baptiste, Claude le Pape, and Wim Nuijten. *Constraint-Based Scheduling*. Number 39 in International Series in Operations Research & Management Science. Kluwer Academic Publishers, 2001.
2. Nicolas Beldiceanu and Mats Carlsson. Sweep as a generic pruning technique applied to the non-overlapping rectangles constraint. In Toby Walsh, editor, *Principles and Practice of Constraint Programming – CP 2001, 7th International Conference*, volume 2239 of *Lecture Notes in Computer Science*, pages 377–391. Springer Verlag, 2001.
3. Nicolas Beldiceanu and Evelyne Contjean. Introducing global constraints in CHIP. *Mathematical and Computer Modelling*, 12:97–123, 1994.
4. Yves Caseau and François Laburthe. Improved CLP scheduling with task intervals. In Pascal van Hentenryck, editor, *Proceedings of the Eleventh International Conference on Logic Programming, ICLP'94*, pages 369–383. MIT Press, 1994.
5. Yves Caseau and François Laburthe. Cumulative scheduling with task intervals. In Michael J. Maher, editor, *Proceedings of the 13th Joint International Conference and Syposium on Logic Programming - JICSLP 1996*, pages 363–377. MIT Press, 1996.
6. Matthias Hoche, Henry Müller, Hans Schlenker, and Armin Wolf. firstcs - A Pure Java Constraint Programming Engine. In Michael Hanus, Petra Hofstedt, and Armin Wolf, editors, *2nd International Workshop on Multiparadigm Constraint Programming Languages – MultiCPL'03*, 29th September 2003. Online available at **uebb.cs.tu-berlin.de/MultiCPL03/Proceedings.MultiCPL03.RCoRP03.pdf**.
7. Petr Vilím. $\mathcal{O}(n \log n)$ filtering algorithms for unary resource constraint. In *Proceedings of the International Conference on Integration of AI and OR Techniques in Constraint Programming for Combinatorical Optimisation Problems – CP-AI-OR'04*, volume 3011 of *Lecture Notes in Computer Science*, pages 335–347. Springer Verlag, 2004.
8. Petr Vilím, Roman Barták, and Ondřej Čepek. Unary resource constraint with optional activities. In Marc Wallace, editor, *Principles and Practice of Constraint Programming – CP 2004, 10th International Conference*, volume 3258 of *Lecture Notes in Computer Science*, pages 62–76. Springer Verlag, 2004.
9. Armin Wolf. Pruning while sweeping over task intervals. In Francesca Rossi, editor, *Principles and Practice of Constraint Programming – CP 2003, 9th International Conference*, volume 2833 of *Lecture Notes in Computer Science*, pages 739–753. Springer Verlag, 2003.
10. Armin Wolf and Hans Schlenker. Realizing the alternative resources constraint. In D. Seipel, M. Hanus, U. Geske, and O. Bartenstein, editors, *15th International Conference on Applications of Declarative Programming and Knowledge Management, INAP 2004, and the 18th Workshop on Logic Programming, WLP 2004, Potsdam, Germany, March 4-6, 2004, Revised Selected Papers*, volume 3392 of *Lecture Notes in Artificial Intelligence*, pages 185–199. Springer Verlag, 2005.

Inductive Logic Programming:
Yet Another Application of Logic

Akihiro Yamamoto

Graduate School of Informatics
Kyoto University
Yoshida-Honmachi, Sakyo-ku, Kyoto 606-8501 Japan
akihiro@i.kyoto-u.ac.jp

Abstract. This paper presents a brief introduction of the relation between logic programming and machine learning. The area researching the
relation is usually called Inductive Logic Programming (ILP, for short).
In this paper we will give the details of neither ILP systems nor ILP theories. We explain how to substitute concepts used in logic programming
to items needed in formulating learning theories. We also show some
theoretical applications to which the substitution are contributing.

1   Introduction

Inductive Logic Programming (*ILP*, for short) is the research area where systems
and theories for machine learning are developed with mathematical logic and
logic programming. *Machine learning* is mechanization of learning, which is an
intellectual human activity, and has been investigated in Artificial Intelligence
for a long time. Recently Machine learning has become one of foundations of
knowledge discovery and data mining, for discovering useful knowledge from
huge amount of data.

Mathematical logic is a formalization of *deductive inference* by human beings.
It is closely related to computation and gives a theoretical foundation of Computer Science. Logic programming is one of precise representation of the relation
between logic and computation. In mathematical logic consequences are derived
from premises by applying logical rules. Learning can be regarded as deriving
general rules from concrete examples given by teachers. In other words, learning
is an *inductive inference*, which is usually regarded as the converse of deductive
inference. This is one of the reasons why machine learning with mathematical
logic is investigated.

However, we should note that computation is activity done by one person or
one computer, after input data is provided, while learning is interactive activity
of at least two types of agents: teachers providing examples and learners generating rules from the examples. In ILP, examples and rules are corresponded with
logical consequences and logical premises, respectively. Derived rules by learners
may change in the process of learning, as the total amount of provided examples increase. Therefore we should call the rules conjectures or hypotheses, and
have to give some methods for ensuring that the conjectures are correct. The

M. Umeda et al. (Eds.): INAP 2005, LNAI 4369, pp. 102–116, 2006.
© Springer-Verlag Berlin Heidelberg 2006

concept of correctness in mathematical logic is useful to define that of learning, but correctness of learning would be quite different because of the nature of mathematical logic and learning.

We start this tutorial with a simple example of learning a concept, in the next section. In Section 3 we explain a traditional formalization of learning and substitute each of the items in the formalization with a concept used in logic programming. In Section 4 we introduce a kind of deductive inference which is called refinement and useful for generating hypotheses in learning. Section 5 presents a famous concept called common generalization or anti-unification in the context of learning from positive presentations. We show some application of the substitution in Section 6, and conclude with some remarks in Section 7.

2   An Example of Learning Process

Let us start with assuming agents of two types, a *teacher* and a *learner*. The teacher is assumed to have something to tell the learner, and the learner should get something which the teachers know. In order to make our discussion simple, what the teacher is teaching is a concept, called *the target concept* and the learner is making his/her effort to get the concept.

Generally speaking, the activity *learning* becomes necessary in the case that the teacher cannot send the whole of the target concept in finite time or that the learner cannot receive it in finite time. In stead the teacher sends examples of the target, and the learner conjectures the target from the given examples and represents its conjecture in the form of a hypothesis. The teacher may give more and more examples, and in such situations, the learner must be able to change his/her current hypothesis, at least when it notices that the hypothesis is not appropriate for the added examples.

Let us consider a situation that a human teacher is teaching the concept of even numbers to a human learner, e.g. a child. The teacher will give the learner examples like:

> 4 is an even number.
> 3 is not an even number.
> 2 is an even number.
> 6 is an even number.
> 1 is not an even number
> 5 is not an even number.
> . . .

The teacher expects the learner to find a rule representing the whole of even numbers. The rule may depend on the language the learner has. For example, if the learner knows the division operation, he/she may derive a sentence for even number such as:

> A number is even if it can be divided by 2.

If the learner does not know the operation, he/she must derive a more complicated sentence.

Now let us suppose we have a *learning machine* which uses logic programs for its input and output. A *logic program* is a finite set of definite clauses and a *definite clause* is a logical formula either of the form $A \leftarrow B_1, B_2, \ldots, B_n$ or of the form $A \leftarrow$, where all of $A, B_1, B_2, \ldots$, and B_n are *atomic formulae(atoms)*. It is well-known that, for a logic program P, there is the *least Herbrand model*, which is denoted by $M(P)$. A natural number $n \geq 0$ is represented with a term

$$\overbrace{\mathsf{s(s(\cdots(s(\,0))))))}}^{n \text{ times}}.$$

When we would like to teach the learning machine the concept of even numbers, the input would be as follows:

$$\mathsf{even(s(s(s(s(0)))))},$$
$$\leftarrow \mathsf{even(s(s(s(0))))},$$
$$\mathsf{even(s(s(0)))},$$
$$\mathsf{even(s(s(s(s(s(0))))))},$$
$$\leftarrow \mathsf{even(s(0))},$$
$$\leftarrow \mathsf{even(s(s(s(s(0))))))},$$

. . . .

The formula $\leftarrow A$ means the negation of a ground atom A. We are expecting, as a teacher of the learning machine, that the machine should generate a logic program like

$$P_{\mathsf{even}} = \left\{ \begin{array}{l} \mathsf{even(0)} \\ \mathsf{even(s(s(X)))} \leftarrow \mathsf{even(X)} \end{array} \right\}.$$

In ILP concept learning is called *learning from interpretations*. Off course, learning from interpretations is one type of learning and we could consider different types of learning. For example, in *learning from proofs,* a teacher gives a learner not only what are examples but also how to prove the examples.

3   Formalization of Learning

According to the traditional theory of machine learning, which has been called the theory of *inductive inference* [3,14], we introduce items needed in formalizing machine learning procedures. We substitute each of the items with a concept in logic programming, and then define machine learning procedures and its correctness. At first we fix a first-order language $\mathcal{L}$.

3.1   Objects, Concepts, Hypotheses, and Languages

Objects: We fix the set $\mathcal{U}$ of all possible objects or observations. Every object in $\mathcal{U}$ has exactly one representation in a language $\mathcal{L}_O$, called the *observational* language. We identify an object and its representation with assuming that every object has exactly one representation. In the learning of even numbers by children, objects are natural numbers, while for the learning machine with logic programming we let an object to be a ground atom **even**(t) where t is a ground term constructed of the function symbol **s** and the constant symbol 0. More generally speaking, $\mathcal{L}_O$ is the *Herbrand base*, the set HB of all ground atoms.

Concepts: We define a *concept* as a subset of U to be considered. The set of all concepts is called the *concept class* and denoted by $\mathcal{C}$. Fixing the concept class $\mathcal{C}$ realizes the assumption that the teacher and the learner share the definition of concepts. The teacher chooses a concept from $\mathcal{C}$ for the *target concept*, and provides examples for it to the learners. For the child explained in the last section the target concept is the set of all even numbers, and for the learning machine it is the set

$$M_{\mathbf{even}} = \left\{ \mathbf{even}(t) \;\middle|\; \begin{array}{l} t \text{ is a gound term constructed of } \mathbf{s} \text{ and } 0, \\ \text{and } s \text{ occurs in } t \text{ in } 2n \text{ times } (n \geq 0) \end{array} \right\}.$$

In the setting of learning from interpretations, a concept is the least Herbrand model $M(P)$ of a logic program P. Here we have to stress that $M(P)$ is defined with a program P called a hypothesis. In other words the concept $M(P)$ is parameterized with a hypothesis P. We require this parameterization of concepts in general.

Hypotheses: We introduce a *hypothetical language*, denoted by $\mathcal{L}_H$, in order to represent each concept in a sentence. Every sentence in the language is called a *hypothesis*. We require that every hypothesis h should represent exactly one concept $C(h) \in \mathcal{C}$ and that every concept $C \in \mathcal{C}$ must be represented by at least one hypothesis h. However, we do not require that every concept should be represented by exactly one hypothesis. We allow two hypotheses h and h' such that $C(h) = C(h')$.

The child would represent the set of even numbers in their natural language, e.g. English, while the rule generated by the learning machine is a logic program P the least Herbrand model of which coincides to the set $M_{\mathbf{even}}$. One of such programs is $P_{\mathbf{even}}$.

3.2 Examples, Learning Procedures, and Correctness of Learning

Training Examples: A *training example* (an *example*, for short) for a target concept C is positive or negative. A *positive example* for C is an element of C provided to the learner with a sign showing that it is in C. A *negative example* for C is an element of $U - C$ with a sign showing that it is not in C. Off course examples are represented in the natural language for the children. In concept learning with logic programming, as is shown in the last section, it is often assumed that every positive example is provided in the form of ground atom A and every negative is provided in the form of $\leftarrow A$.

Learning Procedures: At the beginning of learning a teacher fix a target concept $C \in \mathcal{C}$. A *learning procedure* must at least take examples as its inputs and make outputs by using the inputs. Variations of learning procedures are from what the inputs are and what the outputs are. A simple procedure generates and outputs just hypotheses in $\mathcal{L}_H$ as conjectures. Some procedures would be allowed to give queries to the teacher. It is usually assumed that the learning procedure successfully generates a hypothesis at each step, that is, the hypothesis generation process must terminate.

Correctness of Learning: In order to ensure the activity of learning procedures, we introduce two types of criteria for inference.

A *local* criterion is defined as a relation between E_n and h_n, where $E_n = \{e_1, e_2, \ldots, e_n\}$ is the set of examples given to the current inference algorithm from the starting of the inference to some moment and h_n is a hypothesis generated from E_n. A *global criterion* restricts the properties of sequence of hypotheses h_1, h_2, ... output by the inference algorithm, whether or not the sequence is finite or infinite.

An example of local criteria is *consistency*. We say that a learning procedure has the *consistency property* if every h_n explains the set E_n of examples. It is advantage of using logic programming that this criterion can be represented in terms of mathematical logic. A logic program P_n used as a hypothesis explains E_n if $P_n \models A_i$ for every positive example $e_i = A_i$ in E_n and $P_n \not\models A_i$ for every negative example $e_i = \leftarrow A_i$ in E_n.

If a partial order of concepts is defined, we can add another local criterion that every hypothesis must explain minimal in the partial order. An example of global criteria is *identification in the limit* explained in the following subsection.

3.3   Identification in the Limit

In this subsection we explain a general learning procedure which satisfies consistency and identification in the limit.

We treat a simple learning procedure which just takes examples one by one from a teacher and generates hypotheses from the examples. The teacher feeds examples perpetually and the procedure must make hypotheses perpetually. Under this setting we define a *presentation* for a target concept $C \in \mathcal{C}$ as an infinite sequence of examples for C.

We can consider at least two types of feeding examples. The first one is to feed all positive and negative examples, and the second one is to give only positive examples. A presentation σ for C is *complete* if any element in C occurs in σ at least once as a positive example and any element in $U - C$ occurs at least once as a negative example. The presentation σ is *positive* if any element in C occurs in σ at least once as a positive example and no negative example appears in it.

The learning procedure *identifies C in the limit* if, for *any* complete representation σ of C, after accepting finite number n of examples from σ, it outputs a hypothesis h_n such that $C = C(h_n)$ and never outputs other hypotheses any more. Note that $C = C(h_*)$ for some hypothesis h_* but that the definition above does

Procedure Learn_by_Enumeration_and_Test
Assume an enumeration $P_1, P_2, \ldots, P_k, \ldots$ of all programs in $\mathcal{H}$
$k := 1;$
for $n = 1$ **forever**
    take an example $e_n = A_n$ or $\leftarrow A_n;$
    $i = 1;$
    while $(i \le n)$
        if $(e_i = A_i$ and $A_i \notin M(P_k))$ or $(e_i = \leftarrow A_i$ and $A_i \in M(P_k))$ **then**
            $k + +; i = 1 ;$
        else
            $i + +;$
    output P_k as a hypothesis;

Fig. 1. A learning procedure based on the enumeration-and-test strategy

not require $h_* = h_n$. This means that the machine learns concepts, not hypothesis. The procedure identifies $\mathcal{C}$ in the limit if it identifies every concept C in it.

In Fig. 1 we illustrate in terms of ILP an example of learning procedures which identifies $\mathcal{C}$ in the limit. The procedure is based on the *enumeration and test* principle, under the following assumptions for the hypothetical language $\mathcal{L}_H$:

1. There is a procedure enumerating all logic programs in $\mathcal{L}_H$, that is, there is an effective enumeration $P_1, P_2, P_3, \ldots$ of logic programs in $\mathcal{L}_H$ and every elements occurs in the enumeration at least once.
2. For every program $P_i \in \mathcal{L}_H$ and for every ground atom A in HB, it is decidable whether or not $A \in M(P_i)^1$.

The set of all *linear logic program* [6,35] is an example of such hypothetical languages. Another example is defined with *Datalog programs* [19,37]. A Datalog program may contain negations in the bodies of clauses in it. The set of Datalog programs containing no negation satisfies the two assumptions above.

4   Refiniment of Hypotheses by Deductive Inference

We show that deductive inference can be used for generation of hypotheses in the procedure in Fig. 1. The deductive inference is called *refinement* of hypotheses.

Let us assume that a partial order $\succeq$ on the hypothetical language $\mathcal{L}_H$ is defined so that $P \succeq Q$ implies $M(P) \supseteq M(Q)$, and we define $P \equiv Q$ iff $M(P) = M(Q)$. A *refinement operator* is a recursive mapping $\rho : \mathcal{L}_H \longrightarrow 2^{\mathcal{L}_H}$ satisfying the following conditions [21,29,35]:

- For every $P \in \mathcal{L}_H$, $\rho(P)$ is a finite set.
- If $Q \in \rho(P)$, $P \succeq Q$.
- For every $P \in \mathcal{L}_H$, no infinite sequence $P_1, P_2, P_3, \ldots$ starting with $P_1 = P$ satisfies $P_i \in \rho(P_{i+1})$ for all $i = 1, 2, \ldots$.

---

[1] An example of this realization is by *h-easiness* of P_i introduced in [35].

We inductively define an operator $\rho^n(P)$ for $n = 0, 1, 2, \ldots$ and $\rho^*(P)$ as:

$$\rho^0(P) = \{Q \mid Q \equiv P\},$$
$$\rho^{n+1}(P) = \rho^n(P) \cup \{Q \mid Q \equiv R \text{ for some } R \in \rho^n(P)\} \quad (n \geq 0), \text{ and}$$
$$\rho^*(P) = \bigcup_{n \geq 0} \rho^n(P).$$

The refinement operator ρ is *semantically complete* if for every logic program P it holds that

$$\{M(Q) \mid Q \in \rho^*(P)\} = \{M \in \mathcal{C} \mid M \subset M(P)\}.$$

We define a logic program $\top$ as

$$\top = \left\{ \begin{array}{l} p_1(x_1, \ldots, x_{n_1}) \leftarrow \\ p_2(x_1, \ldots, x_{n_2}) \leftarrow \\ \cdots \\ p_k(x_1, \ldots, x_{n_k}) \leftarrow \end{array} \right\},$$

where $p_1, p_2, \ldots, p_k$ be the list of all predicate symbols used in $\mathcal{L}_H$ and $x_1, x_2, \ldots$ are mutually distinct variables. The logic program is the most general one in $\mathcal{L}_H$ because $M(\top) = HB$. We can generate at least one hypothesis for every concept in $\mathcal{C}$, by applying a semantically complete refinement operator to $\top$ and generating the sets $\rho^0(\top)$, $\rho^1(\top)$, $\rho^2(\top)$, ... This means that such a refinement operator can be used for enumeration of hypotheses in the learning procedure in Fig. 1.

In order to define a concrete refinement for logic programs, we define the subsumption relation of clauses with the inference rules shown in Fig. 2. The names (W), (I), and (U) of the rules respectively represents *Weakening*, *Instantiation*, and *Unification*. In the case a clause D is derived from a clause C by using the rules, we write $C \succeq_c D$ and say that C *subsumes* D [2]. We define the set

$$\rho_c(C) = \left\{ D \ \middle| \ \begin{array}{l} D \text{ is derived from } C \text{ with applying one of} \\ \text{the rules (W), (I), or (U) exactly once} \end{array} \right\}.$$

With the subsumption relation of definite clauses, the subsumption relation of logic programs is defined as the inference rules is shown in Fig. 3. The names (E) and (D) represent Extension and Deletion, respectively. We write $P \succeq_s Q$ if Q is derivable from P with the inference rules (E) and (D) and say that P *subsumes* Q.

Note that the subsumption relation is not equivalent to the logical entailment relation. More precisely, $P \succeq_s Q$ implies $P \models Q$ but the converse does not hold in general.

As is explained in the last section, we cannot adopt such a hypothetical language that can have all logic programs. When we give some restriction to the

---

[2] We follow the usual notation in the ILP area. In the notation of mathematical logic, we should write $C \vdash D$.

$$\frac{A \leftarrow B_1, \ldots, B_m}{A \leftarrow B_1, \ldots, B_m, p(x_1, \ldots, x_n)} \text{ (W)}$$

p is a predicate symbol, and $x_1, \ldots, x_n$ are mutulaly distinct variables which do not appear in $A \leftarrow B_1, \ldots, B_m$.

$$\frac{A \leftarrow B_1, \ldots, B_m}{(A \leftarrow B_1, \ldots, B_m)[x := f(x_1, \ldots, x_n)]} \text{ (I)}$$

f is a function or constant symbol, and $x_1, \ldots, x_n$ are mutulaly distinct variables which do not appear in $A \leftarrow B_1, \ldots, B_m$.

$$\frac{A \leftarrow B_1, \ldots, B_m}{(A \leftarrow B_1, \ldots, B_m)[x := y]} \text{ (U)}$$

x and y are variables which occurs in $A \leftarrow B_1, \ldots, B_m$

Fig. 2. Inference rules for the subsumption relation of definite clauses

$$\frac{P}{P \cup \rho_c(C)} \text{ (E)} \qquad\qquad \frac{P}{P - \{C\}} \text{ (D)}$$

C is a clause in P

Fig. 3. Inference rules for the subsumption relation of logic programs

hypothetical language, we need to modify the refinement operators. In order to illustrate the modification we introduce the hypothetical language $\mathcal{L}_{LMIS}$, in which definite clauses $A \leftarrow B_1, B_2, \ldots, B_n$ must satisfy the followings:

- None of the atoms $B_1, B_2, \ldots, B_n$ has any function symbol.
- The variables occurring in $B_1, B_2, \ldots, B_n$ must occur also in A.

The language was used in the early ILP system MIS [34]. Figure 4 shows the inference rules for refinement operator for the refinement ρ_{LMIS} of logic programs in $\mathcal{L}_{LMIS}$.

5   Anti-unification and Learning from Positive Data

An early investigation of inductive inference [14] showed the difficulty of learning from positive representations under the criteria of identification in the limit, but rich results have been proposed for overcoming the difficulties. The fundamental results were given by Angluin [2]. Fortunately, we can explain the results with the hypothetical language $\mathcal{L}_{ATOM}$ of all atoms in $\mathcal{L}$, with regarding every atom A as a logic program $\{A \leftarrow\}$. In this section the program is denoted by A if no confusion is caused. For example, the least Herbrand model $M(\{A \leftarrow\})$ is denoted by $M(A)$.

$$\frac{A \leftarrow B_1, \dots, B_m}{A \leftarrow B_1, \dots, B_m, p(x_1, \dots, x_n)} \quad \text{(W-LMIS)}$$

p is a predicate symbol, and $x_1, \dots, x_n$ are variables occurring in A.

$$\frac{A \leftarrow}{(A \leftarrow)[x := f(x_1, \dots, x_n)]} \quad \text{(I-LMIS)}$$

f is a function or constant symbol, and $x_1, \dots, x_n$ are mutulaly distinct variables which do not appear in A.

$$\frac{A \leftarrow B_1, \dots, B_m}{(A \leftarrow B_1, \dots, B_m)[x := y]} \quad \text{(U)}$$
x and y are variables occurring in $A \leftarrow B_1, \dots, B_m$.

Fig. 4. Inference rules for the subsumption relation of clauses appearing in $\mathcal{L}_{L-MIS}$

Algorithm Anti-Unify(E)
/* E is a finite set of ground atoms */
Return Refine($E, p(x_1, x_2, \dots, x_n)$);

Algorithm Refine(E, A)
if there exists $B \in \rho_c(A)$ s.t. $E \subseteq M(B)$ **then**
    select such a B and return Refine(E, B);
else
    return A;

Fig. 5. The least general generalization (anti-unification) algorithm

We show that the concept class $\mathcal{C}_{ATOM} = \{M(A) \mid A \in \mathcal{L}_{ATOM}\}$ is inferable from positive representations. The inference procedure is easily constructed by using Plotkin's *least general generalization* algorithm [30], which is also called *anti-unification* algorithm [22].

We give some definitions. We assume that at least one function symbol and one constant symbol are provided in $\mathcal{L}$. A *generalization* or *anti-instance* of an atom A is an atom B such that $B\theta = A$. Note that $B \succeq_s A$ if we regard A and B as logic programs $\{A \leftarrow\}$ and $\{B \leftarrow\}$, respectively. An atom B is a *common anti-instance* of a finite set E of atomic formulae if B is an anti-instance of every atom in E. It is shown that, for every finite set of atom, there is a common anti-instance L of E, unique up to variant, such that $B \succeq_s L$ for any other common anti-instance B of E. The atom L is called the *least general generalization* or the *least common anti-instance* (*lca*, for short) and denoted by $lca(E)$. The algorithm illustrated in Fig. 5 derives the lca of E.

The learning procedure is very simple: Let $\sigma = B_1, B_2, \dots$ be any positive representation for $M(A)$. The learning procedure returns $lca(\{B_1, B_2, \dots, B_n\})$ with the anti-unification algorithm, when $B_1, B_2, \dots, B_n$ are fed to it. In the following we show that the learning algorithm identifies $\mathcal{C}_{ATOM}$ in the limit.

At first note that C_{ATOM} has *finite thickness* [2], that is, for every ground atom B, there is only finite number of such concepts $M(A)$ in C_{ATOM} that $B \in M(A)$. Also we can easily show that, for sets F and G of ground atoms,

$$F \supseteq G \Longrightarrow lca(F) \succeq_s lca(G).$$

With letting $E_n = \{B_1, B_2, \ldots, B_n\}$, the sequence of the hypotheses generated by the learning procedure is $lca(E_1)$, $lca(E_2)$, $lca(E_3)$, ..., and it holds that

$$lca(E_1) \preceq_s lca(E_2) \preceq_s lca(E_3) \preceq_s \cdots.$$

Because of the finite-thickness of C_{ATOM}, there is a number N such that

$$lca(E_N) = lca(E_{N+1}) = lca(E_{N+2}) = \cdots.$$

Then $A \succeq_s lca(E_N)$ because $A \succeq_s B_i$ for every $i = 1, 2, \ldots, N$. If $lca(E_N) \not\equiv A$, there must exists B_m in the positive presentation such that $m > N$ and $lca(E_N) \not\succeq B_m$. Such B_m can be easily constructed from A and $lca(E_N)$ but this causes contradiction.

We have to note that finite thickness is sufficient for a concept class C to be identifiable in the limit from positive presentation [2], and that subsumption ordering is not needed. Finite thickness is not a necessary condition of the identifiablity.

The success of the learning procedure can be interpreted in another manner. For every non-ground atom A, there exists a pair of ground atoms A_1 and A_2 such that $A \equiv lca(A_1, A_2)$. Of course, both A_1 and A_2 are in $M(A)$. The procedure stops changing conjectures if such A_1 and A_2 appears in σ. If both A_1 and A_2 are in $M(A')$, then $A' \succeq_s A$, and therefore, $M(A)$ is the minimal concept containing the set $T(A) = \{A_1, A_2\}$. For a ground atom A, the set $T(A) = \{A\}$ has the same property. The set $T(A)$ is a *finite tell-tale* of $M(A)$.

Generally speaking, a finite tell-tale of a concept $C(h)$ in a given concept class of C is a finite subset $T(h)$ of $C(h)$ such that $T(h) \subseteq C(h')$ implies that $C(h')$ is not a proper subset of $C(h)$. It was shown [2] that the concept class of C is identifiable in the limit from positive presentation iff every concept $C(h)$ has a finite tell-tale $T(h)$ and there is a procedure which takes a hypothesis h as its input and enumerates the elements of $T(h)$.

The concept class C_{ATOM} is too simple, but the finite thickness property is not appropriate to extension of concept classes: even if both of two concept classes C and D have finite thickness, the concept class

$$C \dot\cup D = \{C \cup D \mid C \in C \text{ and } D \in D\}$$

does not always have the same property. Therefore we cannot use the finite thickness property of C_{ATOM} to show that the class $C_{ATOM} \dot\cup C_{ATOM}$ is identifiable from positive representations. The hypothetical language for $C_{ATOM} \dot\cup C_{ATOM}$ consists of logic programs which is a set of at most two clauses of the form $A \leftarrow$. Some other conditions have been found for showing that $C \dot\cup D$ is identifiable from positive representations. One of such conditions is that both C and D have *finite elasticity* [26,38].

6   Theoretical Applications of ILP

6.1   Procedural Semantics of Σ_2-Formula

The identification in the limit requires that, with finite numbers of change of hypotheses, the inference algorithm must find exact representation of every concept. Apart from learning we can find such a type of problems, and finding solutions for them can be represented with Σ_2-formula. A Σ_2-*formula* is a formula of the form

$$\exists x_1 \exists x_2 \cdots \exists x_n \forall y_1 \forall y_2 \cdots \forall y_m \Phi(x_1, x_2 \ldots, x_n, y_1, y_2, \ldots, y_m),$$

where Φ is a formula without any quantifiers and $x_1, x_2 \ldots, x_n, y_1, y_2, \ldots, y_m$ are all of the variables occurring in Φ.

Let us consider the least element c of a set d of natural numbers. The specification of the number c is represented as

$$\forall y (nat(c) \wedge d(c) \wedge (d(y) \rightarrow c \leq y)),$$

where nat is the definition of natural numbers. Because such a constant c must exists for any set of d,

$$M \models P_{nat} \wedge P_{\leq} \rightarrow (\exists x \forall y (nat(x) \wedge d(x) \wedge (d(y) \rightarrow x \leq y)))$$

holds if M is any Henkin model of d.

Another example is more practical. Let us assume that a logic program P_{parent} represents the parent-child relation in a family, and $P_{ancestor}$ gives the recursive definition of the *ancester* relation using the parent-child relation. Then, for any set d of members in the family, a Σ_2-formula

$$P_{parent} \wedge P_{ancestor} \rightarrow (\exists x \forall y (family(x) \wedge (d(y) \rightarrow ancestor(x, y))))$$

represents looking for a member of the family who is the common ancestor of the members in d.

RichProlog [24] is an extended logic programming system which accepts Σ_2-formulae as queries and returns candidate of the value for the variables $x_1, \ldots, x_n$. For the execution only finite number of elements in d are given, and the answers are changed if the set of elements is changed. Hayashi and Akama also investigates the relation identification in the limit and logical formula in another class [1,28,16].

6.2   Amalgamation of ILP and Statistical Inference

Amalgamating Inductive Logic Programming and statistical inference is now attracting many researchers. De Raedt and Kersting [11] have given an excellent survey on the area. Sato [33] gave a theoretical foundation of the amalgamation and is now distributing a practical system PRISM. In this subsection, we do not introduce these works but we just show that the correspondence between ILP and maximum-likelihood estimation of parameters of probability distributions.

In maximum-likelihood estimation we fix a class of distributions each of which are characterized with a tuple θ of parameters. We regard every distribution as a concept and the tuple of parameters as a hypothesis. A positive example is a number drawn according to a unknown target distribution, and estimating the parameters of the distribution is generating hypotheses. Examples are values $x_1, x_2, ..., x_n$ of random variables $X_1, X_2, \ldots, X_n$. The likelihood function is

$$L(\theta) = f(X_1, X_2, \ldots, X_n; \theta).$$

If $X_1, X_2, \ldots, X_n$ are independent random variables, the function is represented as

$$L(\theta) = \prod_{i=1}^{n} f_i(X_i, ; \theta).$$

A maximum-likelihood estimator of θ is the value which maximizes $L(\theta)$.

In textbooks of statistics several criteria are introduced for parameter estimation but we could not use criteria other than *statistical consistency* because others depend on expectation and variants, which cannot be found in ILP. Statistical consistency would fit identification in the limit in the sense that providing examples more and more to learning procedure leads to the target concepts correctly.

As an example we apply the items in Section 3 to the point estimation of binary distribution. Let $\mathcal{C}_{Bin}$ be the class of binary distribution $Bin(p)$ and $\mathcal{L}_{Bin}$ be the value of the parameter p such that $0 \leq p \leq 1$. When we sample n elements $X_1, X_2, \ldots, X_n$ from $Bin(p_*)$ with p_* being the unknown (target) parameter, the most likelihood estimation is

$$\frac{X_1 + X_2 + \cdots + X_n}{n}$$

and this satisfies the statistical consistency criterion.

6.3   Computational Algebra

In this subsection we treat the algebraic structure *ring*. We assume that every element of a ring R is represented in a finite sequence of symbols, that both of the operations $+$ and $\cdot$ are computable, and that every ideal is recursive.

Angluin[2] treated ideals of the set of integers (as a ring) for discussing the identification in the limit from positive presentation. Stephan and Ventsov[36] showed that the class of all ideals of a ring R is identifiable in the limit from positive presentation iff R is *Nötherian*. This result shows that a finite basis of every ideal I acts as a finite tell-tale of I. In particular, for learning ideals of the polynomial ring $\mathbf{Q}[x_1, x_2, \ldots, x_n]$, we can construct a learning procedure by using Buchberger's algorithm which generates Gröbner basis, just as using the anti-unification algorithm in learning atomic formulae.

Kobayashi et al. [20] showed that the class of all ideals of a ring R is identifiable in the limit from positive presentation iff the class has finite elasticity. The equivalence does not hold in general and would characterize the data structure ring. De Brachet et al [10] analyzed the equivalence on the viewpoint of universal algebra.

7   Concluding Remarks

In this paper we explained ILP in the general framework of learning, with showing the role of refinement and anti-unification under the criteria identification in the limit. Readers who would like more precise definitions on refinement and anti-unification should consult textbooks on the area, e.g. [29]. The book [18] should be referred for results on learning under identification in the limit.

Learning logic programs are being investigated under various types of protocols, query learning, PAC learning and so on [4,7,9,19,12]. Learnability in such protocols have been analyzed in the context of Elementary Formal Systems (EFS) [5,25,32], which are logic programs treating strings with patterns as arguments of predicate symbols. Recently kernel method or the Support Vector Machine (SVM) method has applied to ILP, e.g. in [23].

Application of ILP to practical data sets is investigated under the name of *relational datamining* [13]. From a theoretical point of view, the well-known datamining algorithm can be regarded as learning with logic [15]. Applying ILP to Web-mining is found in [39].

As is shown in the last section, ILP has a good correspondence to both statistical inference and computational algebra. We expect that this observation would read us to new interesting application areas of ILP.

Acknowledgements

The author would like to express his thankfulness to Dr. Oskar Bartenstein for invitation to the INAP 2005 conference. This research was partially supported by Ministry of Education, Culture, Sports, Science, and Technology, Grant-in-Aid for Scientific Research on Priority Areas (C) No. 16016246.

References

1. Akama, Y., Berardi, S., Hayashi, S., Kohlenbach, U.: An Arithmetical Hierarchy of the Law of Excluded Middle and Related Principles. *Proc. of LICS 2004*, 192–201 (2004).
2. Angluin, D.: Inductive Inference of Formal Languages from Positive Data, *Information and Control* 45, 117–135 (1980).
3. Angluin, D. and Smith, C. H.: Inductive Inference: Theory and Methods, *Computing Surveys*, 15:237–269 (1983).
4. Arias, M. and Khardon, R.: Learning Closed Horn Expressions, *Information and Computation*, 178(1), 214–240 (2002).
5. Arikawa, S., Miyano, S., Shinohara, A., Shinohara, T., and Yamamoto, A. : Algorithmic Learning Theory with Elementary Formal Systems, *IEICE Trans. Inf. & Syst.*, E75-D(4), 405–414 (1992).

6. Arimura, H.: Completeness of Depth-Bounded Resolution for Weakly Reducing Programs, Nakata, I. and Hagiya, M. (eds.) *Software Science and Engineering* (*World Scientific Series in Computer Science* Vol.31), 227–245 (1991).
7. Arimura, H.: Learning Acyclic First-Order Horn Sentences from Entailment, *Proc. of 8th International Conference on Algorithmic Learning Theory* (*LNAI* 1316), 432–445 (1997).
8. Arimura, H., Shinohara, H., Otsuki, H., and Ishizaka, H.: A Generalization of the Least General Generalization, *Machine Intelligence* 13, 59–85 (1994).
9. Arimura, H. and Yamamoto, A. : Inductive Logic Programming : From Logic of Discovery to Machine Learning, *IEICE Trans. Inf. and Syst.* E83-D(1), 10–18 (2000).
10. De Brecht, M., Kobayashi, M., Tokunaga, H., and Yamamoto, A.: Inferability of Closed Set Systems From Positive Data, *Working Note of LLLL 2006*, 11–17, JSAI (2006).
11. De Raedt, L. and Kersting, K.: Probabilistic Inductive Logic Programming, *Proc. of the 15th International Workshop on Algorithmic Learning Theory* (*LNAI* 3244), 19–36, Springer-Verlag (2004).
12. De Raedt, L. and Džeroski, S.: First-order *jk*-clausal theories are PAC-learnable, *Artificial Intelligence* 70(1-2): 375–392 (1994).
13. Džeroski, S. and Lavrač, N.: *Relational Data Mining*, Springer (2001).
14. Gold ,D.: Language Identfication in the Limit, *Information and Control* 10, 447–474 (1967).
15. Gunopulos, D., Khardon, R., Mannila, H., Saluja, S., Toivonen, H., Sharma, R. S.: Discovering all most specific sentences. ACM Trans. Database Syst. 28(2): 140–174 (2003).
16. Hayashi, S.: Mathematics Based on Learning, *Proc. of the 13th International Workshop on Algorithmic Learning Theory* (*LNAI* 2533), 7–21, Springer-Verlag (2002).
17. Hayashi, S.: Can Proofs Be Animated By Games? *Proc. of the 7th International Conference on Typed Lambda Calculi and Applications* (*LNCS* 3461), 11–22, Springer-Verlag (2005).
18. Jain, S., Osherson, D., Royer, J. S. and Sharma, A.: *Systems That Learn: 2nd Edition*, MIT Press (1999).
19. Khardon, R.: Learning Function-Free Horn Expressions, *Machine Learning*, 37(3), 241–275 (1999).
20. Kobayashi, M., Tokunaga, H., and Yamamoto, A.: Ideals of Polynomial Rings and Learning from Positive Data (in Japanese), *Proc. of IBIS 2005*, 129–134 (2005).
21. Laird, P. D.: *Learning from Good and Bad Data*, Kluwer Academic Publishers (1988).
22. Lassez, J.-L., Maher, M. J. and Marriott, K.: Unification Revisited, in Minker, J. (ed): *Foundations of Deductive Databases and Logic Programming*, 587–626, Morgan-Kaufman (1988).
23. Lloyd, J. W.: *Logic for Learning: Learning Comprehensible Theories from Structured Data*, Springer (2003).
24. Martin, E., Nguyen, P., Sharma, A., and Stephan, F. : Learning in Logic with Rich-Prolog, *Proc. of the 18th International Conference on Logic Programming* (*LNCS* 2401), pp. 239–254, Springer-Verlag (2002).
25. Miyano, S., Shinohara, A. and Shinohara, T.: Polynomial-time Learning of Elementary Formal Systems, *New Generation Computing* 18(3): 217–242 (2000).
26. Motoki, T., Shinohara, T. and Wright, K.: The Correct Definition of Finite Elasticity: Corrigendum to Identification of Unions, *Proc. of COLT 1991*: 375 (1991).
27. Muggleton, S.: Inverse Entailment and Progol, *New Generation Computing* 13: 245–286 (1995).

28. Nakata, M. and Hayashi, S. : A Limiting First Order Realizability Interpretation, *Scientiae Mathematicae Japonicae*, Vol. 55, No. 3, pp. 567–580 (2002).

29. Nienhuys-Cheng, S.-H. and de Wolf, R.: *Foundations of Inductive Logic Programming (LNAI* 1228), Springer (1997).

30. Plotkin, G.: A Note on Inductive Generalization, *Machine Intelligence 5*, Edinburgh University Press (1970).

31. Reynolds, J. C.: *Transformational Systems and the Algebraic Structure of Atomic Formulas*, Machine Intelligence **5**, 135–152 (1970).

32. Sakamoto, H., Hirata, K., and Arimura, H.: Learning Elementary Formal Systems with Queries, *Theoretical Computer Science*, 298(1), 21–50 (2003).

33. Sato, T.: Parameterized Logic Programs where Computing Meets Learning, *Proc. of FLOPS2001 (LNCS* 2024), 40–60 (2001).

34. Shapiro, E. Y.: Inductive Inference of Theories From Facts, Technical Report 192, Department of Computer Science, Yale University (1981). Also in Lassez, J.-L. and Plotkin, G. (eds.) *Computational Logic*, pp. 199–254, The MIT Press (1991).

35. Shapiro, E. Y.: Alternation and the Computational Complexity of Logic Programs, *The Journal of Logic Programming* 1(1), 19–33 (1984).

36. Stephan, F. and Ventsov, Y.: Learning Algebraic Structures from Text, *Theoretical Computer Science* 268, 221–273 (2001).

37. Ullman, J. D.: *Princeples of Dadabase and Knowledge-base Systems, Volume* I, II, Computer Science Press (1988).

38. Wright, K.: Identification of Unions of Languages Drawn from an Identifiable Class. *Proc. of COLT 1989*: 328–333 (1989).

39. Yamamoto, A., Ishino, A., Ito, K. and Arimura, H.: Modelling Semi-structured Documents with Hedges for Deduction and Induction, *Proc. of the 11th International Workshop on Inductive Logic Programming (LNAI* 2157), 240–247, Springer (2001).

Railway Scheduling with Declarative Constraint Programming

Ulrich Geske

Fraunhofer FIRST, Berlin
geske@first.fraunhofer.de

Abstract. Simulation of train scheduling is a highly complex problem. Classical methods in this field are mainly designed for conflict resolution, which means that a solution or partial solution is generated and subsequently tested to determine whether the conditions are met (generate-and-test procedure). The main advantage of the proposed paradigm, Constraint Processing, is that its basic strategy is avoidance of conflicts. The use of the conflict-avoiding CP paradigm is advantageous, for example, in scheduling trains (track selection, global temporal situations, reservations), where strongly branched decision trees arise. Some examples are given illustrating the innovative aspects of the Constraint Processing paradigm. However, the size of real problems, in terms of track length, number and type of trains, different disposition rules, optimization or quality criteria, make it necessary to explore other methods to deal with the amount of data, to reduce the remaining search spaces, to ensure short response times and interactivity and to guarantee high-quality solutions.

We describe possible ways of coping with the above mentioned problems, especially to reducing the lateness of trains: automatic decomposition of large rail networks and distributed train scheduling, using a slice technique to improve the systems backtracking behaviour with a view to finding faster, better solutions, and combining constraint processing and genetic algorithms to find alternative tracks in a station.

1 Introduction

If we look at simulation procedures used in the transport domain and particularly in the area of timetable simulation for rail applications, we find that little basic research has be done the past using Constraint Programming for the generation and simulation of rail timetables. A constraint-based system was studied at RTRI in 1995, and was to yield solutions much faster than other approaches [1]. A constraint-based approach for train rescheduling was discussed in a paper from the Chinese University of Hong Kong in 1997 [2]. It deals with a 600 km stretch of the Chinese rail network between Zhengzhou and Wuhan and considers planning changes in the case of traffic jams, taking into account different criteria. Practical examples confirmed the efficiency of the theoretically investigated algorithms. None of the papers presented at the 1997 "World Congress on Railway Research" (WCRR) dealt with constrained-based train simulation.

M. Umeda et al. (Eds.): INAP 2005, LNAI 4369, pp. 117–134, 2006.
© Springer-Verlag Berlin Heidelberg 2006

More recently there has been a slight increase in the number of constraint approaches. Rodriguez from INRETS [3], for example describes such an approach for scheduling at train junctions; Indra-payong [4] uses constraint-based local search for container freight rail scheduling; and Oliveira [5] uses it for single-track railway scheduling. Various papers from the Swedish SICS institute deal with train scheduling and capacity problems on the basis of the SICSTUS system, e.g. [6; 7]. A number of research projects, as well as our own studies and applications, have shown that constraint-based (CP) methods are suitable for achieving results highly efficiently and with good optimality properties [8, 9, 10, 11, 12]. In addition, such methods can be easily combined with interactivity (online access of experts) and rule processing (integration of background knowledge). The theoretical possibility of exponential runtimes for large problems still remains, but the size of problems being dealt with can be extended considerably by using CP methods.

2   Constraint-Based Programming (CP)

2.1   The Basic CP Paradigm

The main advantage of constraint-based methods is that an admissible value is assigned to a variable leads directly to a reduction of the search space and that an inadmissible value for a variable is immediately recognized and rejected. Unlike in the conventional programming, this is achieved by setting equality or disequality constraints early on in the program (and during program execution), even if they are not yet computable because the included variables have not been assigned (see also Figure 1). Correct treatment of these conditions is possible by extending the classical procedure-call mechanism, e.g. "call by value" or "unification" known from the logic programming language Prolog. Treatment of conditions that are not computable is delayed, while execution of the rest of the program continues. The delayed constraints are put in a so-called constraint store, where they form a constraint net, the arcs being labelled with the constraints and the nodes being variables that occur in the constraints. Conditions that are computable are executed immediately, but the effects of this execution are also examined (propagated) for the set of delayed constraints. If an inconsistency is found during this propagation procedure, backtracking is performed to assign other values to the variables. The processing of constraints appears costly, but in fact it improves efficiency compared with classical methods. The result of the execution of a CLP program can be a ground (variable free) solution or a set of not further simplifiable constraints. The way the constraints are processed leads to significant reductions in the search space. Nevertheless, the remaining search space may still be exponentially complex. Supplementary technologies - like global constraints, backtrackable domain reduction, layered backtracking, constraint hierarchies with nontrivial error functions, and the application of redundant constraints - are necessary to solve simulation and scheduling problems. We confine ourselves here to describing the effects of the basic constraint technology and the above-mentioned extension by global constraints.

2.2 Application of the Basic CP Paradigm for Conflict Avoidance

The classical approach, which consists in local conflict recognition and manual conflict resolution, must be replaced by efficient, more automated methods. The goal is conflict avoidance, which can be achieved by global considerations and early recognition of possible dead ends. Different alternatives for the scheduling of a train (track choice, running on wrong line, train speed, stopping time, time for changing, etc.) result in strongly branched decision trees. Based on the principle of Constraint Programming, procedures can be developed for potential conflict avoidance in such situations. By way of an example, we consider the reservation of block sections by three trains, a fast train (ICE), a medium speed train (RE), and a slow train (IR) (see also Figure 1).

Action	Constraints, Disposition rules	Reservation times for blocks		
		ICE	RE	IR
1st: Definition of variables and their domains	ICE := {1,...,20} RE := {1,...,20} IR := {1,...,20}			
2nd: Propagation	ICE + 5 < RE	14 / 14+5<20	7 / 1+5<7	
	IR + 10 < ICE	12 14 / 1+10<12	18 20 / 7+10<18	1 3 / 3+10<14
3rd: Search	RE := 18 ICE := 14 IR := 2	12 14 13	18 20 19	1 3 2

Fig. 1. Search space restriction using Constraint Programming

The problem may be described in terms of inequations like $Start_i + Duration_i < Start_j$ (the time at which train i enters a block section plus the duration of occupation of the block section by train i is smaller than the time at which train j enters the same block section) and equations like $Start_i := Time$. Let us assume the times for Start to be between 1 and 20 (in time units for each of the three trains). The inequation $ICE + 5 < RE$ then means that the RE can enter the block at the earliest 5 time units after the ICE has entered the block. This inequation immediately leads by constraint propagation to the restriction of the admissible value for the start times of all trains. For example, the start time of the ICE is restricted to the interval of 1 to 14 time units. In the last step ("Search") of Figure 1, propagation causes the values of the remaining start times to be finally fixed by assigning the value 18 to the start time of RE (from the possible interval of 18 to 20 time units).

2.3 Extended CP Paradigm: Global Constraints

Global constraints use domain-specific knowledge to obtain better propagation results and can be applied to large problems. Complex conditions on sets of variables can be modelled declaratively by such constraints and used in multiple contexts. Global constraints with specialized consistency methods can greatly improve efficiency in solving real-life problems. The basic ideas behind the global constraints *diffn* and *cumulative* are treated in the rest of this section.

The *cumulative constraint* was orginally introduced to solve scheduling and placement problems [17]. The simplified form of this constraint is

$$cumulative([S_1, S_2, \ldots, S_n], [D_1, D_2, \ldots, D_n], [R_1, R_2, \ldots, R_n], L)$$

where $[S_1, S_2, \ldots, S_n], [D_1, D_2, \ldots, D_n]$, and $[R_1, R_2, \ldots, R_n]$ are nonempty lists of domain variables (or natural numbers) and L is a natural number. The usual interpretation of this constraint is a single-resource scheduling problem: each S_i represents the starting time of some event, D_i is the duration and R_i the amount of resources needed by the event. L is the total amount of resources available at each relevant point in time. The cumulative constraint ensures that at each time point in the schedule the amount of resources consumed does not exceed the given limit L. The mathematical interpretation of this constraint is:

$$\text{Cumulative constraint: for each } k \in [\min\{S_i\}, \max\{S_i + D_i\}\text{-}1]$$
$$\text{it holds that: } \Sigma R_j \leq L \text{ for all } j \text{ with } S_j \leq k \leq S_j + D_j - 1$$

The *diffn* constraint was included in CLP to handle multidimensional placement problems, like job-shop problems with groups of equal machines. The basic *diffn* constraint takes as its arguments a list of n-dimensional rectangles, where the origin and length can be domain variables with respect to each dimension. An n-dimensional rectangle is represented by a tuple $[X_1, \ldots, X_n, L_1, \ldots, L_n]$, where X_i is the origin and L_i the length of the rectangle in the ith dimension:

$$diffn([[X_{11}, \ldots, X_{1n}, L_{11}, \ldots, L_{1n}], [X_{21}, \ldots, X_{2n}, L_{21}, \ldots, L_2n], \ldots])$$

This constraint ensures that the given n-dimensional rectangles do not overlap. Figure 2 gives an example of three two-dimensional rectangles with the non overlapping constraint. The largest rectangle, for instance, is determined by the second list [1,2,3,2], where the origin is the point (1,2) and the lengths of the two dimensions are 3 and 2. For job-shop problems, the interpretation of the x-axis would be the time and that of the y-axis the different machines. The advantage of using this global constraint in the latter context is that a placement of a task at a machine is computed by the constraint and need not be fixed to a special machine before or at the beginning of execution.

2.4 Use of Global Constraints for Line Blocking

By way of an example, let us demonstrate the application of the global constraints cumulative and diffn. The example considers the running of 37 trains

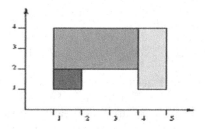

Fig. 2. diffn([[1,1,1,1],[1,2,3,2],[4,1,1,3]])

over a sequence of blocks. To simplify matters, all trains run in the same direction. Each block comprises a series of block sections, which are either always covered completely by a train or are not covered. Typical limitations for blocks are signals of different types: mandatory signals, distant signals, etc. Unlike blocks, single block sections are not limited by signals. We assume that for each train z_i the minimal time for line-blocking $mind(z_i, t_j)$ is given for each block t_j, the earliest time $mins(z_i)$ the train enters the first section of the block, and the latest time $maxe(z_i)$ the train leaves the last section of a block. The topology consists of 27 block sections: $t_1, \ldots, t_5, t_{6.1}, t_{6.2}, t_{6.3}, t_7, \ldots, t_{11}, t_{12.1}, t_{12.2}, t_{13}, \ldots, t_{16}, t_{17.1}, t_{17.2}, t_{17.3}, t_{18}, \ldots, t_{22}$. The blocks $t_{6.1}, t_{6.2}$ and $t_{6.3}$ are parallel, i.e. each train must use exactly one of these three blocks. The blocks $t_{12.1}$ and $t_{12.2}$ as well as the blocks $t_{17.1}, t_{17.2}$ and $t_{17.3}$ are also parallel blocks. The individual blocks are used from left to right in the sequence shown in Figure 3, top line.

Actually, other blocks should also be presented in more detail to reflect the different track lengths. We omit these details because the line-blocking times will be the same. For trains z_i and blocks t_j with $i \geq 1$ and $1 \leq j \leq 22$, the domains of possible values can be initially fixed as follows:

- $S_{ij} = \{mins(z_i), \ldots, maxe(z_i)\}$: start of line blocking
- $D_{ij} = mind(z_i, t_j)$: duration of line blocking
- $T_{ij} = 1$ for all t_j without $j = \{6, 12, 17\}$: block formed by parallel tracks
  $T_{ij} = \{1, 2\}$ for t_j with $j = \{12\}$
  $T_{ij} = \{1, 2, 3\}$ for t_j with $j = \{6, 17\}$

The above-mentioned global constraints can be used to advantage to model the lines and stations in the example. One assumption made here is that traffic is allowed in one direction only. A block on the open track, which allows trains to run in one direction only, is comparable to a machine that can be busy with a number of tasks in a certain time interval. If this number equals 1, a machine can process not more than one task in a given time interval. In this respect, a task in job-shop scheduling is comparable to a train in railway scheduling and a machine to a block, i.e. it is suitable, in this special situation, to use the cumulative constraint for specification. For each block t_j, where j is not in

$\{6, 12, 17\}$ and all relevant trains $z_1, \ldots, z_n$, $n \leq 37$, a cumulative constraint of the following type is generated:

$$cumulative([S_{1j}, \ldots, S_{nj}], [D_{1j}, \ldots, D_{nj}], [1, \ldots, 1], 1).$$

A train may use different tracks in a station. This situation corresponds to a placement problem in job-shop scheduling, where a task can be processed by different machines of a machine group. Since track selection must take place for the three blocks t_6, t_{12} and t_{17}, a diffn constraint for these blocks and for all relevant trains $z_1, \ldots, z_n$, $n \leq 37$, must be generated:

$$diffn([[S_{1j}, T_{1j}, D_{1j}, 1], \ldots, [S_{nj}, T_{nj}, D_{nj}, 1]])$$

The assignment of the global constraints is illustrated in Figure 3, lower part.

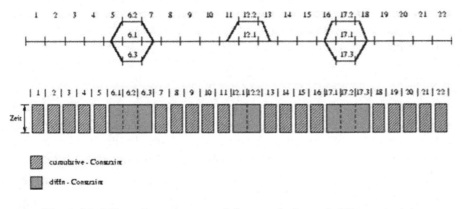

Fig. 3. Modelling of a train network by cumulative and diffn constraints

In the example (Figure 3), tracks in a station can be selected from two or three possible values. The diffn constraint ensures that exactly one of these values is selected, thus ensuring that the parallel sections are covered by one train only in a conflict-free manner. The constraints remove forbidden values from the value domain of the variable describing the problem. The remaining values of all variables form the search space for a solution. A (heuristic) search procedure is needed to find a solution. This procedure is monitored by the constraints so that search dead ends are recognized very early and efficiently and only conflict-free solutions are generated.

3   Scheduling

The above-described techniques were used in a study [12] to derive conflict-free timetables for given disposition rules (see Figure 4) and for trains of different speeds in a rail network. The network is divided into blocks. A train is run from its start to its destination is described by the concatenation of all the blocks the

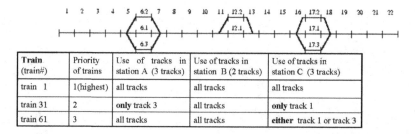

Train (train#)	Priority of trains	Use of tracks in station A (3 tracks)	Use of tracks in station B (2 tracks)	Use of tracks in station C (3 tracks)
train 1	1(highest)	all tracks	all tracks	all tracks
train 31	2	**only** track 3	all tracks	**only** track 1
train 61	3	all tracks	all tracks	**either** track 1 or track 3

Fig. 4. Disposition rules (track selection in stations)

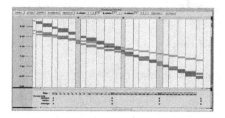

Fig. 5. Initial schedule (conflicts marked by red boxes with a red diagonal strip)

Fig. 6. Constraint-based schedule (without conflicts)

train uses. The blocks are modelled using constraint variables for the starting times and durations, which are connected by arithmetic equations. Figures 5 and 6 show this network with different block sections (blue/grey zones) and two stations (yellow/light zones).

In the stations, there are a sufficient number of tracks to allow trains to pass. Figure 5 shows the time-distance lines of a given initial timetable. The (red) framed boxes indicate block sections where conflicts arise. Using Constraint Programming methods, we immediately obtain a schedule that avoids all these conflicts (Figure 6) by delaying the starting times of the trains at the beginning of the considered network, by extending departure times at stations and varying train speeds on the open track. For reduced train delays, train speeds on the open tracks were adjusted (marked by a white diagonal strip). This technique, previously explained for abstract networks, was used to simulate part of Germanys real rail network (Figure 7) with about 1,000 trains per day, some 43,000 train kilometres per 24 hours and about 100 different-sized stations (see also Table 1, left). The CHIP system [17] was used as implementation basis. Simulations on a 3GHz computer were performed for 6-hour intervals with about 200 trains in each interval (see also Table 1, right). The execution times, including the travelling time recomputations in case a train path is changed in a station, are less than 2 min for each interval. About 25-33% of the total computation time is needed for the recomputation of paths, which happened on average about 4 times.

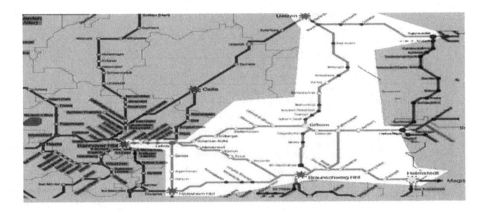

Fig. 7. Real rail network

Table 1. Some figures for the simulated railway network

left: network   right: schedule

	Example	Germany
sum track length [km]	1,006	65,005
stations	104	
number of blocks	7,111	
avg. #trains/day	1,118	34,950
avg. #trains/station	123	
avg. stations/train	11	
avg. track sections/train	266	
avg. train km/day	47,452	

Time Interval (Monday)	#Trains and Exec Time incl. path changes	#Path changes and Time for pure schedule computation
03 - 09	202 / 93sec	6 / 32.6sec
09 - 15	245 / 51sec	3 / 12.7sec
15 - 21	263 / 13sec	5 / 35.0sec
21 - 03	170 / 90sec	5 / 30.8sec

4 Distributed Scheduling

The reasons for decomposing a railway network into smaller parts for distributed simulation are manifold: the mass of data is too large for processing; independent neighbouring nets should rather be simulated; or the efficiency of planning, simulation and optimization should be increased by using more than one computing node. For our investigations [16], we divided the network into k parts, such that the sum of blocks in all parts is about the same. This partitioning is the basis for problem distribution (see Figure 9). The described partitioning ensures that the size of the different subproblems is uniformly distributed, and the workload of the computing nodes thus balanced, and that the number of crossing trains that have to be communicated between different nodes is minimized, reducing communication and recomputation costs. Each part can be simulated separately (and consists in perhaps simultaneously) in less time and with less memory capacity. The problem to be solved is the need for consistent information at the

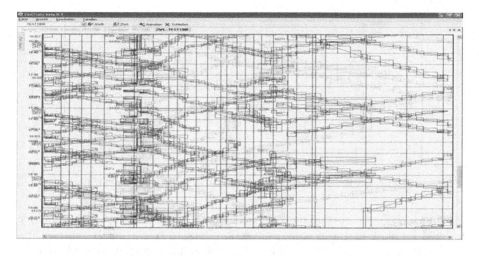

Fig. 8. Generated conflict-free time-distance diagram for the real rail network

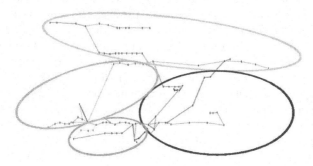

Fig. 9. Decomposition of a rail network

interfaces between neighbouring parts. The times and velocities of trains leaving one part should equal the times and velocities of the same train as it enters the next part of the overall network. As soon as a simulation of a part of the complete network is finished, the entering and leaving times of all crossing trains are communicated to the nodes neighbours. Thus, each part can locally determine which trains simulation is globally inconsistent. The local times for incoming and outgoing trains must be *greater than or equal* to the times given by the neighbours. In the case of inconsistency, a new solution to the updated CSP is computed, leading to new entering and leaving times. All *new times that are different from previous solutions*are considered (globally) inconsistent and are therefore communicated to the neighbours. Since each train that crosses parts may trigger recomputations of local simulations, their number should obviously be kept to a minimum.

Note that the computations of the local simulations can be done in an interleaved manner: while one node **a** is computing, its neighbour **b** can be finished,

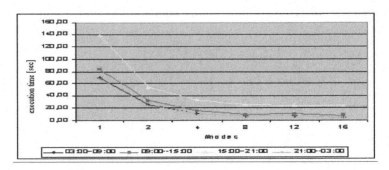

Fig. 10. Execution times for distributed scheduling (cf. [15])

sending a the new crossing data. Some moments before, **bs** other neighbour **c** finished its work and sent some connection data to **b**, so that **b** can now immediately recompute its local simulation, taking into account **cs** work. It does not have to wait until a part has finished. This approach makes maximal use of available computing resources. It is not, however, deterministic: two (global) simulation runs on the same problem may not produce the same results, depending on the order in which the local simulation jobs have been executed.

There could be a strict requirement (from rail experts) that simulations *have to be done deterministically.* We have made allowance for by synchronizing the simulation processes: all local simulations wait for each other after they have finished their local computations. When the simulations of all parts are finished, all of them communicate and then all of them recompute (if necessary). This algorithm is deterministic, and thus always yields the same results. The drawback here is that computational resources are used less optimally.

We theoretically proved the termination property together with the correctness of the algorithm theoretically [16]. Its baseline is as follows: The trains are sequenced according to some predefined global priority and treated accordingly in each local simulation part. This means that no two trains can displace each other forever: every pair of trains consists of a major and a minor train, the major train invariably superseding the minor one. Furthermore, the simulated departure times of all trains always advance. Thus, although the timeline is potentially infinite, the global consistency algorithm always converges and terminates finitely.

Figure 10 shows some empirical results: we have simulated the whole example. We simulated separately the trains from 3 a.m. to 9 a.m. (03:00-09:00), from 9 a.m. to 3 p.m. (09:00-15:00), from 3 p.m. to 9 p.m. (15:00-21:00), and from 9 p.m. to 3 a.m. (21:00-03:00). We did not simulate the whole day, but different 6-hour time slices. And, we tried this on 2, 4, 6, 8, and 16 computing nodes. Each node is equipped with 1GB of memory and 2 AMD K7 processors working at 1.2 GHz. As is evident from (Figure 10), the computing times for simulating the whole network may differ greatly from time slice to time slice. This is mainly due to the problems differing complexity: there are 199 trains in time slice 03:00-09:00, 243 in 09:00-15:00, 259 in 15:00-21:00, and 199 in 21:00-03:00. But although the number of trains in 09:00-15:00 and 15:00-21:00 dos not differ much, the latter takes about twice as long as the former. Sometimes there are local problems that are hard to solve, e.g. when there are many time-distance curves of trains very close together. And the situation is not necessarily the same in all time slices. Obviously, then, there is some exceptional problem in the 15:00-21:00 time slice. We generated and compared different problem partitions with 16, 30 and 50 parts. The decomposition into 30 parts proved out to be best for most of the problems. The above test is therefore based on this partitioning. We have already mentioned that the system can operate in synchronized or non-synchronized mode here we used the synchronized mode since it always produces the same simulation result for a given problem and is likely to be preferred by most users. In fact, the non-synchronized mode is slightly faster (about 10 to 25%, according to other experiments we conducted). Additionally, we could use central or de-central control. Our implementation allows synchronized operation only in combination with central control, so this is the one we used.

Our example is not very complex, nor did we try to find an optimal schedule for the trains. So, very few searches were needed to find the simulation solutions. The 03:00-09:00 time interval took 486 backtracking steps, the 09:00-15:00 1,635, the 15:00-21:00 1,485, and the 21:00-03:00 only 320 steps. Note that these are not average counts because we used the synchronized mode, in which each simulation is done deterministically, independent of execution sequences or even the number of computing nodes!

5   Interval Technique

There is a disadvantage in simulating train schedules over a long time interval: the trains are planned sequentially and if a conflict arises for one of the last trains, its time-distance curve is moved to a latter position. Either the lateness

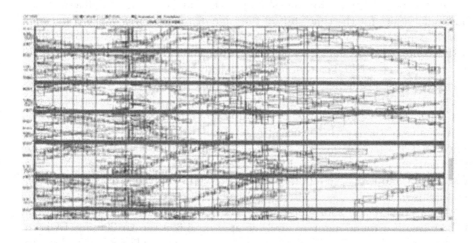

Fig. 11. Partitioning of the scheduling problem into time intervals

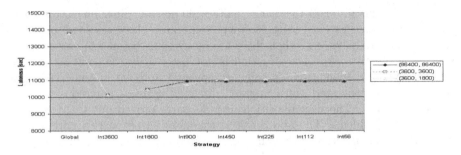

Fig. 12. Lateness of trains for interval labelling compared to global labelling (cf. [13])

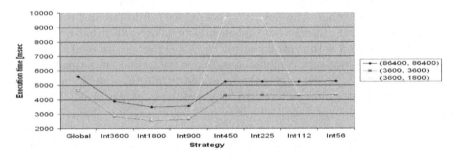

Fig. 13. Execution times for interval labelling (cf. [13])

of the train could increase dramatically because all positions near to the plan are already occupied by other trains. Or, if there is a maximum time defined for the delay of a train, an unlimited backtracking could occur to find another suitable train to move. One possible way to reduce the strong increase in lateness is to decompose the simulation horizon into smaller intervals (see also Figure 11).

We have looked into the optimal size for such a time interval, as well as at what maximum values for the time shift of the time-distance curves of the trains and what maximum value for additional stopping times in stations should be applied in this context before backtracking will occur. The expected effect is that only those trains are scheduled that are located at least partly in the considered time interval. The smaller domains of the trains starting time variables of the trains means that a conflict may be recognized quite early, while scheduling the first train of the sequence in the interval, the system may notice that one of the domains of the starting times of later trains will be empty. In this case the time-distance curve of the first train can already be moved. The results of the investigations are presented in Figures 12 up to 15. In these figures, "Global" denotes the complete scheduling horizon, "Int3600" to "Int56" intervals of 3,600 sec to 56 sec.

Actually, there are some interval sizes which show the expected reduction of lateness. We found interval sizes of approx. 3,600 sec to 900 sec to be a good choice. These values are keeping with the practice of train companies to

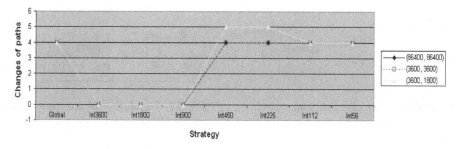

Fig. 14. Number of calls (both successful and failed) for changing the path of a train (cf. [13])

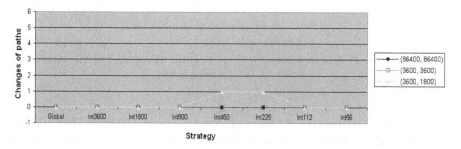

Fig. 15. Number of successful calls for changing the path of a train (cf. [13]

cancel trains that are more than one hour late. The increase in lateness for smaller interval sizes (Figure 13) could be explained by the increasing number of changed train paths in stations to avoid conflicts. This changing operation is time-consuming because it requires recomputation of the occupation times of the blocks.

6   Alternative Paths in Stations

Selecting alternative paths in stations is an optimization task to reduce lateness and to find a conflict-free solution. It is well known that local search methods like Genetic Algorithm (GA), Simulating Annealing Algorithm (SAA), Ant Algorithms (Ant), and Flood Algorithm (FA) are good candidates for such optimization tasks. The aim of the investigation (cf. [14]) was to find out in which situation which of the different methods, or what combination of constraint processing and one of the local-search algorithms, will yield better results than pure constraint methods. The selected methods were tested as their ability to find solutions for the two basic conflicts:

A) two trains travelling in the same direction would occupy a number, of same blocks at the same time (see also Figures 16 and 17) and

B) two trains travelling in opposite directions would at some point in a station or at the open track, use the same block (see also Figures 18 and 19).

Fig. 16. Conflict of trains (same direction)

Fig. 17. Resolution of the conflict in Figure 16

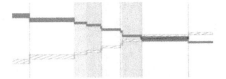

Fig. 18. Conflict of trains (opposite directions)

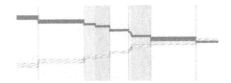

Fig. 19. Resolution of the conflict in Figure 18

The results of the tests for the two cases are presented in Table 2. For the finite-domain method of constraint programming a large initial size of the domains of starting times for the trains is no difficulty. The local search algorithms, besides GA, produce a lot of lateness both for conflict type A and conflict type B. The initial lateness denotes the shift of the schedule compared to the original plan at the edge of the considered network. The relative lateness denotes the shift of the time-distance curve to avoid conflicts by extending stopping times or making additional stops at stations, and changing travelling times on the open track. The absolute lateness is the sum of both the above times.

The initial idea in investigating local-search methods was not to replace CP by local search algorithms but to combine the two. CP methods were thus used to reduce the large domains before calling a local search algorithm. Using this method, the results of the local search methods are greatly improved (see also Table 3). The Flood algorithm does not appear to be very well suited for type B, but GA, Ant and SAA appear to be good candidates for cooperation with CP. One of them, GA, was selected for a further comparison of CP and local search methods in a more complex train scheduling example for 25 trains, with a larger number of conflicting trains (Table 4).

For the complex scheduling example, the both algorithms CP and GA were applied separately. The number of trains was gradually increased. The results are presented in Fig. 20 and Fig. 21. The execution time for CP is essentially better, but the smaller the number of trains considered, the smaller the difference in the execution time for the two algorithms. The quality of the generated plan in terms of lateness is fairly comparable for both algorithms, CP offering a slight advantage when the number of trains is greater than 3. This result is in keeping with the result of the previous two-train example, where GA shows a slight

Table 2. Lateness computed for conflict types A and B (see Figures 16 and 18) without prior domain restriction (cf. [14])

Lateness	CP		GA		Ant		SAA		FA	
Conflict type	A	B	A	B	A	B	A	B	A	B
initial	2	3	19	0	706	1493	257	1141	494	207
relative	0	0	1	13	0	455	0	0	1718	0
total	2	3	20	13	706	1948	257	1141	2212	207

Table 3. Lateness computed for conflict types A and B (see Figures 16 and 18) with prior domain restriction (cf. [14])

Lateness	CP		GA		Ant		SAA		FA	
Conflict type	A	B	A	B	A	B	A	B	A	B
initial	2	3	2	0	2	0	2	0	2	21
relative	0	0	0	1	0	1	0	1	0	0
total	2	3	2	1	2	1	2	1	2	21

Table 4. Scheduling example containing conflicts of type A and B (see also Figures 16 and 18)

Conflict type	Number of conflicts	Conflicts for pairs of trains
A	16	(3;11), (6;7), (6;23), (7;23), (8;13), (9;12), (9;16), (9;17), (9;21), (12;16), (12;17), (12;21), (16;17), (16;21), (17;31), (18;22)
B	15	*(1;20)*, (2;9), (2;12), (2;16), (2;17), (2;21), (3;4), (3;14), (4;11), (5;8), (5;13), *(10;19)*, (11;14), (14;15), *(24;25)*

advantage, especially for conflict type B. For this reason, the complex scheduling example was run in the CP paradigm, without the three marked pairs of trains that have conflicts of type B. The three pairs of trains are given sequentially to the GA algorithm with the additional knowledge of the reduced value sets for their possible starting times, derived from the result of the set of (25-3*2) trains.

Table 5 shows that the expectations are met. The column CP shows the delays to trains when applying the CP paradigm to all trains, and to the three pairs of trains. The column CP/GA shows the result of combining the CP and GA methods. The conflicts of the three pairs of trains are solved in GA better than in CP, and the total lateness of all trains is reduced. The third column shows the benefits of combining the two methods.

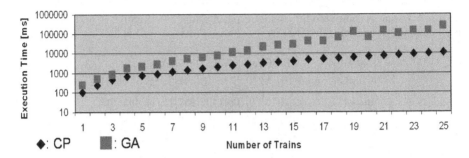

Fig. 20. Execution time for the scheduling example (Table 4) computed by CP and GA (cf. [14])

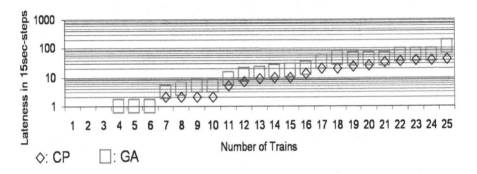

Fig. 21. Lateness of trains for the scheduling example (Table 4) computed by CP and GA (cf. [14])

Table 5. Reduction of lateness of trains by combining CP and GA algorithms

Trains	Delays to trains in 15sec-steps								
	CP			Combination: CP/GA			Gain: CP - CP/GA		
	initial	relative	total	initial	relative	total	initial	relative	total
1 - 25	31	12	43	29	8	37	2	4	6
(1;20)	3	0	3	0	1	1	3	-1	2
(10;19)	0	3	3	0	1	1	0	2	2
(24;25)	0	3	3	1	0	1	-1	3	2

7   Conclusion

Train scheduling is a highly complex problem with very large search spaces. The advantages of constraint technology compared with classical generate-and-test algorithms are its conflict avoiding and a-priori search space reduction strategies. Our investigations and applications show that Constraint Processing (CP) is highly efficient and yields high-quality solutions. We describe different additional techniques to improve the results obtained using this technology.

We are able to demonstrate that distributed constraint-based train scheduling either greatly enlarges the size of networks to be computed or significantly reduces the execution time of train simulation. We were able to verify that a fairly small number of computers running in parallel are sufficient to obtain considerable gains.

Another technique to reduce the complexity of the train scheduling problem is breaking down a large time period into time intervals. Another positive result is the improved quality in schedules, i.e. lateness of trains can be reduced using this technique. We found that a further reduction of lateness compared to the original not error-free plan is possible by combining Constraint Processing with Local-Search methods. These methods seem to be particularly useful and efficient for solving very local conflicts, e.g. the conflict of two trains in a station.

In addition, interactivity and rule processing can be combined very well with Constraint Processing, i.e. the on-line accessing of experts and their knowledge and integration of background knowledge are possible.

To sum up, the CP technology results in:

- greater flexibility: conflict avoidance rather than conflict resolution; closer integration of simulation and planning
- high efficiency: avoidance of wrong alternatives (dead ends); combination with other techniques to reduce complexity
- generation of good solutions in most cases; combination of automatic and interactive simulation; avoidance of time-consuming optimization procedures.

References

1. Tsuchiya, R. & Osada, H.: A Constraint Satisfaction Method for Train Assignment Problem. RTRI Report, Vol.9, No.5, 1995.
2. Chiu,C.K., Chou, C.M., Lee, J.H.M., Leung, H.F. & Leung, Y.W., A Constraint-Based Interactive Train Rescheduling Tool. CS-TR-96-07. The Chinese University of Hong Kong.
3. Rodriguez, J.: A constraint-programming model for real-time trains scheduling at junctions. 1st Inter- national seminar on Railway operations Modelling and Analysis, RailDELFT2005, The Netherlands, June 2005.
4. Indra-payong, N.: Constraint-based Local Search for Container Freight Rail Scheduling. Doctoral Thesis, Univ. of Leeds, 2005.
5. Oliveira, E.S.: Solving Single-Track Railway Scheduling Problem Using Constraint Programming. Doctoral Theses, Univ. of Leeds, 2001.
6. Forsgren, M.: Computation of Capacity on railway Networks. SICS, 2003.
7. Aronsson, M.: Efficient Utilisation of Resources in the Railway Industry by Levelling Departures and Arrivals of Trains. In: ERCIM News No. 56, January 2004.
8. Aggoun, A. & Beldiceanu, N.: Extending CHIP in order to solve complex scheduling and placement problems. J. Math. and Computer Modelling, 17(7):57–73, 1993.
9. Wallace, M.: Survey: Practical applications of constraint programming. Constraints Journal, 1(1,2), S.139-168. Kluwer Academic Publishers. September 1996.

10. Fr¨uhwirth, T. & Brisset, P.: Optimal Placement of Base Stations in Wireless Indoor Communication Networks, Special Issue on Practical Applications of Constraint Technology. In. M. Wallace and G. Freuder, Eds., IEEE Intelligent Systems Magazine Vol. 15(1), IEEE Press, USA, January/February 2000.

11. Geske, U.; Goltz, H.-J.; Matzke, D.: A technology for avoiding conflicts in multi-train simulation. In: Computers in Railways VII; WIT Press Series: Advances in Transport Volume 13, Southampton 2002.

12. Geske, U.; Goltz, H.-J.: Using CHIP for multi train simulation Proc. CHIP User Club Meeting, Paris, Nov. 2002.

13. Schutt, A.: Reduction of delays of trains in simulation of train scheduling based on Constrained-based Programming. (In German). Study. Humboldt-University, Berlin, 2005.

14. Rengert, F.: Investigation of the Combination of Constraint-based methods and Meta Heuristics (in German). Diploma thesis, University of Potsdam, 2005.

15. Schlenker, H.: Distributed Constraint-based Train Simulation (in German). Thesis, Technical University of Berlin, 2004.

16. Schlenker, H; Geske, U.: Simulating Large Railway Networks Using Distributed Constraint Satisfaction. 2nd IEEE International Conference on Industrial Informatics. Conference Proceedings, ISBN 0-7803-8514-4. 2004.

17. CHIP: http://www.cosytec.fr

User Profiles and Matchmaking on Mobile Phones

Thomas Kleemann and Alex Sinner

{tomkl|sinner}@uni-koblenz.de

Abstract. During the past few years mobile phones have become an ubiquitous companion. In parallel the semantic web provides enabling technologies to annotate and match information with a user's interests. This paper presents a thorough definition of annotations and profiles. The optimizations of annotations and profiles make the mobile phone a first class participant of a semantic environment rather than a mere displaying client of services running elsewhere. The implementation of the system – including a first order model generating theorem prover and a description logic interface – renders the idea viable in the real world. The choosen solution even enables explanations within the matchmaking process. The profile does not have to leave the personal device and ensures privacy by doing so. An additionally benefit is the independence from communication with any reasoning backends.

1 Introduction

Mobile phones were up to now mainly used for messaging and phone calls but they have become powerful devices with much more potential. Still, todays smart phones are at most used as dumb clients to more or less sophisticated mobile services.

Our goal is to show how this potential can be used for description logic (DL) based reasoning on the mobile devices themselves for personalization of mobile messaging services. To reach this goal, we define a unique framework called 'Semantic Mobile Environment', where the matchmaking between the user's profile and incoming semantically annotated messages is defined as a deduction task to be solved on the mobile device. The mobile reasoner, Pocket KRHyper, uses a transformation of DL concept expressions of expressivity $\mathcal{ALCHIR}+$, which is also described in this paper.

Because of their limited resources, mobile devices were generally not considered able to perform such reasoning tasks. An empirical evaluation of our implemented system shows the contrary, namely that today's smart phones are indeed suitable devices for intelligent services.

This paper is organized as follows: it starts with a thorough description of the framework which motivates this work. We continue with the formalization of different semantic mobile environment components, namely the semantic annotation of messages, the semantic user profile, and the matchmaking algorithm with limited resources in mind. We show how we used the Pocket KRHyper system to perform the description logic reasoning required for the matchmaking and explanations to matches. Finally we empirically evaluate our approach and compare it to related prior work.

M. Umeda et al. (Eds.): INAP 2005, LNAI 4369, pp. 135–147, 2006.

2   A Semantic Mobile Environment

The IASON project aims at providing mobile users with location-aware personalized information. Motivated by the development of powerful mobile devices and the semantic web, we define a *Semantic Mobile Environment*. In such an environment, so-called service nodes are installed at chosen points of interest. These service nodes broadcast semantically annotated messages (see Sect. 3.2) to nearby mobile users using bluetooth wireless technology. Because the service nodes are based on the same technology as the mobile phones the phones may become a service node themselves. Thus peer-to-peer services are established.

Such a semantic mobile environment is characterized by its independence from the internet and any cellular network. Only free ad-hoc bluetooth connections between service nodes and mobile devices have to be established to receive messages. Location-awareness is given implicitly by being in the wireless range of a service node. A *Semantic User Profile* describing the user's interests and disinterests is managed on her mobile device. This user profile is used to sort out unwanted messages by performing matchmaking between the semantic annotation of the messages and the user profile with respect to a common ontology (see [19]). The profile data never needs to be transmitted to any other device. This protects the privacy of mobile users.

The independence from the internet as well as our privacy policy come however at a cost: we cannot use existing reasoning systems like FaCT [12] or RACER [11] to perform the description logics [2,3] reasoning required for matchmaking. To take advantage of the existing work in ontologies we still think that description logics is the formalism of choice for semantic web applications, so we implemented a first order logic automated theorem prover (ATP), Pocket KRHyper [18], which also comes with a description logic interface. Pocket KRHyper is the first full-featured ATP system running on Java 2 Mobile Edition (J2ME[1]) cellular phones.

3   Semantic Personalization

Personalization is essential for all kinds of mobile services. The most obvious reason is that spam messages are generally not wanted. Another less obvious reason is that if mobile users want information, they only want information that is of interest to them. Or, to put it differently, mobile services will only be widely accepted if mobile users are relieved from the tedious task of sorting out irrelevant information. In our approach we use a description logic as a semantic language to perform personalization, which is discussed in the following.

3.1   Description Logics as Semantic Language

The idea of using description logics as a semantic language is not new [3]. There is good reasoning support for most expressive description logics and they are compatible to current W3C standards like OWL [1]. In this paper we use the expressiveness of the DL $\mathcal{ALCHIR}+$, which is the standard DL $\mathcal{ALC}$ extended with role hierarchies,

---

[1] http://java.sun.com/j2me

transitive and inverse roles. Syntax and semantics of $\mathcal{ALCHIR}+$ are amply described in [2]. This is a subset of the DL $\mathcal{SHIF}$ underlying OWL lite without the limited number restrictions.

In our mobile environment, we consider semantic services, semantic user profiles and concepts to which the services and profiles refer. This means that we have a common vocabulary ontology about the concepts in the real world, which is used to describe the annotation of semantic messages and the user profile. In addition a separate service ontology is used to describe the capabilities of services and user profiles. We expect all participants of the service to incorporate these ontologies. Figure 1 shows a sample movies vocabulary ontology in DL notation, where $\top$ is the universal concept and U the universal role.

$$
\begin{aligned}
Thing &\sqsubseteq \top \\
Movie &\sqsubseteq Thing \\
Genre &\sqsubseteq Thing \\
Medium &\sqsubseteq Thing \\
DVD &\sqsubseteq Medium \\
VCR &\sqsubseteq Medium \\
CinemaScreen &\sqsubseteq Medium \\
Epic &\sqsubseteq Genre \\
Fantasy &\sqsubseteq Genre \\
SciFi &\sqsubseteq Genre \\
Chess &\sqsubseteq Game \\
hasGenre &\sqsubseteq U \\
hasMedium &\sqsubseteq U
\end{aligned}
$$

Fig. 1. A Simple Movie Ontology

This simplistic movie ontology provides us with the necessary vocabulary to express a semantic annotation for a service which describes an offer of a Movie of genre SciFi on a DVD:

$$\exists offer.(Movie \sqcap \exists hasGenre.SciFi \sqcap \exists hasMedium.DVD)$$

3.2 Semantic Messages

In the semantic mobile environment every message is annotated with a DL concept expression that determines the semantics of the message. Because the mobile devices and service nodes can be used in a commercial and a peer-to-peer environment, the annotation has to distinguish between producers and consumers of goods and services. Additionally general and social interests lacking a producer-consumer separation shall

$$
\begin{aligned}
share &\sqsubseteq U \\
offer &\sqsubseteq share \\
request &\sqsubseteq share
\end{aligned}
$$

Fig. 2. The Service Ontology

be possible. These different types of services are specified through a role hierarchy in the service ontology (see Fig. 2).

This ontology is intentionally kept simple for clarity's sake, but could easily be extended by subroles of *offer* and *request*. Using these roles in combination with the vocabulary ontology, we can express complex annotations of the form:

$$annotation \equiv \exists R.C \tag{1}$$

$$R \in \{offer, request, share\} \tag{2}$$

Where C is a concept based on the vocabulary ontology. This ontology may change for specialized scenarios like trade fairs, tourism, and so on. The task to differentiate producers and consumers of objects is arranged by the two roles *offer* and *request*. Every producer is required to send an annotation starting with $\exists offer$. A consumer will send annotations starting with the quantified role $\exists request$. Because these roles are associated with every single message a participant may be a consumer of some kind of service, while offering some other services at the same time.

For those that do not adapt the consumer-producer scenario but prefer to look e.g. for a partner of a chess match, a more generic role expressing an undirected statement of interest has to be used. $\exists share$ has to be used in these cases. Additionally share may be used to define the interest of both *directions* in a topic C. Because *share* subsumes *request* and *offer* (see Fig. 2) it will match annotations that start with the *share* role as well as the *offer* and *request* role.

3.3 Semantic User Profile

On the receiving end for semantic services, we have a mobile device which manages a semantic user profile. This user profile stores the positively marked interests and the disinterests determined by rejected topics. The interests and disinterests in the profile are defined as follows:

$$profile \equiv interests \sqcap \overline{disinterests} \tag{3}$$

$$interests \equiv \bigsqcup_{i=1}^{n} positive_i \tag{4}$$

$$positive_i \equiv \exists R_i.C_i \tag{5}$$

$$disinterests \equiv \bigsqcup_{i=1}^{m} negative_i \tag{6}$$

$$negative_i \equiv \exists R_i.C_i \tag{7}$$

$$R_i \sqsubseteq share \tag{8}$$

From the definition, we see that the interests and disinterests are a collection of DL concepts that follow the definition of the annotations.

The user's interests and disinterests are updated from his/her responses to messages and allow for the use of ontological knowledge to generalize the annotation. The procedure of these updates is beyond the scope of this paper. An initial profile is generated from a short questionaire.

In the *Semantic Mobile Environment* every receiver of messages may also transmit these. A producer/consumer of goods or services is likely to be interested in requests/offers that correspond to his/her own messages. To enable the automatic update of the users profile a positive entry is generated for his/her outgoing messages. The annotation of the outgoing message $\exists R.C$ with $R \sqsubseteq share$ generates a positive entry in the profile $\exists R_p.C$ where R_p replaces R according to the table below. Thus a sender of messages will also positively match messages with an *inverse* annotation. The topic is preserved.

R in outgoing message	R_p in the profile
offer	*request*
request	*offer*
share	*share*

3.4 Matchmaking

The main motivation behind the DL formalization was to be able to compare the semantic annotation of incoming messages with the interests and disinterests stored in the semantic user profile. This is what we call matchmaking following the ideas in [16].

The decision whether a message matches a users interests is based on concept satisfiability and subsumption of the DL in use. Because the mobile clients provide limited computing power, the decision of a match is performed with at most two queries for arbitrarily complex profiles.

$$profile \sqcap annotation \not\equiv \perp \tag{9}$$

$$annotation \sqsubseteq profile \tag{10}$$

If the annotation satisfies test (9) the annotation is *compatible* with the profile.

The second test (10) will give a better *match degree* for those annotations that are subsumed by at least one of the *positive$_i$* terms. We call these annotations a *match*. This second test is only performed for *compatible* messages.

The satisfiability test (9) will fail for every annotation that is subsumed by the disinterests of a user. As a result we translate all *negative$_j$* concepts into a constraint on the models, see Sect. 5.

Unlike other approaches [16,17] these two queries are sufficient to answer the compatibility of an annotation with the profile. A large profile containing many interests and disinterests does not impose more tests. Thus this approach scales well even in the context of limited resources.

Avoiding Spam. As in all open communication systems there is a risk of unsolicited messages. Our approach has been designed to reject these annoying messages. The first test avoids spam carrying unsatisfiable annotations. If not rejected by this test these messages would be subsumed by the profile and considered a *match*.

The subsumption test avoids spam annotated with $\top$ or something close to $\top$ that will overcome the satisfiability test.

3.5 Example

The example shall illustrate the match decisions with respect to a user, who is interested in SciFi-movies and every information concerning cars. Messages covering

Table 1. Example Messages and Annotations

Message Text	
Annotation	Matchdegree
Car dealer buys all cars with diesel engine and 4wd	
$\exists request.(Car \sqcap \exists hasEngine.diesel \sqcap \exists hasDrive.fourwheel)$	match
Movierental offers 'Bladerunner' DVDs	
$\exists offer.(Movie \sqcap \exists hasGenre.SciFi \sqcap \exists hasMedium.dvd)$	match
I'm looking for a chess partner	
$\exists share.Chess$	mismatch
Museum of Modern Art shows Picasso exhibition	
$\exists offer.(Museum \sqcap \exists exhibits.Art)$	compatible

games are not of interest to the user. The profile contains the interests $\exists share.Car \sqcup \exists offer.(Movie \sqcap \exists hasGenre.SciFi)$ and the disinterest $\exists share.Game$. We have to mention here that a user requesting movies is interested in offers of movies.

On her walk through the city, the mobile user passes four service nodes and receives the messages listed in Tab. 1. Assuming the given profile the messages of the car and the DVD are matched, the exhibition is compatible with the profile, but the chess related message is rejected.

I would like to explain two cases in more detail. Because the annotation $\exists share.Chess$ of the third message is subsumed by the disinterest $\exists share.Game$, the first test of the matchmaking algorithm for the satisfiability of *profile* $\sqcap$ *annotation* fails. This renders the message/annotation to be a mismatch. No further testing is performed in this case.

In the case of the car dealer this first test is successful. So far this message would be compatible with the profile. The subsequent test for the subsumption *annotation* $\sqsubseteq$ *profile* is successful too, because $\exists request.(Car \sqcap ...)$ is subsumed by $\exists share.Car$ and therefore by the *profile*. Consequently this message is matched by the profile.

4 Mobile Reasoning

In Sect. 3, we have described how to formalize the semantic personalization problem for use on mobile devices. Messages are annotated with description logics semantics and the user profiles are similarly formalized using the same language. In the following, we will show how to perform the actual description logics reasoning needed for matchmaking on mobile devices.

4.1 Pocket KRHyper

Pocket KRHyper [18] is a J2ME software library for automated reasoning. It can be embedded in applications on mobile devices like PDAs, smartphones, and cell phones to perform first order logics reasoning.

The reasoning engine is based on the hyper tableau calculus [6] and can be considered as a resource optimized version of the KRHyper [23] system.

Pocket KRHyper was developed explicitly for use in mobile devices with modest resources, and is actually the first reasoner for mobile devices able to tackle useful first order logics problems. The main motivation behind the implementation of a mobile reasoner was the use case described in this paper, so Pocket KRHyper comes with a description logics interface. The transformation of DL expressions to first-order clausal form is described in Sect. 4.2.

Before describing how to perform this transformation, we will give some insights into the underlying calculus and its implementation.

The hyper tableau calculus is a first-order logic clausal tableau procedure described in [6,4]. A complete description of the calculus is beyond the scope of this paper, so we will only give a brief overview, focusing on some of the features of Pocket KRHyper.

Pocket KRHyper can tackle first order logic problems in clausal form. Clauses are considered as rules, where the head is a disjunction of all positive literals and the body a conjunction of all negative literals. Rules with an empty body are called facts. Rules with empty heads represent constraints on the models.

In each hyper tableau reasoning step, new instances of rule heads are derived in a bottom-up manner from input and derived facts. In hyper tableau, disjunctions are handled by exploring the alternative branches in a systematic way. If a hyper tableau derivation terminates without having found a refutation, the derived facts form a representation of a model of the input clauses.

To use the Pocket KRHyper system, a knowledge base of first-order logic clauses has to be provided. The hyper tableaux reasoning engine uses this knowledge base to compute either a refutation or a model. The reasoning algorithm performs an iterative deepening search for a model, expanding the proof tree in each iteration step up to a certain term weight. To ensure termination, the algorithm may be parameterized with either a timeout limit or a maximum term weight limit. If either limit is reached, the reasoner stops without a proof.

Ideally, the reasoning algorithm terminates when it has found either a model or a refutation. Found models can be retrieved and analyzed in the reasoning application. The reasoning algorithm may however also terminate abnormally if it has either been interrupted manually or by reaching a timeout or term weight limit, or if the virtual machine has run out of memory. All these abnormal cases are caught safely without causing the application to crash.

In comparison to the desktop KRHyper system [23], Pocket KRHyper lacks some features like default negation and term indexing, but it still provides all the main features that made the original KRHyper a useful tool. The new implementation of the calculus was necessary because the programming languages of previous ones are not supported on mobile devices. In addition convenient access to the reasoning services could be implemented.

4.2 Description Logics Transformation

The terminology, profile, and annotations are considered to be a finite set of axioms $C \sqsubseteq D$ and $C \equiv D$, where C, D are concepts of the DL ALC extended by inverse and transitive roles and role hierarchies (see Sect. 3.)

The transformation into sets of clauses introduces subconcepts to reduce the complexity of the concept expression or axiom. As an example the axiom $\exists R.C \sqsubseteq \forall S.\forall T.D$ is decomposed into $\exists R.C \sqsubseteq sub_i$ and $sub_i \sqsubseteq \forall S.sub_j$ and $sub_j \sqsubseteq \forall T.D$ to comply with

Table 2. Translation Primitives

description logic	first order formula	clauses
$C \sqcap D \sqsubseteq E$	$\forall x.C(x) \wedge D(x) \rightarrow E(x)$	e(x) :- c(x), d(x).
$C \sqcup D \sqsubseteq E$	$\forall x.C(x) \vee D(x) \rightarrow E(x)$	e(x) :- c(x).
		e(x) :- d(x).
$C \sqsubseteq \neg D$	$\forall x.C(x) \rightarrow \neg D(x)$	false :- c(x), d(x).
$\exists R.C \sqsubseteq D$	$\forall x \forall y.R(x,y) \wedge C(y) \rightarrow D(x)$	d(x) :- c(y), r(x,y).
$\forall R.C \sqsubseteq D$	$\forall x.(\forall y.R(x,y) \rightarrow C(y)) \rightarrow D(x)$	d(x); r(x,f_{R-C}(x)). *
		d(x) :- c(f_{R-C}(x)).
$C \sqsubseteq D \sqcap E$	$\forall x.C(x) \rightarrow D(x) \wedge E(x)$	e(x) :- c(x).
		d(x) :- c(x).
$C \sqsubseteq D \sqcup E$	$\forall x.C(x) \rightarrow D(x) \vee E(x)$	e(x); d(x) :- c(x).
$\neg C \sqsubseteq D$	$\forall x.\neg C(x) \rightarrow D(x)$	c(x); d(x). *
$C \sqsubseteq \exists R.D$	$\forall x.C(x) \rightarrow (\exists y.R(x,y) \wedge D(y))$	d(f_{R-D}(x)) :- c(x).
		r(x,f_{R-D}(x)) :- c(x). **
$C \sqsubseteq \forall R.D$	$\forall x.C(x) \rightarrow (\forall y.R(x,y) \rightarrow D(y))$	d(y) :- c(x), r(x,y).
$R \sqsubseteq S$	$\forall x \forall y.R(x,y) \rightarrow S(x,y)$	s(x,y) :- r(x,y)
$R^- \equiv S$	$\forall x \forall y.R(x,y) \leftrightarrow S(y,x)$	s(y,x) :- r(x,y).
		r(x,y) :- s(y,x).
R^+	$\forall x \forall y \forall z.R(x,y) \wedge R(y,z) \rightarrow R(x,z)$	r(x,z) :- r(x,y), r(y,z).

the transformation primitives. Table 2 gives the transformation primitives in abstract DL syntax, a corresponding first order formula, and the generated clauses.

The clauses marked with * share variables in a disjunctive head, they are not range-restricted. As an extension to previous work [18] Pocket KRHyper now handles these clauses by generating all ground instances up to the given term weight. Doing so often causes timeouts of the prover due to the limited resources. Clauses marked with ** are suitable for reasoning tasks in acyclic terminologies. Decidability commonly requires the tableau procedure to engage a blocking technique. The blocking techniques found in [10] may be adapted to the transformation as shown in [5].

The effective test for satisfiability of a concept C temporarily inserts a single fact C(a). into the knowledge base. C is satisfiable if the Pocket KRHyper finds a model for the knowledge base. A refutation indicates the unsatisfiability of the concept.

Subsumption of $C \sqsubseteq D$ is reduced to a test for satisfiability of $C \sqcap \neg D$. If this expression is not satisfiable, i.e. Pocket KRHyper finds a refutation, the subsumption holds. In clausal form the fact C(a). and a constraint :-D(a). are temporarily inserted into the knowledge base.

5   Optimizations to Save Resources

With these DL transformations Pocket KRHyper is able to detect satisfiability and subsumption of concepts. The requirements are currently limited to these tasks (see Sect. 3.4 and [19,16].)

Managing the Knowledge Base. In order to reduce the workload introduced by the translation of DL axioms into clausal form, the knowledge base is split into three parts.

The ontology is assumed to be stable throughout the runtime of the application. Thus this part is transformed once at the start of the mobile Java application (MIDlet). The profile is transformed only when it is updated. Solely the annotations of messages and the associated queries are transformed as they emerge.

The knowledge base keeps track of these parts by setting a mark at each such step, so it is possible to revert it to the state it had before an update or query.

Transformation of the Profile. The transformation of the user profile to the clausal knowledge base is performed according to Sect. 4.2 as far as the transformation of the individual *positive* and *negative* concepts are affected. To enhance the performance of Pocket KRHyper in the context of matchmaking, the interests and disinterests are treated differently. The equivalence of *interests* is reduced to subsumption. The *negative* concepts that make up the *disinterests* are transformed as constraints. Thus the closing of branches within the tableau is performing better.

$$positive_i \sqsubseteq profile \qquad\qquad i \in \{1,...,n\} \qquad\qquad (11)$$

$$negative_i \sqsubseteq \perp \qquad\qquad i \in \{1,...,m\} \qquad\qquad (12)$$

These changes do not vary the results with respect to the matching decisions (Sect. 3.4). Due to the structure of annotations and the profile, i.e. always starting with an existentially quantified subrole of *share*, the satisfiability of $annotation \sqcap profile$ is tested by the satisfiability of *annotation* with all $negative_i$ translated as mentioned above (12). A satisfiable *annotation* will fail this test if it is subsumed by one of the *disinterests*.

The subsumption $annotation \sqsubseteq profile$ has to be tested after the satisfiability test. At that point a subsumption of *annotation* by *disinterests* is known to be false. The reduction of the equivalence to subsumption does not influence this test.

Both simplifications lead to a reduced number of clauses. The effect is a reduced memory consumption of the knowledge base itself and the hyper tableau generated for the tests.

6   Towards Explaining Matches

Especially with a large profile made up of many interests a user may need a hint why a message is considered a match. Our suggestion is to point out the previously positively marked annotations or messages that generated the positive entry in the profile.

Unfortunately the subsumption is checked by a refutation. Opposed to that the first test in matchmaking provides a model based on the annotation. This model shall be used to find the relevant parts of a profile, namely the positives of the profile. A model generated by Pocket KRHyper is a set of ground or non-ground facts:

top(X0), *annotation(a)*, sub1(sk3(a)), offer(a,sk3(a)), share(a,sk3(a)),
... , *positive1(a), profile(a)*

This model is actually taken from the output of Pocket KRHyper with a slightly different notation. As can be seen in this example the model contains – in case of a match – the initial individual a of the predicate *annotation* in the predicate *profile*. Otherwise the subsumption will not hold (as this is the source of the clash.) Because the *profile* is a consequence of $positive_i$ at least one of the $positive_i(a)$ terms must be present in the model.

Of course there may be more positives in the model. To explain the match only those positives are relevant that are predicates of the initial individual a. This is opposed to the generated/skolemized individuals triggered by existential quantification, e.g. $sk3(a)$ in the example.

The set of $positive_i(a)$ is complete but not sound. The completeness is a consequence of the definition of subsumption. The subsumption $annotation \sqsubseteq positive_i$ holds iff in all models I the interpretations meet the condition $annotation^I \subseteq positive_i^I$.

The missing soundness is a consequence of disjunctions like $annotation \sqsubseteq positive_i \sqcup positive_j$. In these cases one of the $positive_i$, $positive_j$ will be part of the model, but neither subsumption $annotation \sqsubseteq positive_i$ nor $annotation \sqsubseteq positive_j$ holds. Some additional tests are needed to regain soundness, but the tests are limited by the model. Because the explanation is not the focus of this paper further details are postponed. However the ease of explanation is an advantage of the model generating paradigm in the context of DL reasoning.

7   Related Work and Evaluation

Some aspects described in this paper have been thoroughly investigated before, especially in the context of personalization in semantic web scenarios. To our knowledge, the use of automated reasoning on mobile devices for personalization in a semantic mobile environment is new.

A propositional tableaux-based theorem prover for JavaCard, CardTAP [8], has been implemented long before Pocket KRHyper. But unlike Pocket KRHyper, this was considered a toy system and was too slow and too restricted for real applications.

The capabilities of the presented DL transformation extend those of the Description Logic Programs (DLP) [9] subset of DL and LP. DLP captures the DAML+OIL fragment of RDFS. DLP is limited to the Horn-fragment of a logic like most Rule languages (e.g.RuleML [7]). According to our experience with non toy-problems the restriction to OWL-Horn or DLPs lacks the justification, because – as our implementation shows – disjunctive logic programs can be evaluated successfully, even on mobile devices.

The combination of disjunctive OWL lite knowledgebases and Horn-rules according to the SWRL proposal [13] is an obvious extension wrt. rules of the demonstrated approach. First results are available in [14].

A similar approach to matchmaking is described in [16]. We adapted that approach to reduce the number of reasoning steps needed for deciding a match degree to a maximum of two for arbitrarily complicated profiles. Another approach [17] to DL matchmaking using abduction also depends on multiple tests.

The integration of the distinction between producers and consumers within the annotation was a *must* in the mobile environment to reduce the number of reasoning steps.

Server-based marketplaces [22] tend to organize this differentiation on a meta-level. Opposed to these marketplaces we also support the generic *sharing* of interests that is required in peering settings of the system.

A performance evaluation of Pocket KRHyper with respect to a selection of TPTP [20] problems can be found in [18]. This evaluation shows that the reasoner performs reasonably well to be used in real applications. The matchmaking process on a contemporary phone is performed in about one second with an ontology of about two hundred concepts. The execution time of the same reasoner running on a desktop computer with a J2SE virtual machine is about fifty times faster than on our mobile phones, and is comparable to the execution time of the RACER [11] system for the given tasks. For more general tasks this performance may not be expected, because the mobile implementation is intentionally kept small without most of the indexing and caching techniques used in systems like RACER. A comprehensive comparison is available in [15].

Beyond our messaging scenario a mobile reasoning or matchmaking task may be a useful contribution in maintenance scenarios as described in [21].

8   Conclusions

In this paper, we have described how to perform matchmaking on mobile devices for personalization in a semantic mobile environment. In such an environment, semantically annotated messages are sent to nearby mobile users. The personalization task is performed on the user's mobile device by matching the annotation of incoming messages against the semantic user profile on the device.

We have shown how to formalize the semantics of messages and user interests and disinterests using description logics in a resource friendly fashion. The messages and user profiles are described using a common ontology, which allows us to propose an efficient matchmaking algorithm using standard description logics checks. An additional service ontology allows to specify the semantics of the type of service offered.

To bring the theory to life, we have implemented the described system including the Pocket KRHyper first order logic theorem proving system for mobile devices. A brief overview about the calculus and some implemented features is given. Since our personalization problem is specified in description logics, we also propose a transformation from DL terminologies to first order knowledge bases.

Both the management of the user profile and the decision support using the Pocket KRHyper reasoner are handled on the mobile device, which has not been done in other systems so far. This implies that no personal information ever has to leave the mobile device, which ensures the privacy of the user.

Decision support on mobile devices is no longer fiction, but from now on we expect a range of new reasoning-supported mobile applications to emerge.

Acknowledgments. This work has partly been performed with the support of "Stiftung Rheinland-Pfalz für Innovation" for the IASON project.

References

1. G. Antoniou and F. van Harmelen. Web ontology language: Owl. In S. Staab and R. Studer, editors, *Handbook on Ontologies in Information Systems*. Springer-Verlag, 2003.
2. F. Baader, D. Calvanese, D. L. McGuinness, D. Nardi, and P. F. Patel-Schneider. *The description logic handbook: theory, implementation, and applications*. Cambridge University Press, 2003.
3. F. Baader, I. Horrocks, and U. Sattler. Description logics as ontology languages for the semantic web, 2003.
4. P. Baumgartner. Hyper Tableaux — The Next Generation. Technical Report 32–97, Universität Koblenz-Landau, 1997.
5. P. Baumgartner, U. Furbach, M. Gross-Hardt, and T. Kleemann. Model based deduction for database schema reasoning. In S. Biundo, T. Frühwirth, and G. Palm, editors, *KI 2004: Advances in Artificial Intelligence*, volume 3238, pages 168–182. Springer Verlag, 2004.
6. P. Baumgartner, U. Furbach, and I. Niemelä. Hyper Tableaux. Technical Report 8–96, Universität Koblenz-Landau, 1996.
7. H. Boley and et. al. RuleML, www.ruleml.org, 2005.
8. R. Goré, J. Posegga, A. Slater, and H. Vogt. System description: cardtap: The first theorem prover on a smart card. In *CADE-15: Proceedings of the 15th International Conference on Automated Deduction*, pages 47–50, London, UK, 1998. Springer-Verlag.
9. B. N. Grosof, I. Horrocks, R. Volz, and S. Decker. Description logic programs: Combining logic programs with description logic. In *Proc. of the Twelfth International World Wide Web Conference (WWW 2003)*, pages 48–57. ACM, 2003.
10. V. Haarslev and R. Möller. Expressive ABox Reasoning with Number Restrictions, Role Hierarchies, and Transitively Closed Roles. In *KR2000: Principles of Knowledge Representation and Reasoning*, pages 273–284. Morgan Kaufmann, 2000.
11. V. Haarslev and R. Möller. RACER system description. *Lecture Notes in Computer Science*, 2083:701, 2001.
12. I. Horrocks. The FaCT system. *Lecture Notes in Computer Science*, 1397:307–312, 1998.
13. I. Horrocks, P. F. Patel-Schneider, S. Bechhofer, and D. Tsarkov. OWL rules: A proposal and prototype implementation. *J. of Web Semantics*, 3(1):23–40, 2005.
14. T. Kleemann. Towards mobile reasoning. In *proc. of the workshop on Knowledge Engineering and Software Engineering*. Bremen, 2006.
15. T. Kleemann. Towards OWL reasoning with SWRL. In *proc. of the Description Logic workshop*. ceur-ws.org, 2006.
16. L. Li and I. Horrocks. A software framework for matchmaking based on semantic web technology. In *Proceedings of the Twelfth International World Wide Web Conference (WWW'2003)*, pages 331–339. ACM, 2003.
17. T. D. Noia, E. D. Sciascio, F. M. Donini, and M. Mongiello. Abductive matchmaking using description logics. In *Proc. of IJCAI'03*, pages 337–342, 2003.
18. A. Sinner and T. Kleemann. Krhyper - in your pocket, system description. In *proc. of Conference on Automated Deduction, CADE-20*. Springer Verlag, 2005.
19. A. Sinner, T. Kleemann, and A. von Hessling. Semantic user profiles and their applications in a mobile environment. In *proc. of Artificial Intelligence in Mobile Systems*, 2004.
20. G. Sutcliffe and C. Suttner. The TPTP Problem Library: CNF Release v1.2.1. *Journal of Automated Reasoning*, 21(2):177–203, 1998.
21. H. Takahshi and O. Yoshie. Ubiquitous maintenance - defining invocation of plant maintanance agents in real workspace by spatial programming. In D. Seipel, M. Hanus, U. Geske, and O. Bartenstein, editors, *Applications of Declarative Programming and Knowledge Management INAP/WLP*, volume 3392 of *Lecture Notes in Artificial Intelligence*. Springer Verlag, March 2004.

22. D. Veit, J. Muller, M. Schneider, and B. Fiehn. Matchmaking for autonomous agents in electronic marketplaces. In *5th international conference on Autonomous agents AGENTS'01*, pages 65–66. ACM, 2001.
23. C. Wernhard. System Description: KRHyper. Fachberichte Informatik 14–2003, Universität Koblenz-Landau, 2003.

A Design Product Model for Mechanism Parts by Injection Molding

Tatsuichiro Nagai[1], Isao Nagasawa[1], Masanobu Umeda[1], Tatsuji Higuchi[2],
Yasuyuki Nishidai[2], Yusuke Kitagawa[3], Tsuyoshi Tsurusaki[1],
Masahito Ohhashi[2], and Osamu Takata[1]

[1] Graduate School of Computer Science and Systems Engineering,
Kyushu Institute of Technology, Japan
[2] Olympus Corporation, Tokyo, Japan
[3] NaU Data Institute Inc., Fukuoka, Japan

Abstract. Recently, design support tools have been used to improve the efficiency of design work. These tools support design verification at each design stage, and succeed to some extent in improving the efficiency of the design work. However, the management of scattered design information and data conversion have lately become difficult because designers often require two or more tools. In this paper, we focus on the detailed design of mechanism parts made by injection molding and used in precision consumer products. We propose a design product model which describes the detailed design of such parts. The model describes the mechanism parts based on sets of faces, which are basic units in design work. In this way, the model can express design information in both two- and three-dimensional forms. We also define the procedures used to operate the model. Finally, the effectiveness of this model is shown by applying it to an experimental system.

1 Introduction

Recently, there has been an increased demand for small size and high performance in precision consumer products such as cameras, cellular phones, and PDAs, and thus it has become important to reduce the number of parts within these devices. Accordingly, component parts[1] in which two or more functions are combined are seeing increasing use.

The product life-cycle of these precision consumer products has recently become shorter, and consequently the design period has shortened. On the other hand, much manpower is needed to design component parts that have complex forms. The result has been an insufficient number of detailed checks at each design stage, including checks on parts interference, assembly, operation performance, mass production, etc. This, in turn, has frequently resulted in design deficiencies, and has thus posed an obstacle in shortening the device's design period and reducing its cost.

---

[1] These parts are made using the injection molding method[1], a technique for forming molded goods by injecting high temperature melt materials into metal molds, followed by cooling to solidify them.

M. Umeda et al. (Eds.): INAP 2005, LNAI 4369, pp. 148–160, 2006.
© Springer-Verlag Berlin Heidelberg 2006

Currently, the design period has been shortened by the use of individual design-support tools. For instance, the rapid prototyping process (stereolithography) omits formation of the mold in the experimental stage, reducing both the design period and the cost. Other examples include CAE, CAM, and the use of 3D CAD to perform interference checks.

The injection molding method discussed in this paper has the following features with respect to the part's form. These parts' forms can be designed by synthesizing the form definition in each direction in which the mold is pulled out. Until recently, the part form viewed from the direction in which the part is pulled from a mold has been drawn using 2D drafting CAD. The dimension settings and the manufacturing notes are included in 2D drafting CAD. However, assembly cannot be verified in this environment. Recently, parts have been designed using 3D CAD, and part of the design verification has also been performed using 3D CAD. However, the present 3D CAD cannot sufficiently support the design of mechanism parts produced using the injection molding method. Moreover, 3D CAD cannot effectively represent and handle the part's function and dimension settings. Therefore, 3D CAD cannot continuously support the mechanism parts design from the mechanism unit design.

Increasingly, design divisions are demanding design support environments that can continuously support the mechanism parts design from the mechanism unit design. Several studies have considered the modeling of design objects by using enhanced feature-based models [2,3,4,5] that express function and assembly. Such models enable us to describe a part's form and function. However, they are inadequate at modeling the dimension setting and the restriction of the injection molding method.

We previously proposed an attribute model[6,7,8] of the design object that uniformly expressed information regarding the design proposal of consumer products based on sets of attributes. In addition, we devised a technique that enables us to analyze tolerance through the use of this model. Finally, by enhancing the attribute model we represented information regarding the detailed design of a welding vessel and its manufacturing design.

In this paper, we propose a model in which both 2D and 3D forms are uniformly represented. We pay attention to the direction in which a part is pulled from a mold in injection molding. This is 3D form creation technology using the attribute model for the injection molding method. When the function of mechanical components is added to this model, the accuracy of the assembly and mechanism can be verified. As a result, the greater part of design verifications become possible on the computer in the design section, and the design period and the design cost can be reduced.

2   An Overview of the Production of Mechanism Parts by Injection Molding

In the production of a device's mechanism parts by injection molding, metal molds[1] composed of a cavity and a core are used, as shown in Fig.1. First,

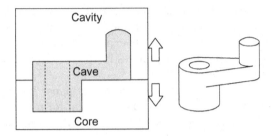

Fig. 1. Example of a metal mold used in injection molding

the cavity and the core are matched to each other, and the melt resin is then injected into the cave formed in the metal mold and press-fit to the shape of the cave. Second, the cavity portion is pulled out after the press-fit resin cools and hardens. Finally, the molded products that are attached to the core portion are pushed out by ejector pins.

3   Requirement for the Design Object Model

The following are required for a model that can describe the form and function of a mechanism part produced by injection molding.

Range of representation of the design product model
Mechanism's parts produced by injection molding, called simply **mechanism parts** hereafter, are widely used for precision consumer products, such as cameras, cellular phones, and PDAs. Therefore, the model should describe the mechanism parts using a general method which is applicable to those cases.

Representation of function and form creation [2]
The model should describe the functions of the mechanism and assembly operation, and should also describe the form of the mechanism parts created by injection molding.

Flexibility in design changes
In the development of precision consumer products, the design is frequently changed in order to improve the mechanism's operation and avoid interference with its form. Therefore, the model should be flexible regarding modifications of dimension, tolerance, and form.

Automatic generation of three-dimensional form
The model should be able to automatically generate a three-dimensional form of the mechanism parts, allowing inspection of the form in regard to parts interference and confirmation of the results of the injection molding process.

---

[2] This paper targets the part design performed in the design section, but does not concern itself with the type molding done in the experimental section.

4 Assembly Structure of Mechanism Parts by Injection Molding

When mechanism parts are designed, the designer describes their form by using a ruler and a compass. In addition, the designer specifies the properties of the important faces of the mechanism parts in terms of the part's dimensions and manufacturing notes. Surface characteristics, position, posture, and the final processing method are all properties of a part. In light of the above, we propose the following. Mechanism parts can be structurally defined by using the part's basic figures, faces, views, and form. The basic figure is a generic name for point, straight line, curve, and so on. The face is composed of the face's properties and the contours of its surface. The view is a form seen from the direction in which the mold is pulled out and is composed of sets of faces. The part form is composed of two or more views. The model defined above is called the **assembly structure**[3]. The assembly structure is a kind of the attribute model.

The basic figure, face, view, and part form that compose the assembly structure are generically called an **assembly object**. The assembly object has attributes of position, dimension, form, and so on. The assembly object depends on other assembly objects. In the following, this relationship is called the **dependence**.

4.1 Arrangement Coordinate System and Dimension Setting

The data structure that expresses the position and the direction of the figure and parts is called an **arrangement coordinate system**. As a simple example, we consider an arrangement system of coordinates in two dimensions. The arrangement coordinate system expresses a position and an angle by a set[4] $\{x, y, r\}$ where x and y are its origin and r is its angle. In addition, the arrangement coordinate system is dependent on another arrangement coordinate system, which is called **dimension setting** (Table 1).

In the following, we explain the arrangement coordinate system by using the examples shown in Fig.2 . In (a), the coordinate system $C0$ is the arrangement coordinate system that becomes the standard at the position. $C1$ is an arrangement coordinate system in which $C0$ was rotated by 30° . $C2$ is an arrangement coordinate system in which $C1$ was transferred along the x-axis by 50. The lower side in (b) shows the assembly structure of these arrangement coordinate systems and dimension settings. The ovals $(C0, C1, C2)$ in Fig.2 show the assembly objects of the arrangement coordinate systems, called **coord** in the following. A circle shows an attribute of an assembly object. An arrow shows dimension setting of an assembly object. Here, $r2$ and $t2x$ show the dimension settings by a rotation of 30° and a transfer along the x-axis by 50, respectively.

---

[3] The functional element was designated as a component of the assembly structure in [6,7,8]. However, in this paper a basic figure is a component of the assembly structure, and the functional element is not.

[4] Actually, this has been expressed by the coordinate transformation matrix [9].

Table 1. Dimension settings

Type	Name	Description
2D transfer	t2x,t2y	transfer to X or Y direction.
2D rotation	r2	rotate.
3D transfer	t3x,t3y,t3z	transfer to X, Y, or Z direction.
3D rotation	r3x,r3y,r3z	rotate on X axis, Y axis, or Z axis.

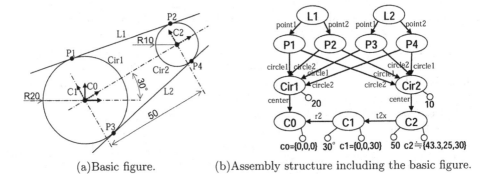

(a)Basic figure.   (b)Assembly structure including the basic figure.

Fig. 2. Assembly structure including the basic figure

In figures of assembly structure, we use the drawing $b \xleftarrow{R} a$ to show that an assembly object a depends on another assembly object b because of dependence R.

4.2 Basic Figure

The assembly object that shows a point, a straight line, and a circle is called a **basic figure**. In Table 2, the **point** is a basic figure whose position in two dimensions is shown for the x and y coordinates. The **line** and the **circle** are basic figures in which a straight line and a circle in two dimensions are shown. These depend on the other basic figures and are arranged with attributes such as coordinate value and radius.

In the following, we explain the assembly structure including the basic figure by using the example shown in Fig.2 . This figure was made using the following procedures. First, circle $Cir1$ of radius 20 and $Cir2$ of radius 10 were arranged a center on the arrangement coordinate systems $C0$ and $C2$, respectively. Next, two common tangents between $Cir1$ and $Cir2$ were temporarily drawn and their contact points were defined as $P1, P2, P3$, and $P4$, while the lines on these points were defined as $L1$ and $L2$, as shown in Fig.2 (a). In (b), **Circle $Cir1$ depends on coord $C0$** because of the dependence *center*. **Point $P1$** depends on **Circles** $Cir1$ and $Cir2$ because of the dependencies *circle1* and *circle2*. **Line $L1$** depends on **Points** $P1$ and $P2$ because of the dependencies *point1* and *point2*. **Circle** $Cir2$, **Points** $P2, P3$, and $P4$, and **Line** $L2$ are also similar to those mentioned above.

Table 2. Examples of basic figures

Type	Name	Description	Attribute	Dependence
Point	coordsys	arrangement coordinate system	$\{x, y, r\}, t, \theta$	t2x, t2y, r2
	point_2L	intersection of two lines	$\{x, y\}$	line1, line2
	point_tan_2C	contact point on tangential line of 2 circles	$\{x, y\}$	circle1, circle2
Line	line_1P	line provided for at one point and angle	$intercept X, Y, \theta$	point
	line_2P	line that passes by two points	$intercept X, Y$	point1, point2
Circle	circle_1P	circle provided for at center point and radius	$\{x, y\}, radius$	center
	circle_2P	circle provided for at two points and radius	$\{x, y\}, radius$	point1, point2

4.3 Contour Element

The segment and the circular arc together are called the **contour element**. A contour element has the attributes of length and angle, and a contour element depends on basic figures (Table 3).

In the following, we explain the assembly structure including contour elements by using the example shown in Fig.3 . In this figure, **Arc** $A1$ and **Segment** $S1$ depend on **Points** $P1 \sim P3$, **Circle** $Cir1$, and **Line** $L1$. Some basic figures are omitted from the figure for simplicity.

4.4 Face

One of the features of the face is called the surface. The surface includes a plane, a cylinder, and a sphere as shown in Table 4. The closed path is made of connected contour elements. The closed path is called the loop. The face is composed of the surface and the loops. The surface is attached to the loops. In the loop of the face, the number of outside contours, hereafter called the **OutLoop**, is one, and the number of inside contours, hereafter called the **InLoop**, is 0 or more.

Table 3. Examples of contour elements

Type	Name	Description	Attribute	Dependence
Segment	lineseg	segment provided for by two points on a line	length	line, point1, point2
Arc	arc	arc provided for by two points on a circle	open angle	circle, point1, point2

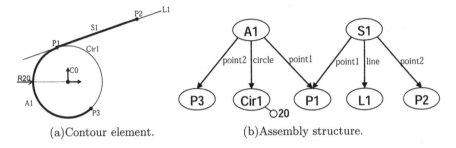

(a)Contour element.　　　　　(b)Assembly structure.

Fig. 3. Assembly structure including contour elements

Table 4. Examples of surfaces

Type	Name	Description	Attribute
Plane	plane	horizontal plane by height specification	height
Cylinder	cylinder	cylinder by center axis and radius	center axis,radius
Sphere	sphere	sphere by center point and radius	center point,radius

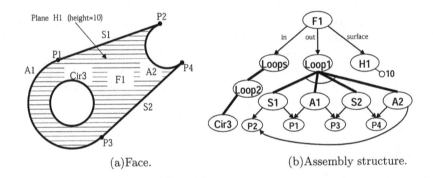

(a)Face.　　　　　　　　(b)Assembly structure.

Fig. 4. Assembly structure including the face

In the following, we explain the assembly structure including the face by using the example shown in Fig.4. In this figure, **Face** $F1$ has a **Plane** $H1$ with a height of 10. **Face** $F1$ is composed of **OutLoop** $Loop1$ and **InLoop** $Loop2$. **OutLoop** $Loop1$ is composed of **Arc** $A1$, **Segment** $S2$, **Arc** $A2$, and **Segment** $S1$. **InLoop** $Loop2$ is composed of **Circle** $Cir3$[5] . Some basic figures are omitted in this figure. In (b), $Loops$ is an object that shows a set of **InLoops**. The thick line shows the set.

4.5　View

The part's form seen from the direction in which the part is pulled out of the mold is called the **View**. The assembly structure of the **View** is composed of the

---
[5] A **Circle** is considered to be the **loop**.

standard arrangement coordinate system and all assembly objects that depend on this arrangement coordinate system. The **View** is then represented in terms of this arrangement coordinate system. The **coord** $C0$ in Fig.2 is a representative of the **View**.

4.6 Part Form

The **Part form** is a synthesis of two or more **Views** centered on the part's standards. The mold of the Slider is set to a direction different from those of the Cavity and the Core. The position and the posture of the **View** can then be defined by using the coordinate arrangement system in three dimensions. Up to now, we have focused on an arrangement coordinate system in which the view is represented in two dimensions. However, the arrangement coordinate system can also be interpreted in three dimensions. The arrangement coordinate system in three dimensions showing the part's center is the representation of the **Part form**. All **Views** depend on this arrangement coordinate system.

Fig.5 shows the part form used to synthesize two **Views** of the cavity and the core. The representation of the cavity is made based on the arrangement coordinate system $C0$. The representation of the core is made based on the arrangement coordinate system $C0'$. Fig.5 (a) shows the relation between the actual parts and the **View**. Fig.5 (b) shows the assembly structure of the **Part form**. The dotted lines with arrowheads are dependencies that omit assembly

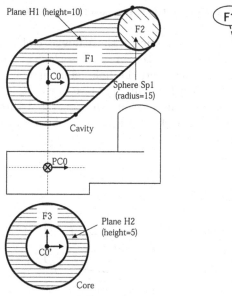
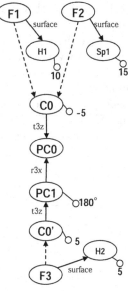

(a)Actual parts and the view.   (b)Assembly structure.

Fig. 5. Part form

object further down the assembly chain. $PC0$ is an arrangement coordinate system showing the part's center. **View** $C0$ is arranged at the position that moved from $PC0$ in the Z-direction by -5. The **coord** $PC1$ is arranged at the position in which **coord** $PC0$ was rotated around the X-axis by 180° . In addition, **coord** $C0'$ is arranged at the position in which **coord** $PC1$ was moved in the Z-direction by 5.

5 Three-Dimensional Form Generation

The three-dimensional form of a mechanism part can be generated based on the assembly structure of the **Part form**. A rectangular solid larger than the part's form is first prepared. The rectangular solid is reduced to the positions of the **Faces** in the **View**. When the rectangular solid is reduced to the position of the **Faces** of all **View**s, the **Part form** of the 3D form can be generated.

A mechanism part actually has parting lines where it touches the metal mold when made by injection molding. When the **View** is made, faces where the cavity and the core of the metal mold touch are arranged as the **Face** of the assembly object. As a result, we can easily enhance the model to include the parting line is considered.

Fig.6 shows a three-dimensional form generated from the assembly structure shown in Fig.5 . Fig.6 (a) is the three-dimension form on the **View** of the cavity generated by reducing the rectangular solid. In addition, the **Part form** is generated by reducing this according to the core's assembly structure, as shown in Fig.6 (b).

In Fig.6 (a), the shaded portion is not a **Face** of the **View** assembly structure. Rather, when the View is formed, this side face is created as a logical consequence of View formation. The gear, the shaft, and the hole, etc., that are made by injection molding become the surface where this side face functions.

The assembly simulation can be done by using the generated three-dimensional forms. Moreover, the interference checks of parts can be done. These can decrease the failure of the design.

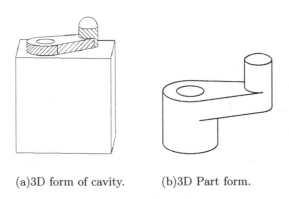

(a)3D form of cavity.   (b)3D Part form.

Fig. 6. 3D form of a part

6   Assembly Structure Operation

The assembly structure is edited by using the basic operations shown in Table 5. These basic operations include the procedures that generate each assembly object, such as **Basic figure**, **Contour element**, **Face**, **View**, and **Part form**.

Table 5. Examples of basic operations for assembly structure

operation type	operation name	operation meaning
generate an instance of assembly object	make_instance($Class,Obj$, attributes($a_1(v_1),\dots,a_n(v_n)$), relation($r_1(Ob_1),\dots,r_n(Ob_n)$)))	To make instance Obj from the $Class$. $a_i(v_i)$ means attribute a_i with the initial value or the expression v_i.
refer to a object by dependence	$Obj.R$	To refer to the assembly objects that assembly object Obj depends on them by the dependence R.
inversely refer to a object by dependence	$Obj.inv(R)$	To refer to the assembly objects that depend on assembly object Obj by the dependence R.
change attribute value	set_attribute(Obj, a, v)	To change the value of attribute a of assembly object Obj.
get attribute value	$Obj.a$	To refer to the value of attribute a of Obj.

```
make_line_2p(Obj, Point1, Point2):-
    point1.y =\= point2.y,
    point1.x =\= point2.x, !,
    make_instance(line_2p, Obj,
        attributes(
            interceptX(
                (point2.x*point1.y-point1.x*point2.y)
                            /(point1.y-point2.y)), ···(1)
            interceptY(
                (point1.x*point2.y-point2.x*point1.y)
                            /(point1.x-point2.x))),···(2)
        relation(point1(Point1),point2(Point2))).      ···(3)
```

Fig. 7. A procedure for generating line_2P

Fig.7 shows examples of the procedure that generates the assembly object of **line_2P**. In this figure, the expressions (1), (2), and (3) define $interceptX$, $interceptY$, and the dependence ahead, respectively. When $interceptX$ of **line_2P** is referred to, expression (1) is evaluated. The description form shown in Fig.7 includes the addition of an object-oriented feature to Prolog [10] . Other assembly

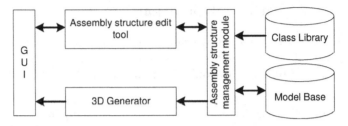

Fig. 8. System overview

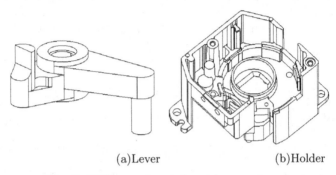

(a)Lever   (b)Holder

Fig. 9. 3D forms of parts input by experiment

objects can be similarly defined. The kind of class used when generating the assembly object is 'part_form', 'view', 'face', or the item 'Name' in Tables 2,3, and 4 .

7   Experimental Edit System of Design Product Model for Mechanism Parts

To demonstrate the effectiveness of our model, we developed an experimental system based on the model. The assembly structure can be edited using this system. Fig.8 shows an overview of the system at its present stage of development. This system includes 'GUI' that corresponds to the operation of 2D CAD. The 'Assembly structure edit tool' edits the assembly structures of parts through GUI. The 'Assembly structure management module' manages the assembly structures of the mechanism parts. The 'Class Library' is used to refer to the information necessary for generating and editing the assembly structure. The 'Model Base' saves the assembly structure of the designed mechanism parts. The '3D Generator' automatically generates the three-dimensional form of mechanism parts based on the assembly structure. The '3D Generator' is powered by Parasolid (Unigraphics Solutions Inc.)[11] .

Certain mechanism parts of precision consumer products were used to evaluate the experimental system, and it was confirmed that the parts' three-dimensional forms could be generated based on the assembly structures. Fig.9 shows three-dimensional forms of the parts input to the system. (a) is a part of easy shape, and (b) is a part of complex shape. In addition, when the assembly structures of the mechanism parts changed, their three-dimensional forms changed automatically.

The input time was shorter than a general CAD system just a little. However, the input time of parts was not too important because it was a confirmation of an effectiveness of the model this time. Time to generate three-dimensional form from the model was 1 second or less.

8   Conclusion

In this paper, we have focused on the detailed design of mechanism parts for precision consumer products created by means of injection molding, and have proposed an assembly structure that manages design information. The mechanism parts are described based on the faces that are expressed in terms of the two dimensional figure and their surfaces. The two dimensional figure and that of the surface are classified into primitive objects. And, the assembly structure is constructed by using them. The proposed model can treat the direction in which a mold is pulled during injection molding. This paper has also proposed a technique that can generate the three-dimensional forms of mechanism parts. Finally, this paper demonstrated the effectiveness of the model by constructing an experimental model system and applying it to design examples.

In the future, it will be necessary to enhance the model and to develop a design support system that can verify assemblies and mechanism operation. It will also be necessary to apply the model system to actual design projects.

References

1. Japanese Society of Die and Mould Technology, editors. *DIE & MOULD*. THE NIKKAN KOGYO SHIMBUN,LTD., 1989.
2. J. J. Shah and M. T. Rogers. Assembly modeling as an extension of feature-based design. *Research in Engineering Design (USA)*, 5:218–237, 1993.
3. V. Allada and S. Anand. Feature-based modelling approaches for integrated manufacturing: state-of-the-art survey and future research directions. *Int. J. Computer Integrated Manufacturing*, 8(6):411–440, 1995.
4. M. Martti, N. Dana, and S. Jami. Challenges in feature-based manufacturing research. *Comm. ACM*, 39(2):77–85, 1996.
5. F.-C. Yang and M.-T. Wang. An object-oriented feature-based computer-aided design system for concurrent engineering. IEEE Cat. No.92TH0500-9, 393-8, xvi+711, 1992.
6. M. Mochizuki, I. Nagasawa, M. Umeda, T. Higuchi, and T. Ojima. A knowledge representation language for tolerance analyses and its programming techniques. *Transactions of Information Processing Society of Japan*, 35(9):1922–1935, 1994.
7. T. Ojima, I. Nagasawa, T. Higuchi, M. Mochizuki, M. Umeda, and Z.H. Zhang. Design support system for lens case units of camera. *Transactions of Information Processing Society of Japan*, 38(1):131–145, 1997.

8. Z.H. Zhang, I. Nagasawa, M. Mochizuki, H. Yamaguchi, and M. Umeda. A design object model for manufacturing design of welding vessel objects. *Transactions of Information Processing Society of Japan*, 41(1):123–135, 2000.

9. David F.Rogers and J.Alan Adams. *Computer Graphics*. THE NIKKAN KOGYO SHIMBUN,LTD., 1979.

10. Keiichi Katamine, Masanobu Umeda, Isao Nagasawa, and Masaaki Hashimoto. Integrated development environment for knowledge-based systems and its practical application. *IEICE Transactions on Information and Systems*, E87-D(4):877–885, April 2004.

11. Unigraphics Solutions Inc. *Parasolid V12.0 On-Line Documentation*, June 2000.

A Knowledge-Based System for Process Planning in Cold Forging Using the Adjustment of Stepped Cylinder Method

Osamu Takata[1], Yuji Mure[2], Yasuo Nakashima[3], Masuharu Ogawa[3], Masanobu Umeda[1], and Isao Nagasawa[1]

[1] Kyusyu Institute of Technology, Japan
[2] Kagoshima Prefectural Institute of Industrial Technology, Japan
[3] Japan Hardware Co., Ltd., Japan

Abstract. We report on a knowledge-based system for process planning in cold forging. In this system, a forged product is represented as an aggregation of forming patterns that consists of cylindrical pillar parts. The basic principle of the inference method we propose is to adjust the diameters of neighboring stepped cylinders so that they are identical. Plural deformable process plans are generated using expert knowledge about working limits, die configurations, and metal flow. This system can eliminate ineffective plans by using the knowledge of how to combine plural forming patterns into a single process. Moreover, it can evaluate process plans and interactively select the optimal one by considering production costs, the forming load, the effective strain in the product, the equipment, and other factors. We applied this system to actual forged products. As a result, this system is widely applicable to various shapes and types of equipment and can improve both maintenance and operation.

1 Introduction

Forging is a process of forming steel or non-ferrous metal billets into required product shapes through intermediate products by hammering or pressing as shown in Fig. 1. This process is applicable to mass production and is, therefore, widely used in manufacturing automobile parts.

Process planning in forging is very important because it has great influence on the cost and quality of the final products. However, it is time-consuming and requires considerable experience and knowledge about forming and equipment. Because the number of expert engineers is decreasing, it is essential to create a way for companies to inherit this knowledge by developing systems using a knowledge-based approach that incorporates a knowledge of the forging process and formulates the utilization of this knowledge.

For this purpose, many kinds of knowledge-based systems have been developed [1, 2, 3, 4, 5, 6, 7]. These can be classified into two types. Systems of the first type formulate a new process plan by retrieving previous cases and revising them. Such systems, however, cannot generate a plan if a similar case is not stored in their database. Systems of the second type generate new process plans

M. Umeda et al. (Eds.): INAP 2005, LNAI 4369, pp. 161–174, 2006.

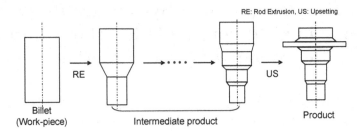

Fig. 1. An example of multi-stage cold forging

by using knowledge of the forming method of one process, its working limits, etc. For this type of system to be applicable to various kinds of products, it is necessary to analyze and formalize a large number of cases in order to build a cumulative knowledge base. For these reasons, neither of these two types of systems is applicable to a wide range of forged products and equipment.

The basic concept of the present study is to faithfully reproduce the thinking processes of expert engineers in process planning in forging. In our approach, expert knowledge of process planning is decomposed into working limits, die configurations, and metal flow. As a result, the decomposition of the knowledge contributes greatly in applying it to a variety of forged products and equipment. Therefore, in our approach various practical process plans and die configurations can be generated by the use of this knowledge. Furthermore, an optimal process plan can be evaluated and selected based on considerations of production costs, forming load, effective strain in the product, equipment, etc.

This paper explains a prototype system based on our basic principles and describes the functions of plan generation and plan selection [8]. In particular, methods to implement plan generation such as data representation, inference method, and knowledge representation are mentioned. We demonstrate the usefulness of our system by applying it to various practical solid and hollow forged products.

2   Outline of FORTEK

For axis-symmetrical solid or hollow cold forged products, including such as bolts and gears, the present system uses knowledge to generate feasible process plans. Next, it selects the optimal process plan, also incorporating a designer. The optimal criteria, which include information such as forming load, effective strain, and the die configuration, are interactively defined by the designer.

First, in the plan generation stage, the system, with knowledge about working limits, die configurations, and metal flow, generates feasible process plans, which consist of a series of single formings combined into a single process. At this time, a plural forming in a single process plan is generated based on a combination of the forming methods.

Next, in the plan selection stage, the system evaluates each process plan based on the stage number of the process, the forming load, and the effective strain, and it selects the optimal one. Designers can select a desirable plan interactively from feasible plans.

3   Plan Generation

We analyzed the thinking processes of expert engineers during plan generation and found that expert engineers gave attention to the differences between cylindrical pillars. As a result, we formulated the operation of process planning in the present system so that the diameters of neighboring cylindrical pillars are adjusted to make them identical. To obtain feasible plans, we apply the method of plural forming in a single process to the plans that are generated by the above operation. In this chapter, we explain the data representation, the inference method of plan generation, and the knowledge representation.

3.1   Data Representation

The shape of a forged product is represented as a series of Basic Elements (BEs), shown in Fig. 2. In a hollow product, the outer and inner (upper-inner and lower-inner) shapes are individually represented.

Each BE includes not only geometrical information such as diameter and height, but also deformation information such as plastic strain and forming load.

For example, the forged solid product shown in Fig. 3(a) is represented by [C1,TL3, C1, TU3, C1, TU1, C1, TU1, C1]. Similarly, the forged hollow product shown in Fig. 3(c) is represented by an outer: [C1, TU3, C1, TU1, C1], by an upper-inner: [C1], by and a lower-inner: [].

In a forming process, a work-piece, i.e., a constructed cylinder part, is deformed into an intermediate product and also a forged product that consists of plural cylinder parts. In our system, a forged product is represented as an aggregation of forming patterns that consists of stepped cylinders. Fig. 3(b) shows a solid product (a) represented as an aggregation of four stepped cylinders [SC1, SC2, SC3, SC4]. Similarly, Fig. 3(d) shows a hollow product (c) represented as

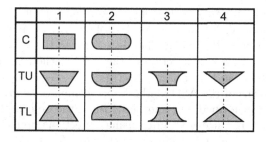

Fig. 2. Data Representation (Basic Elements)

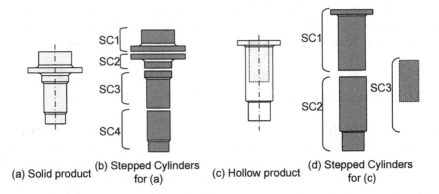

(a) Solid product   (b) Stepped Cylinders for (a)   (c) Hollow product   (d) Stepped Cylinders for (c)

Fig. 3. Input Products

an aggregation of two stepped cylinders [SC1, SC2] for an outer and one stepped cylinder [SC3] for an upper-inner.

In our system, all data such as the basic element, the product, and the stepped cylinder are managed uniformly in an object-oriented framework.

3.2   Inference Method of Plan Generation

We formulated the model of a forged product as consisting of an aggregation of N stepped cylinders. The N stepped cylinders mean that the forged product is deformed through N-1 intermediate products from a work-piece. This process is achieved by the the Adjustment of Stepped Cylinder (ASC) method described below.

To reduce the number of stages in the process plan, combining plural forming into a single process is achieved.

Inference method of the ASC method. For plan generation, we propose the ASC method, in which the basic principle of plan generation involves adjusting the diameters of adjacent stepped cylinders so that they are all identical. By using the ASC method, a forged product is transformed into a pre-formed product. The operation is repeated until the pre-formed product is transformed into a work-piece.

As shown in Fig. 4, part of a target cylinder and a joint is transformed into a shape whose diameter is the same as that of the key cylinder. Fig. 5 shows a schematic illustration of how the method is applied to the forged product shown in Fig. 3(a). Notice that the direction of the ASC method is the reverse of the forging process shown in Fig. 1.

In the mechanisms of the ASC method, our formulations involve one state of an object being transformed into another state of the object. In this operation, FORTEK updates instance attributes using object manipulation functions in order to generate pre-formed products, as shown in Table 1.

The ASC method generates two pre-formed products with different diameters. As shown in Fig. 6, adjusting the diameter of the target cylinder to that of the

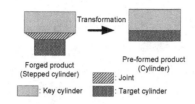

Fig. 4. The ASC method

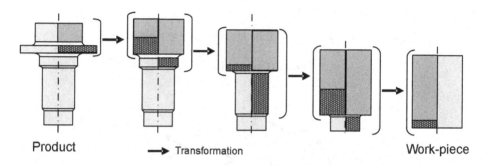

Fig. 5. Schematic illustrations representing the basic principle for plan generation

Table 1. Object manipulation functions

function	explanation	usage
get	refer to an attribute value of an instance	get(class, instance, attribute)
put	store an attribute value of an instance	put(class, instance, attribute, value)
create	generate an instance object	create(class)

key cylinder generates two pre-formed products. Fig. 7 shows the process of applying the ASC method to the forged product shown in Fig. 3(a) and shows that plural intermediate (pre-formed) products and work-pieces with different diameters are generated.

In general, the ASC method generates $2^N N!$ process plans for a forged product that consists of N stepped cylinders. The number of aggregations of the product shown in Fig. 7 is 4, so 384 process plans are generated.

However, the geometrical transformation by the above the ASC method may generate impractical plans. To avoid the generation of ineffective plans, knowledge of plan generation for forming limits, die configuration, and metal flow is introduced [9], as shown in Section 3.3.

Inference method for plural forming combined into a single process.
In practical application, the plural portions of an intermediate product may be simultaneously formed into a single process, while only one portion of an intermediate product is formed in one process using the ASC method.

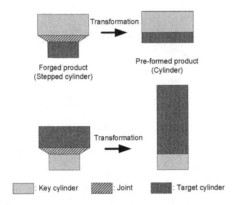

Fig. 6. Generated patterns

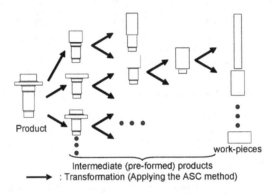

Fig. 7. Schematic illustrations representing key and target cylinder, and plural process plans generated by the ASC method

In the present system, combining plural forming into a single process is achieved by taking into consideration the constraint conditions of plural working limits, the combination of different forming methods, etc. A schematic illustration of the combination of plural forming into a single process is shown in Fig. 8. Section A of the forged product P1 is generated as section A' of the intermediate product P2 by applying the ASC method. Similarly, section B of the intermediate product P2 is generated as section B' of the intermediate product P3. In this example the system combines plural forming into a single process by generating section B' from the A section. The lower part of Fig. 8 shows two stages of plural forming in a single process, i.e., the combination of the forming methods: US + RE and RE + RE.

It is necessary to consider the above constraint conditions simultaneously at this time. If one or more of the intermediate products are eliminated from the original process plan and the targets of the plural forming are achieved within the constraint conditions, new process plans are generated. These constraint conditions are written in the knowledge-base.

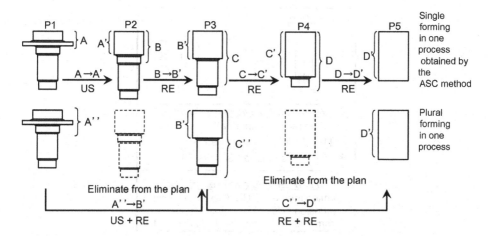

Fig. 8. Schematic illustration representing the plural forming in one process

3.3   The Knowledge Representation of Plan Generation

In the previous system [5], the knowledge of working limits, die configuration, and metal flow was acquired from each case and stored in the system as compiled knowledge [10,11]. In contrast, the present system stores decompiled knowledge such as working limits, die configuration, and metal flow as individual items. For this reason, the system is widely applicable to various shapes and types of equipment.

We classified plan generation knowledge into the three categories of working limits, die configuration, and metal flow and found that the contents of knowledge for each operation are different but that the usage of it is similar, irrespective of each operation. As a result, all the knowledge can be described in the same manner. In order to execute plan generation, the inference method applied to the knowledge manipulates instance attributes using object manipulation functions, as shown in Table 1.

Knowledge is composed of **if-then** rules which have condition and action parts. If the condition parts are satisfied, then the action parts are executed.

Using this knowledge representation, designers can maintain knowledge-bases that are independent and not consistent with other knowledge-bases because knowledge-bases are classified according to their plan generation into three categories.

Knowledge of working limits. Knowledge of the working limits in the forming methods, i.e., rod extrusion (RE), upsetting (US), can extrusion (CE), and shearing (SH), is stored within the system.

Fig. 9 shows an example of the knowledge of the working limits in RE. In this example, the reduction in area and the angle of taper are described as a constraint condition of the working limits. If the condition part is satisfied, the

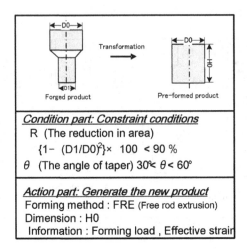

Fig. 9. An example of the knowledge for working limit

説明	*	変数	型	式	
30 =< Alpha2 <=< 60		_	s	when((30 =< Alpha2) and (Alpha2 =< 60))	condition part
Reduction <= 25%		_	s	test(Reduction =< LimitFree)	
		_	s	call(formingRuleREcylinder,[Works,Key],[NewList,NewH,Kh])	
		NewH	r		
		Kh	r		
		FM	a	'FRE'	
generate FR		NewFR	a	fortek_generate(formingRule)	
put formingRule data		NewFM	t	fortek_put(formingRule,NewFR,formingMethod,FM)	action part

Fig. 10. An example of the knowledge representation for working limit

intermediate product will be transformed using the ASC method. In detail, if the reduction in area is smaller than 90% and the angle of taper is between 30 and 60, then the forming method is FRE, and the intermediate product will be transformed. Fig. 10 shows the knowledge representation of Fig. 9 by using the knowledge-based tool DSP [12], which is developed with Inside Prolog [13].

Knowledge of die configuration. If the forming method differs, regardless of whether the intermediate product is the same, the die configuration also differs. Moreover, the die configuration depends on the accuracy of the forged products. If the die configuration becomes complicated, it will become a factor in an unexpected fracture.

The die configurations (upper die, lower die, outer case, etc.) were stored in this system as knowledge of the die configuration. After plan generation, the die configuration is determined using the above knowledge, information about the forged product and the forming method.

Fig. 11 shows an example of the stored knowledge about the decomposition of upper and lower dies. In the example, there are two decomposition patterns.

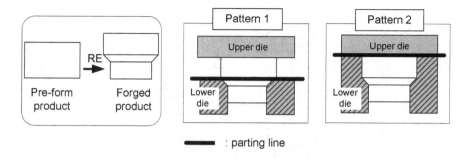

Fig. 11. Example of knowledge for die configuration

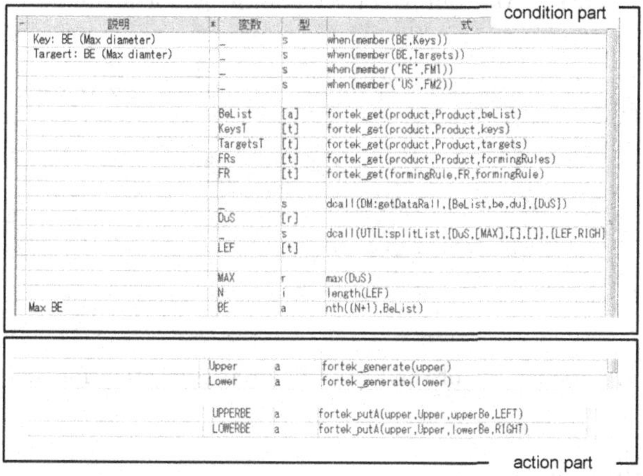

Fig. 12. Example of knowledge representation for die configuration

Fig. 12 shows the knowledge representation for pattern 1 in Fig. 11. First, the knowledge checks the condition of the forming-method and the connectivity of the maximum diameters, refers and calculates values of instances attributes, then generates new instances such as upper and lower dies, and finally puts calculated values on the instances.

Knowledge of metal flow. When based solely upon the above knowledge of working limits and the die configuration, the ASC method may generate poor quality products suffering, for example, from folding and/or dimension faults.

An expert engineer can heuristically evaluate a process plan for metal flow conditions. Knowledge of metal flow is therefore introduced into the present system to eliminate poor quality products. This knowledge describes the condition of a transformation being good or not. Fig. 13 describes the knowledge of the transformation by which the ACS method causes a forging defect and removes it, and Fig. 14 shows the knowledge representation of Fig. 13.

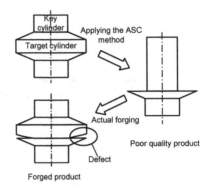

Fig. 13. An example of the knowledge for metal flow

	説明	*	変数	型	式	condition part
			Hworks	a	head(Works)	
			_	s	when(Key = Hworks)	
			_	s	when(not(null(Rights)))	
			Hrights	sa	head(Rights)	
	lowerDieDU		DUdie	r	fortek_getR(be,Hrights,du)	
	lowerDieDL		DLdie	r	fortek_getR(be,Hrights,dl)	
	lowerDieDiameter		Ddie	r	max(DUdie,DLdie)	
	workDiameter		DUkey	r	fortek_getR(be,Key,du)	
			_	s	test(Ddie =< DUkey)	

Fig. 14. An example of the knowledge representation for metal flow

4   Plan Selection

Plural deformable process plans are generated using the ASC method and the method of plural forming combined into a single process. It is difficult to automatically select the optimal process plan because the evaluation factors envisioned by the designer are different from those of any specific production environment. In the present system, a designer interactively selects the optimal plan or the most desirable plans from among the feasible ones on the basis of the organization strategy and other circumstances.

As shown in Fig. 15, the designer inputs an evaluation item and its requirements to the system, and then the system evaluates all feasible plans and screens out ones that cannot satisfy the requirements. The operation is repeated until a desirable plan can be found.

The selection should be made by considering such items as the following:

– Maximum number of stages in the process plan
– Billet size: the diameter and/or the length of work-pieces
– The maximum and/or average forming load in each stage and the total

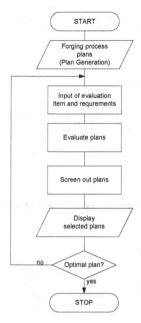

Fig. 15. Procedure of plan selection

- Maximum strain and degree of work hardening in the final product and performs which the accumulated strain in the forged product
- Requirements of the intermediate heat treatment and the lubrication: the number of heat treatments between processes

5   Execution Results

We applied FORTEK to the practical axis-symmetrical solid and hollow products to evaluate the usefulness and effectiveness of the proposed system. The prototype of FORTEK was implemented with the knowledge-based tool DSP and Microsoft Visual Basic.

Once the designer inputs a forged product shape, the system generates the feasible (deformable) plural process plans from the forged product shape to the work-pieces. Subsequently, the system selects the optimal plans from among the feasible plans in the plan selection stage, incorporating a designer. In this case, 15 kinds of plan generation knowledge were stored.

In plan generation for the solid and hollow products shown in Fig. 16, this system generated 612 and 12 process plans, respectively, and the total execution times were 219 and 0.5 seconds. Typical outputs of the process plan are shown in Fig. 17 and Fig. 18.

As shown in these figures, desirable process plans were successfully obtained; thus, we were able to obtain a solution containing a process plan in an actual production.

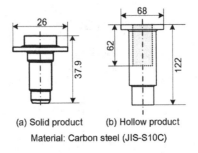

(a) Solid product   (b) Hollow product

Material: Carbon steel (JIS-S10C)

Fig. 16. Examples of the cold forged products

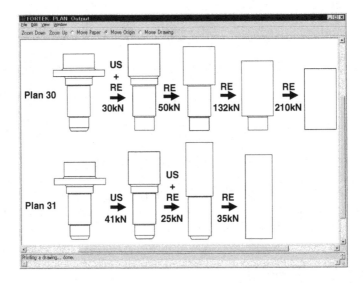

Fig. 17. Typical output of forging sequence plans for solid product

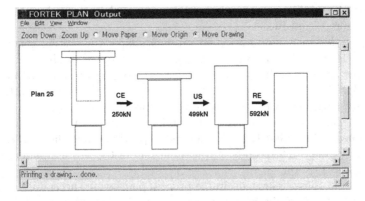

Fig. 18. Typical output of forging sequence plans for hollow product

6   Conclusions

For the purposes of plan generation, we analyzed the thinking processes of expert engineers and formulated an operation of process planning that adjusted the diameters of adjacent stepped cylinders so that they were all identical. In this case, knowledge of the working limits, die configurations, and metal flow was used in identifying and eliminating undesirable plans. To obtain feasible plans, we combined the method of plural forming into a single process and from this created the plans that were generated by the above operation. The system then evaluated all generated plans to interactively select the optimal process plan by screening out those that could not satisfy the requirements.

We developed a prototype system, FORTEK, and applied it to actual forged products; appropriate results, including a practical process plan, were obtained. The knowledge using the ASC method can be widely applicable to various shapes and equipment. Therefore, both maintenance and operation have been improved in the present system.

This system utilizes knowledge of the working limits, die configuration, and metal flow. However, acquiring knowledge of metal flow was found to be difficult. Additional analysis is necessary in the future in order to formulate and incorporate this knowledge of metal flow in conjunction with physical/numerical simulation in designing a detailed die configuration.

References

1. P. Bariani, E. Benuzzi, and W. A. Knight. Computer aided design of multi-stage cold forging process: Load peaks and strain distribution evaluation. *Annals of the CIRP*, 36(1):145–148, 1987.
2. K. Sevenler, P. S. Raghupathi, and T. Altan. Forming-sequence design for multi-stage cold forging. *J. of Mechanical Working Technology*, 14:121–135, 1987.
3. K. Lange and D. Guohui. A formal approach to designing forming sequences for cold forging. *Trans. of the NAMRI/SME*, pages 17–22, 1989.
4. T. Mahmood, B. Lengyel, and T. M. Husband. Expert system for process planning in the cold forging of steel. *Expert Planning Systems*, 322:141–146, 1990.
5. O. Takata, K. Nakanishi, and T. Yamazaki. Forming-sequence design expert system for multistage cold forging: Forest-d. In *Proc. of Pacific Rim International Conference on Artificial Intelligence '90*, pages 101–113, 1990.
6. G. Yang and K. Osakada. A review of expert system for process planning of cold forging. *Manufacturing Review*, 6(2):101–113, 1993.
7. H. S. Kim and Y. T. Im. An expert system for cold forging process design based on a depth-first search. *J. of Materials Processing Technology*, 95:262–274, 1999.
8. Osamu Takata, Yuji Mure, Yasuo Nakashima, Masuharu Ogawa, Masanobu Umeda, and Nagasawa. Knowledge-based system for process planning in cold forging using adjustment of stepped cylinder method. In *INAP-2005*, pages 117–126, 2005.
9. S. J. Russell and P. Norvig. *Artificial Intelligence: A Modern Approach (2nd Edition)*. Prentice Hall, 2002.
10. M. D. Verson. *Impact Machining*. Verson Allsteel Press Company, 1969.

11. JSTP. *Forging Technology (in Japanese)*. Corona Publishing Co., 1995.
12. Masanobu Umeda, Isao Nagasawa, and Tatsuji Higuchi. The elements of programming style in design calculations. In *Proceedings of the Ninth International Conference on Industrial and Engineering Applications of Artificial Intelligence and Expert Systems*, pages 77–86, June 1996.
13. Keiichi Katamine, Masanobu Umeda, Isao Nagasawa, and Masaaki Hashimoto. Integrated development environment for knowledge-based systems and its practical application. *IEICE Transactions on Information and Systems*, E87-D(4):877–885, April 2004.

An Overview of Agents in Knowledge Management

Virginia Dignum

Universiteit Utrecht
P.O. Box 80089, 3508 TB Utrecht
The Netherlands
virginia@cs.uu.nl

Abstract. Current developments in Knowledge Management concern the sharing and usage of knowledge in dynamic environments. The need for systems that both react to and anticipate the needs and expectations of users calls for flexible and adaptable development and implementation frameworks. These are exactly the characteristics that identify software agents and agent societies, which make natural the application of the agent paradigm in KM. This paper attempts to identify both the advantages of agents for KM, and the aspects of KM that can benefit most from this paradigm. Furthermore, the paper describes several current KM projects that use agent technology and identifies open research areas

1 Introduction

The main goal of Knowledge Management (KM) is to provide relevant knowledge to assist users in executing knowledge intensive tasks. KM is about facilitating an environment where work critical information can be created, structured, shared, distributed and used. To be effective such environments must provide users with relevant knowledge, that is, knowledge that enables users to better perform their tasks, at the right time and in the right form. Knowledge Management (KM) has been a predominant trend in business in the recent years. Scaling-up research prototypes to real-world solutions usually requires an application-driven integration of several basic technologies, e.g., ontologies for knowledge sharing and reuse, collaboration support like CSCW systems, and personalized information services.

As it is often mentioned in the literature, knowledge tasks have a collaborative aspect, that is, an individual can best acquire and use knowledge by reusing information already collected and annotated by others or by making use of existing relations among people (communities) [9]. Furthermore, a KM system must be able to adapt to changes in the environment, to the different needs and preferences of users, and to integrate naturally with existing work methods, tools and processes. That is, KM systems must be *reactive* (able respond to user requests or environment changes) and *proactive* (able to take initiatives to attend to user needs). These aspects also characterise intelligent software agents, what seems to indicate the applicability of agent technology in the KM area.

Intelligent agents are a relatively new paradigm for developing software applications and are currently the focus of intense interest on the part of many fields of

M. Umeda et al. (Eds.): INAP 2005, LNAI 4369, pp. 175–189, 2006.

computer science and artificial intelligence [7]. Agents have made it possible to support the representation, co-ordination, and co-operation between heterogeneous processes and their users. Internet technology and software agents make thus possible to build sophisticated, well performing KM systems designed to deliver content, from multiple, heterogeneous sources, to each individual, in the individual's specific context and under the individual's own control. This ability contributes to improve the relationship between knowledge suppliers and consumers by providing both parties more precise control over the interaction.

In order to cope with the inherent complexity of a more comprehensive solution, the concept of Agent-mediated Knowledge Management (AMKM) proposes agent-based approaches to deal with collective aspects of the domain in an attempt to cope with the conflict between desired order and actual behavior in dynamic environments [4]. Inherent to AMKM is a social layer, which structures the society of agents by defining specific roles and possible interactions between them.

In this paper, we intend to show the applicability of agent technology to the development of collaborative KM environments that address the problems highlighted above. The paper is organised as follows: Section 2 provides some generic background on Knowledge Management and software agents. Section 3 discusses the applicability potential of agents to the KM area. In section 4, some current KM projects that make use of agent technology are listed. In section 5, discusses issues related to AMKM design and methodology, on the basis of the OperA framework being developed at our institute. Finally, section 6 presents our conclusions and discusses some open issues and highlights aspects for further research.

2   Background

2.1   Knowledge Management Environments

Business processes are often highly dynamic and unpredictable. This makes it difficult to give a complete a priori specification of all the activities that need to be performed, which their knowledge needs are, and how those activities should be ordered. Within organisations, there is a decentralised ownership of the tasks, information and resources involved in the business process. Different groups within organisations are relatively autonomous, in the sense that they control how their resources are created, managed or consumed, and by whom, at what cost, and in what period [6]. Furthermore, often multiple and physically distributed organisations (or parts hereof) are involved in the business process. Each organisation attempts to maximise its own profit within the overall activity. That is, there is a high degree of natural concurrency (many interrelated tasks and actors are active at any given point of the business process) which makes important to monitor and manage the overall business process (e.g. total time, total budget, etc.). These characteristics call for an environment that integrates the business process aspects of knowledge work with active support for searching, using and adding heterogeneous knowledge sources [15].

The first attempts towards business integration were made at the data level, where distributed computing frameworks have been developed to support distributed computing in heterogeneous environments and provide an interface description language and services that allow objects to be defined, located and invoked across locations and applications. However, knowledge assets available in an organisation are more than data sources alone. Such assets include structured and unstructured information, multimedia knowledge representations and links to people (ex. through knowledge maps or yellow pages). Besides using existing knowledge sources, the environment should be able to create (and store) new knowledge based on its observation of the user's task performance [11]. Furthermore, there is a need to combine formal and informal knowledge representations, as well as heterogeneous multimedia knowledge sources. At knowledge level, integration must be based on the semantics and the context of the problem at hand. A knowledge-level integration framework must be able to create dynamic relationships between knowledge-intensive business processes and knowledge sources that do not compromise the autonomy of the different parts. In order to be able to support the execution of knowledge-intensive tasks, using knowledge from heterogeneous sources, according to diverse user preferences, KM system must be able to provide a common knowledge description. In this way, integration and autonomy are achieved by separating the use of knowledge from the specific characteristics of the knowledge source. KM systems must therefore provide uniform access to a diversity of knowledge and information sources of different degree of formality. Furthermore, knowledge management environments must be able to adapt to the different needs and preferences of users, and integrate naturally with existing work methods, tools and processes. That is, such environments must be *reactive* and *proactive*.

2.2 Intelligent Software Agents

The key issue in software agents is **autonomy**, which refers to the principle that agents can operate on their own, without the need for human guidance. An autonomous agent has the control over its own actions and internal state. That is, an agent can decide whether to perform a requested action. Furthermore, agents are problem-solving entities, with well-defined boundaries and interfaces, designed to fulfil a specific purpose and exhibit flexible and pro-active behaviour. Autonomous agents have the possibility to interact with other agents using a specific communication language, thus creating a sort of social ability that allows them to perceive their environment, respond to its changes or achieve goals by simply adapting and reacting to other players. A Multi-Agent System (MAS) can therefore be defined as: "a collection of possibly heterogeneous, computational entities, having their own problem solving capabilities and which are able to interact among them in order to reach an overall goal" [5].

Agents usually operate in a dynamic, non-deterministic complex environment, in which a single input action can often produce unexpected results. MAS environments assume no global control, data decentralization and asynchronous computation. Furthermore, agents in a MAS are assumed to operate with incomplete information or capabilities for solving the problem. Communication is thus the key for agents to share the information they collect, to co-ordinate their actions and to increase inter-operation. In heterogeneous systems, knowledge sharing is hampered by the lack of common ontologies. Therefore, adequate support for ontology matching and meaning negotiation is of great importance to MAS and to AMKM in special.

3   Agents in Knowledge Management

KM environments can be described as distributed system where different actors, acting autonomously on behalf of a user, and each pursuing its own goals, need to interact in order to achieve their goals. In such environments, the ability to communicate and negotiate is paramount. Furthermore, the number and behaviour of participants cannot be fixed a priori and the system can be expected to expand and change during operation, both in number of participants as in amount and kind of knowledge shared. The choice for multi-agent systems for KM is motivated by the following observations:

- KM domains involve an inherent distribution of data, problem solving capabilities and responsibilities (conforms to the ideas of autonomy and social ability of agents).
- The integrity of the existing organisational structure and the autonomy of its subparts need to be maintained (uses autonomous nature of the agents).
- Interactions in KM environments are fairly sophisticated, including negotiation, information sharing, and coordination (requires complex social skills with which agents are endowed).
- KM domains call for a functional separation between knowledge use and knowledge sources as a way to incorporate dynamic behaviour into information systems design (agents can act as mediators between source and application of knowledge).
- The solution for KM problems cannot be entirely prescribed from start to finish and therefore problem solvers are required that can respond to changes in the environment, to react to the unpredictability of business process and to proactively take opportunities when they arise (requires the reactive and proactive abilities of agents).

In order to cope with the inherent complexity of a more comprehensive solution, the concept of Agent-mediated Knowledge Management (AMKM) proposes agent-based approaches to deal with collective aspects of the domain in an attempt to cope with the conflict between desired order and actual behavior in dynamic environments. Inherent to AMKM is a social layer, which structures the society of agents by defining specific roles and possible interactions between them. Van Elst, Dignum and Abecker argued that "the basic features of agents (social ability, autonomy, re- and pro-activeness) can alleviate several of the drawbacks of the centralized technological approaches for KM" [4]. In that article, we proposed three dimensions to describe agent KM systems: the system development layer (from analysis to implementation of the system), the macro-level structure of the system (single agent and Multi-agents models) and the KM applications area (share, learn, use, distribution and so on). Taking into account the second dimension, a classification of software or experimental models of agent systems was proposed that could support KM. For example,

Personal Information Management (PIM) tools could be considered as single agent systems whose task is to support knowledge workers in their daily work in a way to become "a personal assistant who is collaborating with the user in the same work environment" [13]. Many different examples fall into this category, like Lieberman's Letizia [12] and the OntoBroker developed by Staab and Schnurr [15].

In KM environments, agents can check of the dynamic conditions of the environment, reason to interpret those perceptions, solve problems, draw inferences and determine actions, and finally, act accordingly. The use of agents in KM can be seen in two perspectives. In one hand, agents can be used to model the organisational environment where the KM system will operate and, on the other hand, software agents can be used to implement the functionality of KM systems. Most existing KM projects involving agent technology concentrate on using agents as implementation tool modelling primitives. Agents are used there to support and extend the activity of (human) users. However, more and more interest is arising about the advantages of agent-based modelling of KM environments. In the remaining of this section, we will describe both perspectives in more detail.

3.1 Agent-Based Models for KM Environments

Agent-based models for knowledge management see agents as autonomous entities (like employees in a company) that are endowed with certain behaviours and the interactions among these entities give rise to complex dynamics. In this context, agents can be defined as 'one that acts or has the power or authority to act' or 'one that takes action at the instigation of another'. The concept of agent in this sense is not new, nor restricted to software. In this perspective, agents are autonomous social entities that exhibit flexible, responsive and proactive behaviour.

An organisation can be seen as a set of entities and their interactions, which are regulated by mechanisms of social order and created by more or less autonomous actors to achieve common goals. Business environments must furthermore consider the behaviour of the global system and be able to incorporate collective characteristics of an organisation such as stability over time, some level of predictability, and clear commitment to aims and strategies. While current research often takes individual agents as starting point and looks at interaction from the perspective of an individual agent, that is, how it affects and influences the goals and beliefs of the agent, agent models for organisations must take the perspective of the organisation as a whole. That is, multi-agent systems, or **agent societies**, must therefore be able to define the global aims as well as the roles and responsibilities of participants.

Agent societies represent the interactions between agents and are as such the virtual counterpart of real-life societies and organisations. Individual agents model specific roles in the society and interact with others as a means to accomplish the goals specified by those goals. This perspective makes the design of the system less complex since it reduces the conceptual distance between the system and the real-world application it has to model. Therefore, agent societies are an effective platform for virtual organisations because they provide mechanisms to allow organisations to advertise their capabilities, negotiate their terms, exchange rich information, and synchronise processes and workflow at a high-level of abstraction [15].

From an organisational perspective, the main function of an individual agent is the enactment of a role that contributes to the global aims of the society. That is, society goals determine agent roles and interaction norms. Agents are actors that perform role(s) described by the society design. The agent's own capabilities and aims determine the specific way an agent enacts its role(s). However, the society is often not concerned about which individual agent will actually play a specific role as long it gets performed. Several authors have advocated role-oriented approaches to agent society development, especially when it is manifest to take an organisational view on the application scenario [17], [18].

3.2 Using Agents to Implement KM Systems

Knowledge Management Environments can be implemented as communities of different types of agents that collaborate to provide the required support to users on their knowledge intensive tasks. In agent-based implementations of knowledge management systems, software agents are employed as tools to manage loosely coupled information sources, to provide unifying presentation of distributed heterogeneous components and to personalise knowledge presentation and navigation. Possible agent-based services in a KM system are [8]:

- Search for, acquire, analyse, integrate and archive information from multiple heterogeneous sources,
- Inform us (or our colleagues) when new information of special interest becomes available,
- Negotiate for, purchase and receive information, goods or services,
- Explain the relevance, quality and reliability of that information,
- Learn, adapt and evolve to changing conditions.

These services are often specified in terms of the following types of agents:

- **Personal Assistants** represent the interests of the user and provide the interface between users and the system. They are concerned with user preferences and needs, and will present information in the preferred format, at the right time. A proactive personal assistant agent will not only perform the tasks given to it by the user, but will also suggest knowledge sources or other resources that are not explicitly requested if they match the user's interests.
- **Cooperative Information Agents** (CIAs) focus on accessing multiple, distributed and heterogeneous information sources. A CIA needs to maintain actively its information by communicating with others and reasoning about its own information.
- **Task analysts** are agents that monitor a certain task in the business process, determine the knowledge needs of the task, and gather that knowledge by communicating with other agents. The agent can also monitor the execution of the task and evaluate the applicability of the knowledge provided. The lessons learned here are used to update its internal state and optimising task knowledge.
- **Source keepers** are agents dedicated to maintaining knowledge sources and are responsible for describing the knowledge contained in the source and extract relevant information for a given request. Source keepers can also actively propose

uses for its source to other agents based on its own knowledge of other agents' needs.

– **Mediators** are agents that can provide a number of intermediate information services to other agents. They may suggest collaboration between users with common interests, or provide information about the tools available.

4 Applications of Agents in KM

Knowledge Management systems typically employ a strong organizational perspective. Macro-level questions, such as number of agents or stakeholders, the typology of information flows and the coordination of decisions are therefore of special concern. One possible way of characterize AMKM systems, as proposed in [Springer] is the degree of sociability of its agents:

- *Single-agent architectures*: agents interact with its (information) environment and with the user, but have no (elaborated) interaction with other agents, in special, no cooperative action is expected. Typical examples include agent-based user interfaces and PIM agents.
- *Closed multi-agent architectures*: agents co-operate with other agents in order to solve their tasks. These agents do not necessarily have to have exactly the same goals, but their tasks and capabilities are comparable. Societies are homogenous, and participating agents are known from the beginning. Agent–based collaborative filtering is a typical example for this class of MAS.
- *Open multi-agent architectures*: contain multiple agent classes which may have completely different purposes, knowledge and capabilities. Specialists exist for wrapping information sources, agents for integrating different description schemas, and for adequately presenting information to the users. Up to a certain extent, agents can enter of leave the society at all times, and represent different stakeholders, with possibly conflicting objectives. All these different agent types have to cooperate and bring in their complementary expertise in order to accomplish the overall goal of the system.

Furthermore, AMKM applications are characterized specifically by the knowledge management functionality they are meant to support. In particular, taking in account the well-known KM cycle, we classify AMKM applications by their focus in terms of KM processes:

– *Identification* processes analyze what knowledge exists in an organization, what the knowledge containers are, who the stakeholders are, etc.
– *Acquisition* is the process of integrating external knowledge into an organization.
– *Development* processes generate new knowledge in the organization.
– *Distribution* processes connect knowledge containers with potential users.
– *Preservation* aims at the sustainability of knowledge, i.e., that is accessible and understandable over a period time.
– *Utilization* means to operationalize available knowledge in order to solve actual business tasks better.

From these classical models, several further distinctions have been developed in Knowledge Management research that can be utilized to describe the application area. For example, systems can take a more *process–oriented* or a more *product–oriented* view [10], [14]. The latter emphasizes the management of explicit knowledge contained in "knowledge products" such as databases, documents, formal knowledge bases etc., whereas the former focuses on human beings and their internal knowledge, i.e., the "process of knowing" and the "process of exchanging knowledge" between people. Typical systems that take a product–oriented view are document retrieval agents. Expert finder systems, on the other hand, take a more process–oriented view. Furthermore, a KM system can support individuals and their tasks at hand, it can support teams and groups, or it may take a more global, organizational perspective. The theoretical analysis of Knowledge Management characteristics in Section 1 may be the source of further possible application areas for information technology, e.g., facilitating trust, motivating users to share knowledge, or establishing group awareness. Concrete agent–based KM applications may deal with one or a few of these aspects, or they may be more comprehensive frameworks that try to cover large parts of the KM cycle. In the following section we will analyze existing agent-based KM applications, illustrative for different approaches.

5 AMKM Design and Methodology

Only a few of the existing AMKM systems provide a comprehensive agent-based KM methodology that enables the development of KM support systems in organizational contexts from a software engineering perspective. Agent-Oriented Software Engineering (AOSE) methodologies provide models and methods adequate to represent and support all types of activities throughout all phases of the software lifecycle. AOSE methodologies must be both specific enough to allow engineers to design the system, and generic enough to allow the acceptance and implementation of multi-agent systems within an organization, allowing for the involvement of users, managers and project teams. From an organizational point of view, the behavior of individual agents in a society can only be understood and described in relation to the social structure. Therefore, the engineering of agent societies needs to consider both the interacting and communicating abilities of agents as well as the environment in which agent societies are situated. Furthermore, in open societies the 'control' over the design of participating agents lies outside the scope and design of the society itself. That is, the society cannot rely on the embedding of organizational and normative elements in the intentions, desires and beliefs of participating agents. These considerations lead to the following requirements for engineering methodologies for agent societies [2]:

- Include formalisms for the description, construction and control of the organizational and normative elements of a society (roles, norms and goals).
- Provide mechanisms to describe the environment of the society and the interactions between agents and the society, and to formalize the expected outcome of roles in order to verify the overall animation of the society.

- The organizational and normative elements of a society must be explicitly specified because an open society cannot rely in its embedding in the agent's internal structure.
- Methods and tools are needed to verify whether the design of an agent society satisfies its design requirements and objectives.
- Provide building directives concerning the communication capability and ability to conform to the expected role behavior of participating agents.

A recent proposal for a AMKM design framework and methodology is OperA [1]. OperA uses the agent paradigm to analyse and model organisations and their knowledge needs, and to provide a reusable architecture to build KM systems. Different knowledge intensive tasks need knowledge from different sources and in different presentation formats. Therefore, the framework distinguishes between application, description and representation of knowledge and provides a common, uniform description of knowledge items (both sources and needs). A community of collaborative agents is responsible for the matching of knowledge supply and demand taking in account the user needs and preferences and the knowledge needs of a task. By collaborating with each other and with users, agents will learn and dynamically extend this framework by checking the current conditions of the environment. Agents will collaborate to interpret those perceptions, solve problems, draw inferences and determine actions, and finally, act accordingly. Information agents specialised in the different types of sources can provide this description.

5.1 OperA Model and Methodology

The framework for agent societies we propose models the collective and interaction aspects of the society from an organisational perspective based on the notions of agent, role, norms, communication and goals. We propose a framework for agent societies consisting of three interrelated models each describing different aspects of the society that attempts to cope with the difference between desired order (from an organisational perspective) and actual behaviour (as actually realised by the participants) in dynamic environments [17]:

- The **organisational model** is the result of the observation and analysis of the domain and describes the desired behaviour of an agent society, as determined by the society 'owners' in terms of goals, rules, roles and interactions.
- The **social model** maps organisational roles to specific agents. Agreements concerning the role(s) an agent will play and the conditions of the participation are described in social contracts.
- The **agent model** specifies the interaction agreements between agents as interaction contracts. This model accounts for the actual (emergent) behaviour of the society.

A methodology to analyse a given domain and determine the type and structure of the agent society that best models that domain is described in [3]. Organisation theory shows that different organisations with exhibit different requirements for coordination and interaction. Coordination models are determined by transaction costs and reflect the balance between organisational objectives and activities. For example, the market model fits well in an exchange situation, and the hierarchical model can be used in production settings. The methodology provides generic facilitation and interaction frameworks for agent societies that implement the functionality derived from the co-ordination model applicable to the problem domain. Standard society types as market, hierarchy and network, can be used as starting point for development and can be extended where needed and determine the basic norms and facilitation roles necessary for the society.

5.2 AMKM Architecture

The AMKM architecture based on the model described in [1][3] consists of two layers: **operation** and **facilitation** as depicted in figure 1. At production level, there are basically three types of agents: personal assistants, (business) process task analysts and knowledge source keepers. Depending on the application area, other agent types may be needed what can be determined by the application of the metho-dology introduced in [3]. Each of those agents provides a transparent access to its organisational background. That is, a personal assistant concentrates on the fulfilment and description of its user needs and does not need to know the type and format of knowledge sources, which are encapsulated by source agents, with whom the personal assistant can communicate.

The facilitation level helps agents to locate each other, based on their needs and facilities. That is, at facilitation level, the 'norms' of the society are kept and enforced and interaction is ensured. Furthermore, facilitation agents ensure interaction by monitoring and supporting contract formation, take care of introducing new agents to the rules of the society and keep track of the reputation of trading agents. Typical facilitation agent roles are matchmakers, gatekeepers and reputation agents.

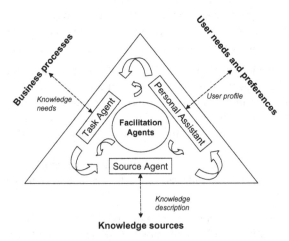

Fig. 1. Generic architecture for Agent-mediated Knowledge Management

5.3   An Application of AMKM Framework

Based on the OperA Model, we are developing a Knowledge Market to support KennisNet members to exchange knowledge according to the requirements expressed in the previous section. This model enables for the incorporation of individual initiative (embodied in personal agents) within organizational processes (described by organizational model of the society). The model is further described in the following subsections.

5.3.1   Organizational Model

The social activity of agents is coordinated at the facilitation level. That is, at facilitation level, the 'norms' of the society are kept and enforced and interaction is ensured. Facilitation agents ensure interaction by monitoring and supporting contract formation, take care of introducing new agents to the rules of the society and keep track of the reputation of trading agents. Typical facilitation agent roles are matchmakers, gatekeepers and reputation agents. Gatekeepers are responsible for accepting and introducing new agents to the knowledge market. Matchmakers keep track of agents in the system, their needs and possibilities and mediate in the matching of demand and supply of knowledge. Notaries register and keep track of collaboration contracts between agents. Finally, monitoring agents are trusted third parties that keep track of the execution of collaboration contracts between agents.

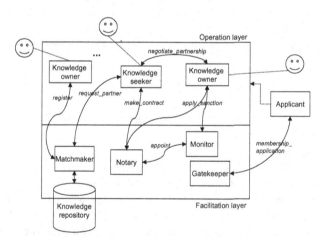

Fig. 2. Knowledge Market architecture

The operational roles identified from the requirements and domain characteristics are knowledge seeker and knowledge owner, which are both specific aspects of personal assistants. The seeker agent provides the interface between the user seeking collaboration and the market and reflects the personal preferences, learning style and work process of the user. Owner agents are responsible to 'advertise' the capabilities of a knowledge worker and vindicate the interests of the knowledge owner. The owner agent can also actively offer the services and skills of its user propose uses for its source to other agents based on its own knowledge of other agents needs or indicated by the matchmaker. Figure 1 depicts the roles and role dependencies in the Knowledge Market.

The interaction structure displayed in figure 2 describes the activity of the user roles (knowledge owner and seeker) in the Knowledge Market. Knowledge seekers and knowledge owners apply to enter the society through the 'Member registration' scene. If the application is successful, the agent proceeds can choose to 'request partner', 'publish' some knowledge item of its own, or 'browse' the repository. In the 'request partner' scene, both seeker and owner agents can initiate an exchange by respectively announcing a need or a skill. In the 'negotiate partnership' scene, seeker and owner discuss the conditions of an exchange. The result is an interaction contract that describes an instance of the 'exchange' scene. Interaction scripts serve as a blueprint for the actual interactions between agents enacting roles. That is, an instantiation of a scene script can adapt the script to accommodate specific requirements of the enacting agents. Scene instances must however, comply with script norms and objectives.

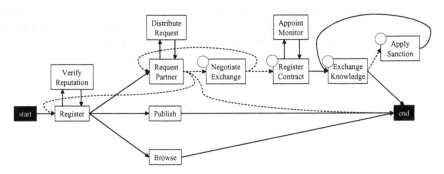

Fig. 3. Interaction structure of Knowledge Market

5.3.2 Social Model

Social contracts describe the agreements between participating agents and the Knowledge Market society. People seeking collaboration can initiate through the user interface of the Knowledge Market a personal agent that will act as their avatar in the system. This agent will use the preferences and conditions specified by the user to find appropriate partners and negotiate exchange terms. Furthermore, factors such as privacy, secrecy and competitiveness between brands and departments may influence the channels and possibilities of sharing and must thus be considered. Matching of supply and demand of knowledge is very complex and requires techniques such as fuzzy matching algorithms, or multi-attribute matching[1]. Due to space restrictions we will not further discuss this here.

Negotiation of social contracts is done between the applicant agent and the Gate-keeper agent, which will watch over the interests of the society itself. For example,

---

[1] That is, how much is a specific piece of knowledge worth, at a specific moment, under the specific circumstances holding and to the specific partners involved in the exchange.

imagine that Anne is a member of the KennisNet group that is seeking knowledge on price policies from the competition. Anne will initiate an agent enacting the knowledge seeker role in the Knowledge Market. During the Member admittance scene, the conditions for Anne's agent will be negotiated and fixed in a social contract. This contract can specify, for instance, which parts of the repository Anne is allowed to access, which are the obligations of Anne concerning the publication of knowledge items received as result of an interaction, and whether Anne allows for items that she provides to be published or not.

5.3.3 Interaction Model

When role enacting agents come together in an interaction scene, the actual interpretation of the scene script that is the interaction protocol to be used must be agreed upon. In OperA, role enacting agents will, for each scene, negotiate an interaction contract that defines their partnership, and fixes the way a specific interaction scene is to be played. Interaction contracts describe instances of scene scripts which inherit the organizational norms and objectives described in the interaction script and possibly extend or restrain it to accommodate the specific needs and desires of the participating agents.

A fictive but typically possible in the domain of non-life insurance contract between two members is, for example, the following. Anne will provide Bob with a report about competition prices, on the condition that Bob will give her comments on the report (that she will have to present to her Unit directors) and eventually share with her his new pricing concept for car insurance. This contract is generated during the 'Negotiate partnership' scene and registered in the 'Register partnership' scene. In this scene, the notary agent will assign a monitor agent to check the fulfillment of the contract between Anne and Bob.

6 Conclusions

Current developments in KM indicate a need for systems that are reactive and proactive in relation to the needs and expectations of its users. In this paper, we have discussed the role of agents in the design and functionality of knowledge management environments. In such environments, the flow of knowledge within an organisation (or organisations) must take in account not only the knowledge needs of business processes, but also the personal preferences and level of expertise of individual users.

Agent concepts, which originated in artificial intelligence but which have further developed and evolved in many areas of computing, hold great promise for responding to the new realities of knowledge management. While there are many conceptions of agents, most have embodied higher levels of representation and reasoning involving knowledge/belief, perception, goal, intention, and commitment. On the one hand, the technical embodiment of these concepts can lead to advanced functionality of KM systems, e.g. personalisation of knowledge presentation and matching supply and demand of knowledge. On the other, the rich representational capabilities of agents as modelling entities allow more faithful and effective treatments of complex organisational processes.

Although several projects are currently taking place that use agents for the design and implementation of KM systems, several research issues are still open that will provide a clear view of the applicability and consequences of using agents in KM. While the agent research area is very active, its concerns towards KM are not yet well covered. Agent concepts could fundamentally alter the nature of knowledge management both in the way KM systems are build as well as the way organisations are analysed and modelled.

Future research in agent-oriented approaches to knowledge management and collaborative systems must include:

- Methodologies are needed that support the analysis of knowledge management needs of organisations and its specification using software agents and agent societies
- Reusable agent-oriented knowledge management frameworks, including the description of agent roles, interaction forms and knowledge description
- Agent-based tools for organisational modelling and simulation that help determine the knowledge processes of the organisation,
- The role of learning in agent-based knowledge management systems, namely, how to use agent learning to support and extend knowledge sharing.

References

[1] V. Dignum: *A Model for Organizational Interaction: Based on Agents, Founded in Logic*. PhD thesis, Utrecht University, (2004).

[2] V. Dignum, F. Dignum: Modeling agent societies: coordination frameworks and institutions. In: Brazdil, P, Jorge, A.: *Progress in Artificial Intelligence*, LNAI 2258, Springer, pp. 191 - 204, 2001.

[3] V. Dignum, F. Dignum, J.J. Meyer: An Agent-Mediated Approach to the Support of Knowledge Sharing in Organizations. *Knowledge Engineering Review*, Cambridge University Press, **19**(2), pp. 147-174, 2004.

[4] L. van Elst, V. Dignum, A. Abecker: Towards Agent-Mediated Knowledge Management. In: L. van Elst, V. Dignum, A. Abecker (Eds): *Agent-Mediated Knowledge Management: Selected Papers*, LNAI 2926, Springer, 2004.

[5] J. Ferber. *Multi-Agent System: An Introduction to Distributed Artificial Intelligence*. Harlow: Addison Wesley Longman. 1999.

[6] Jennings, N., Faratin, P., Johnson, M., Norman, T., O'Brien, P., & Wiegand M.: Agent-based business process management. *International Journal of Cooperative Information Systems*, **5**(2&3), pp. 105 – 130, 1996.

[7] N. Jennings & M. Wooldridge: Applications of Intelligent Agents. In: Jennings, N. and Wooldridge, M. (Eds.): *Agent Technology: Foundations, Applications and Markets*, Springer, 1998, 3 – 28.

[8] Klusch, M. (Ed.): *Intelligent Information Agents: Agent-based Information Discovery and Management in the Internet*. Springer, 1999.

[9] Koch, M.: Knowledge Management and Knowledge Agents in Campiello. In: Lees, B., Müller, H., Branki, C. (Eds.): *Proc. Workshop on Intelligent Agents in CSCW*, Dortmund, Germany, pp. 44-52, 1998.

[10] O. Kühn and A. Abecker. Corporate memories for knowledge management in industrial practice: Prospects and challenges. In U.M. Borghoff and R. Pareschi (Eds): *Information Technology for Knowledge Management*. Springer, 1998.

[11] Leake, D., Birnbaum, L., Hammond, K., Marlow, C. & Yang, H.: Task-Based Knowledge Management. In: P*roc. AAAI Workshop Exploring Synergies of Knowledge Management and Case-Based Reasoning,* AAAI Technical Report WS-99-10, 1999.

[12] H. Lieberman. Letizia: An agent that assists web browsing. In C. Mellish (Ed):, *Proc. IJCAI-95*, Montreal, Canada, August 1995.

[13] P. Maes. Agents that Reduce Work and Information Overload. In *Communications of the ACM*, **37**(7), July 1994

[14] G. Mentzas, D. Apostolou, R. Young, and A. Abecker. Knowledge Asset Management: Beyond the Process-centred and Product-centred Approaches. *Advanced Information and Knowledge Processing*. Springer-Verlag, 2002.

[15] Preece, A., Hui, K.-Y., Gray, W., Marti, P., Bench-Capon, T. Jones D. & Cui Z.: The KRAFT Architecture for Knowledge Fusion and Transformation. *19th SGES International Conference on Knowledge-based Systems and Applied Artificial Intelligence*, 1999.

[16] S. Staab and H.-P. Schnurr. Smart task support through proactive access to organizational memory. *Knowledge–based Systems,* **13**(5): 251–260, 2000.

[17] J. Vazquez-Salceda, V. Dignum, F. Dignum: Organizing Multiagent Systems. *JAAMAS*, Springer, online 29 June, 2005.

[18] F. Zambonelli, N. Jennings, M. Wooldridge: Organizational Abstractions for the Analysis and Design of Multi-Agent Systems. In: P. Ciancarini, M. Wooldridge (eds.): *Agent-Oriented Software Engineering*. LNAI 1957. Springer, 2001.

ubiCMS – A Prolog Based Content Management System

Oskar Bartenstein

IF Computer Japan
5-28-2 Sendagi, Bunkyo-ku, Tokyo 113-0022 Japan
oskar@ifcomputer.co.jp

Abstract. ubiCMS is a commercial internet based CMS application service built around a collection of best practice templates. ubiCMS implements best practice templates, e.g. for XHTML rendering, ease-of-use, browser compatibility, compliance with legal requirements in MINERVA and *.MSS. To maintain best practice templates over time and over evolving standards is a knowledge management task. The paper explains ubiCMS and the importance of knowledge management in CMS both for the application and implementation. It details some advantages of using Prolog for open ended content management and briefly introduces applications, including an application with custom extensions.

1 Motivation

In any learning organization, i.e. an organization with growing explicit knowledge, newly arising information must have a place to go or it will clog desks and get lost, and it must be available to a potential re-user or it will cause double work with consequential inconsistencies.

This holds for simple business documents like invoices just as well as for complex bodies of documentation. Since true semantic processing is still eluding the powers of our otherwise mighty computers, ubiCMS does not attempt semantic processing: it only provides an interface between authors, users, and "content"; meaning is left to people. Content may be text, pictures, programs and so on. In general, authors and users are distant in space, time, and responsibilities. Their cooperation is supported by ubiCMS.

Assumed is a business background: information serves a purpose, information is structured, authors and users have defined roles, resources are limited. Therefore, ubiCMS has to satisfy the following requirements:

maintainable
> changes of content must not require changes to templates.
> changes of templates must not require change to content.
> if a local change requires global updates, these must be automatic.

scalable
> there must not be any hard coded limitations to the scope of an application of ubiCMS with respect to time, space, users, languages, devices or other environmental dimensions

M. Umeda et al. (Eds.): INAP 2005, LNAI 4369, pp. 190–199, 2006.

accessible

      ubiCMS must satisfy W3C/WAI, JIS, Section508 an other accessibility standards   by default and without requiring special author attention

consistent

      site policies must be enforced by default.

      Exceptions to site policies must be explicit and cause extra effort.

compliant

      generated renderings must be compliant with formal (e.g. W3C) and industry (e.g. Internet Explorer) standards for maximal interoperability

auditable

      there must be metrics and measurements for conformance to specification

useable

      email/blog level user expertise must suffice

      expectations must not be violated

extensible

      there must be economic ways to incrementally add service oriented functionality including reasoning, calculation, simulation, recommendation, dialog for non-trivial business, legal, medical, engineering or other professional use.

2 Why Prolog in Content Management Systems?

Many current CMS are based on the combination of a database (e.g. Postgres) with a rendering language (e.g. PHP). They emphasize variations of renderings of database content on web pages. This approach is effective for the presentation side, but it does not help with deeper use or processing of structured knowledge.

ubiCMS is based on the combination of a database (filesystem), a system level engine language (Java) , a business logic level language (MINERVA), and an Internet-oriented rendering language (*.MSS).

Although in general users are not aware of Prolog in ubiCMS, we use Prolog as the main mediation language for four reasons:

1. because Prolog is one of the few major programming languages backed by a very well understood rigorous mathematical theory
2. because there are stable and efficient ISO standard conforming implementations in Java suitable for large scale web programming
3. because it is suitable for parsing, matching, recommendation and similar
4. "intelligent" components of business logic which are not easily implemented in pure database driven CMS systems.
5. because it has a distinguished track record as implementation language for reasoning systems.

This last point is important for us to achieve scalability in "processing depth", e.g. for financial, engineering, medical, legal reasoning as part of commercial or other portal sites with potentially executable knowledge.

In short, ubiCMS uses Prolog to leverage expert systems on CMS, i.e. to open CMS to applications from document management through knowledge management all the way to knowledge processing. The design is based on the strategic assumption that any business content to be "managed" also has parts that are "executable" and can be automated. Building a business system is the process of moving as much operational knowledge as possible through the implementation levels recognized, managed, automated.

3 Related Work

We are not aware of any commercial, accessible, international CMS hosted in Java for standard servlet delivery and extensible with ISO-Prolog programs.

Frank Bergmann: SiteC http://www.fraber.de/sitec/ reports about a site generator in Prolog, where Prolog calls can be embedded in HTML. The site itself appears to be generated batch-style for static delivery and Prolog used only at generation time, not for interactive server side services.

By comparison, ubiCMS is a hybrid system. Pages are generated on user demand, at authoring time, or on schedule, depending on deployment factors which are beyond the scope of this paper. Pages can include interactive custom components, e.g. business rule executives or engineering calculations.

Hajime Yoshino and Seiichiro Sakurai in their studies on legal expert systems http://www.ntt.dis.titech.ac.jp/ICAIL2005/Paper01.pdf and also http:// www.ntt.dis. titech.ac.jp/ICAIL2005/Paper02.pdf describe the need for Prolog in CMS systems. As a possible realization for Prolog in CMS they mention Plone/Zope http://plone.org , a CMS in Python http://python.org, and PyLog, a first order logic library in Python http://christophe.delord.free.fr/en/pylog/ and state that since there is a Python implementation in Java this amounts to a Prolog in a CMS in Java for internet deployment.

ubiCMS meets the need for Prolog in CMS. By comparison its design is based on rigid layers of Java and ISO-Prolog, both mature languages. From a software engineering perspective it could be considered much less experimental.

4 Modules

ubiCMS consists of interacting modules. It manages text, pictures, structure, calendar, events, time, users, sessions, and rendering for mobile, desktop and paper output. User interaction is through web browsers and subscriber email.

Functionally, ubiCMS provides:

structure
> Content is organized in a hierarchical tree structure or outline. The structure is reflected in navigation aids, file system storage, and the external URLs.

reading
> Browsing with mobile and desktop internet clients. System gives navigation and orientation, site maps and other functions to assist efficient access of site content. Default rig renders pages for mobile, desktop and paper devices.

editing
> Authors contribute outline, text, images, other materials. Contributions are always local, with global effects derived automatically.

mail opt-in/opt out subscription
> Community support with email notification based on author request and user request and topical match. Allows for simple workflow support.

local search engine
> flat site access as complement to structure driven built-in site maps and outline.

access control
> user, group, location specific access control for interacting partners. All access is session-specific.

blogs
> threadable contributions to specific topics,

attachments
> multi-media files as part of a topic, for rendering or delivery

photoalbums/slideshows
> organized set of images for rendering as photo album or, depending on client, slideshow.

editable stylesheets
> a typical web template

optional email functions
> with desktop and mobile web interfaces, spam and virus filter, to realize HTTP only convenience.

A Note on Editing with ubiCMS

By design, the programmed parts in MINERVA and *.MSS, and the configuraton files in XML are also under management by the system and it is possible to change them. In many environments, it makes perfect sense to have users change executables on web sites, e.g. to compute a fee, or to add an engineering equation, or to adapt an executable legal regulation to reflect a change in legislation.

However, editing live programs is normally not open to users for security reasons. Also, there is a qualitative difference: broken text or image files cannot cause a correct web server to crash, but a programming mistake can very well cause a whole site to disappear. Since we do not limit programmer freedom there is no mechanical solution to ensure reliability, if live parts of the CMS itself are open to changes.

5 Implementation

Roughly, ubiCMS uses Linux as base machinery, Java as system programming language, MINERVA as business logic programming language, *.MSS as rendering language, HTTP as transport protocol and XML as universal notation language.

These layers reflect a pure Unix/Internet culture. A short look at protocol, system, language and template layers: The most widely supported internet protocol today is HTTP. Therefore, ubiCMS uses HTTP and does not require any other protocol for maximal compatibility across devices.

Client side, mobile phone and desktop browsers [1] are used for display and interaction. For industry standard browsers, client side system administration is not required. Delivered by default is a carefully designed, validated and tested small subset of XHTML and CSS. JavaScript is used minimally to achieve convenience effects only; ubiCMS deals gracefully with non-support of client side JavaScript.

Server side, we use clustered Linux [2] servers running ubiCMS as a set of servlets on Tomcat [3] servlet servers, accessed through Apache [4] reverse proxies for security, ease of administration, scalability and workload distribution. Since Prolog is memory based, a good implementation of Prolog is an excellent companion to servlet based web servers; for example much more responsive than CGI-BIN based configurations. The technical reason for this is beyond the scope of this paper.

Although an external database can be used if data size or existing IT infrastructure requires this, ubiCMS does not use a SQL or similar database. Content source files are stored in the server file system, and MINERVA blackboards are used to index and cache content for fast access and downstream processing. For a non-database-centric applications this has 3 important advantages beyond reduced cost and complexity:

1. filesystems are well supported and benefit directly from advances in OS technologies for performance and reliability
2. filesystems are longer lived than database systems and integral part of server systems. This drastically reduces system administration complexity over extended life cycles
3. MINERVA does the indexing and delivery in memory, so normal operation can be expected to be faster than external DB access calls.

ubiCMS configuration files for site administration and user management are in XML.

The ubiCMS servlets are implemented in *.MSS and MINERVA, which in turn make extensive use of Java libraries for system level tasks, sometimes also outside programs. *.MSS [5] is a Prolog Server Pages language for MINERVA, which allows to embed compiled Prolog into e.g. XHTML page templates. MINERVA [6] is a 100% Java [7] based ISO-Prolog compiler. The following code fragments show the interaction of the templates that request and generate a deliverable,

Example: XML Configuration Template

```
<mss language="jp,en,de">
        <file name="home_$(language).html"
         type="both"
         main="ifc_page(_,_,pg(pc,main,_,$(language)))"
         script="../mss/page_structure.mss" />
</mss>
```

The configuraton fragment requests production of files for Japanese, English and German using a given function of the referenced *.MSS template.

Example: *.MSS Rendering Template

```
<%@ function footer(_Page,Dir,IndexFile) %>
<div class="footer">
<%@ include documentInfo(Dir, IndexFile) %>
</div>
<% end %>

<%@ function documentInfo(Dir,IndexFile) %>
  <% begin
        % we need this to print the URL
        documentRoot(DocumentRoot),
        suckDate(Dir,Date), time_now(Year,Month,Day),
        atom_concat(Dir,IndexFile,Ref),
        atom_concat(DocumentRoot,Ref,Doc),
        % add space after slashes to allow browser to fold it
        substitute_all('(%w+?)/(%w+?)',Doc,'%1/ %2',Doc_)
        %>
document: &Doc_;<br />
published  &Year;/&Month;/&Day;
updated  &Date;
  <% end %>
<% end %>
```

The fragment shows function calls within MSS and integration of Prolog programs into the MSS template, together with the use of MINERVA variables inside the produced XHTML document.

Example: CSS Template for Cosmetics

```
div.footer {
        width: 100%;
        display: block;
        border: 0px solid  #999999;
        border-top-width: 3px;
        border-top-style: solid;
        border-top-color: #ccccee;
        }
```

This is usual web design.

Example: XHTML Result

```
<div class="footer">
document: http://ubicms.com/ home_en.html<br />
published  2005/6/28
updated  2005/6/22
<div>
```

Output of ubiCMS.

Example: Resulting Browser Rendering

Attachment Edit Page Add Folder Update Global Update validate   ubiCMS
document: http://ubicms.com/ home_en.html
published 2005/6/28 updated 2005/6/22

完了

Rendered by a desktop browser.

The tight integration of Apache, Tomcat, Java and Prolog gives the programmer who implements customizations of ubiCMS the chance to address network, system, and business logic issues at the right level of abstraction, up to full scale knowledge based expert systems implemented in Prolog responding to a -on the surface- extremely simple-looking HTTP GET.

Typical uses for Prolog would include e.g. recommendation, dialog components [8] or parsing and matching [9] .

The architecture of ubiCMS allows integration of external web services, and we believe it can be used for delivery of web services in the W3C sense of the term.

6   Applications

As of 2005/8, ubiCMS is in field use for corporate web sites, intranet knowledge bases, document repositories, and product web shops. Users cover a wide range of industries from consumer products over non-profit organizations to professionals. The following examples show two complementary aspects of the role of Prolog within ubiCMS: first, its use as a web programming language, and second, its use as a knowledge processing language. The combination of these two aspects gains weight with increasingly service-oriented web systems.

6.1   Traditional Web Site Applications

An architects use of ubiCMS for his corporate web site

A software company use of ubiCMS for product documentation

These examples are mentioned here to illustrate that ubiCMS is sufficiently general purpose to be used as a mainstream CMS for "usual" corporate web sites. The use of

Prolog here is purely for economical reasons, the specific implementation technology is otherwise irrelevant to the users and owners of these sites.

6.2 Applicatons with Prolog Custom Extensions

The site wadokujt.w3dict.com [9] uses ubiCMS with custom made Prolog components to use a 50MegaByte Japanese-German dictionary of 220.000 entries to render a natural language dictionary-in-text reading aid.

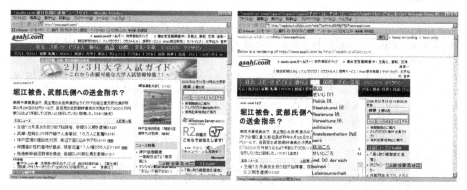

A Japanese online newspaper	same page rendered with dictionary-in-text

Prolog components provide the dictionary cache, the target site cache, the access hash tables, some internet plumbing, and the pseudo natural language parser. The rendering of the roll-over markup is generated with *.MSS, output consists of a pair of XHTML 1.0 strict and CSS1 files.

This application illustrates the benefit of using a CMS with Prolog based calculation and Prolog based rendering for tight integration of originally independent resources: the dictionary, the target documents, the w3dict dictionary-in-text engine.

7 History

ubiCMS is the result of a team effort to generalize and engineer a casual implementation of a document management system to reduce cost and time-to-market of technical documentation of an internationally operating software company. The first version around 1989 [10] produced raw printer codes for early laser printers. Later versions [11] were adapted to render HTML. These systems worked as batch programs to deliver static printer and web pages. Some are still in commercial use today. Positive user feedback, rapid development of web programming technology, and completely new implementation of the ubiCMS kernel software allowed later to put editing and rendering under management by the system, and to optimize execution for caching memory based servlet operation.

Recently, both static and dynamically generated pages are delivered to keep their specific advantages with respect to their use of resources relative to user experience, i.e. response times. Most important limited resources are computing time, routing time, and resident RAM. To a lesser degree relevant are client device specifications and server waste heat and noise.

Experience with commercial web based systems to provide financial and retail services convinced us to put Prolog into the CMS for live computation. Applications of live computations include product recommenders, engineering calculations, and other advice systems.

8 Conclusion

We discussed ubiCMS, a commercial Prolog based Content Management System used to manage not only data and visual appearance, but also system level and business logic level engine programs.

We detailed its implementation as a set of servlets programmed with Java, MINERVA, *.MSS on Linux servers with Apache and Tomcat frontends, and delivery by HTTP to mobile and desktop internet clients. We explained its commercial deployment on corporate and non-profit web sites.

The application service described in this industrial report is commercially available at http://ubiCMS.com .

Personally, I believe that CMS with reasoning capabilities outclass CMS for passive content. Some people read WWW as "whoever wherever whenever", playing on the power of the internet to give everybody access to the same information. But this is only the neccessary infrastructure. Even more important and much more exciting is "Me, Here, Now". Using a web site, I rarely want the massive data of a universal library, but I want to get a specific true answer for "me, here, now" when I confront a technical, medical, legal or any other non-trivial issue.

Therefore reasoning capabilites are very important for service-delivering sites. ubiCMS as a CMS with Prolog as engine is a contribution towards that end. Our field experience indicates that Java as system language and ISO-Prolog are a good combination and firm basis for real-world use.

Acknowledgements

I am grateful to the anonymous reviewers for the effort they spent on the review. I repeat here that this paper does not claim whatsoever that ubiCMS itself does any semantic processing.

Many thanks go to my friends, colleagues and partners at IF Computer Japan for their willingness to discuss and build on our mutual ideas, and for their great contributions to the implementation.

I am very grateful to our customers who contributed the resources and critique to make this work a success

References

[1] XHTML http://www.w3.org/MarkUp/
[2] Linux Kernel http://www.kernel.org

[3] Tomcat http://jakarta.apache.org/tomcat/

[4] Apache http://httpd.apache.org/

[5] *.MSS in International Conference on Declarative Programming and Knowledge Man-
     agement INAP2001
     http://www.ifcomputer.co.jp/inap/inap2001/program/inap_bartenstein.ps

[6] MINERVA http://www.ifcomputer.co.jp/MINERVA/

[7] Javahttp://java.sun.com

[8] in International Conference on Declarative Programming and Knowledge Management
     INAP2003 DialogEngines http://DialogEngines.com

[9] at Workshop wadoku.de March 6-8 2006, National Institute of Informatics, Tokyo, Japan
     Oskar Bartenstein The Japanese-German Dictionary-in-text Internet Reading Help, wado-
     kujt.w3dict.com http://wadokujt.w3dict.com

[10] in Proc Symp. on Industrial Applications of Prolog INAP1990, Ren AssociatesOskar
     Bartenstein "Dynamic Documents"

[11] in Proc 12th Intl Conf on Applications of Prolog INAP1999, Ren AssociatesYuri Saka-
     moto, Oskar Bartenstein "WeaveWeb - 5 Tools For Document Management"

Multi-threading Inside Prolog for Knowledge-Based Enterprise Applications

Masanobu Umeda, Keiichi Katamine, Isao Nagasawa, Masaaki Hashimoto, and Osamu Takata

Graduate School of Computer Science and Systems Engineering,
Kyushu Institute of Technology, Iizuka, Fukuoka, Japan
`umerin@ci.kyutech.ac.jp`

Abstract. A knowledge-based system is suitable for realizing advanced functions that require domain-specific expert knowledge in enterprise-mission-critical information systems (enterprise applications). This paper describes a newly implemented multi-threaded Prolog system that evolves single-threaded Inside Prolog. It is intended as a means to apply a knowledge-based system written in Prolog to an enterprise application. It realizes a high degree of parallelism on an SMP system by minimizing mutual exclusion for scalability essential in enterprise use. Also briefly introduced is the knowledge processing server which is a framework for operating a knowledge-based system written in Prolog with an enterprise application. Experimental results indicated that on an SMP system the multi-threaded Prolog could achieve a high degree of parallelism while the server could obtain scalability. The application of the server to clinical decision support in a hospital information system also demonstrated that the multi-threaded Prolog and the server were sufficiently robust for use in an enterprise application.

1 Introduction

Advanced functions that utilize domain-specific expert knowledge are needed for enterprise-mission-critical information systems (hereinafter called enterprise applications) such as hospital information systems and logistics management systems. Clinical decision support [1] for preventing medical errors and order placement support for optimal inventory management are such examples. A knowledge-based system is suitable for realizing such functions because it can incorporate a knowledge base in which domain-specific expert knowledge is systematized and described.

Production systems in combination with Java technology [2] have been studied as a means to apply a knowledge-based system to an enterprise application [3,4,5]. They provide possibilities of improving the development and maintenance of an enterprise application to separate business rules, which are repeatedly updated, from workflow descriptions, which are rarely updated. However, certain issues involved in applying a production system to large business rules, that is, side effects, combinatorial explosion, and control saturation [6], have not been sufficiently resolved in these systems. On the other hand, Prolog, which

M. Umeda et al. (Eds.): INAP 2005, LNAI 4369, pp. 200–214, 2006.

is suitable for knowledge processing, in combination with Java technology has also been studied with the aim of advancing the development of information systems [7,8,9,10,11]. However, there remain unresolved issues of scalability and transaction processing which are essential to enterprise applications.

The authors have been developing an integrated development environment called Inside Prolog [12], which is dedicated to knowledge-based systems. Various knowledge-based systems, such as design calculation support systems [13,14,15] and health care support systems [16,17], have been developed using Inside Prolog and put to practical use [18]. Inside Prolog provides standard Prolog functionality, conforming to ISO/IEC 13211-1 [19], and also provides a large variety of Application Programming Interfaces (APIs) which are essential for practical application development. These features allow the consistent development of knowledge-based systems from prototypes to practical use. It has been, however, difficult to apply Inside Prolog to an enterprise application as is, because only a stand-alone system was within the scope of Inside Prolog.

Therefore, in order to cope with the scalability issue, the authors initially developed a new Prolog system that was capable of multi-threading by evolving Inside Prolog. The authors then developed the knowledge processing server [20] for operating various knowledge-based systems with enterprise applications by combining this multi-threaded Prolog system with Java technology. The knowledge processing server has been practically applied to clinical decision support [21,22,20] in the hospital information system CAFE [23,24], and it enables validation of contraindications within diseases, drugs, and laboratory results, suggestion of the quantity and administration conditions of a medication order, and the summarization of clinical data such as laboratory results.

This paper describes an overview of Inside Prolog and its multi-thread extension for enterprise use. The knowledge processing server is then briefly introduced. Finally, the multi-thread feature and parallelism of multi-threaded Inside Prolog, and the scalability of the knowledge processing server are evaluated.

2   Overview of Inside Prolog

Inside Prolog is an ISO/IEC 13211-1 compliant Prolog system with various extensions. It is developed over the Prolog abstract machine TOAM, which is based on WAM [25]. Figure 1 illustrates the system architecture of Inside Prolog. It provides several optimization features, such as unification optimization using the matching tree [26] and the translation of determinate predicates to C functions [27]. It also provides advanced APIs, which are required for the development of practical applications, and integration APIs, which are required for integration with existing information systems, in a uniform platform-independent manner [1]. These features allow the consistent development of knowledge-based systems from prototypes to practical use using one programming language, Prolog.

---

[1] Platform-specific functions, such as OLE on Windows, are designed so as to eliminate platform differences from an application program by providing minimal libraries.

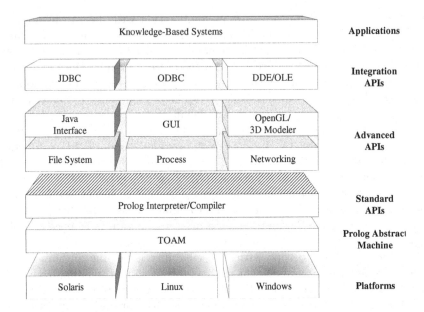

Fig. 1. Architecture of Inside Prolog

The following subsections briefly introduce several topics related to a multi-thread extension of Inside Prolog.

2.1   Memory Model

TOAM has three stacks - a control stack, trail stack, and global stack (or heap) - and a data area (or atom area) for storing global data such as predicate definitions. The data area is divided into two, i.e., a persistent area and a transient area. Data that are never modified dynamically, such as an inference engine and GUI of a knowledge-based system, are stored in the persistent area, while data that can be modified dynamically, such as a knowledge base and execution results, are stored in the transient area. The separation of the data area has the following advantages. That is, the performance of garbage collection can be improved due to the exclusion of the persistent area from its target; the reliability of a system can be improved due to the prevention of unexpected modifications while further optimizations are possible using the immutability of program locations as described in Sect. 2.3.

2.2   Program Code Representation

The components of a knowledge-based system can be classified into several categories. Immutable programs such as an inference engine and GUI, mutable data such as inference rules and clinical information, and programs generated dynamically from these data are such examples. These components can be expressed in a uniform representation of a program code because Prolog's programs and data can be handled in the same manner. However, a program in each category has both advantages and disadvantages if a uniform representation is used. For example, if a program generated from an inference rule, as well as an inference engine are optimized, the program's execution speed can be improved; however, its optimization costs result in the inconvenience of the interactive debugging of inference rules. Therefore, Inside Prolog allows the choice of the most suitable representation of a program code from the following according to its role and scene in an application, and thus enables the development of practical knowledge-based systems.

Static program. A static program is represented as a bytecode generated by an optimizing compiler [26]. It is appropriate to a static predicate whose execution speed is important, and one that is never modified while an application is running. A static program is stored in either the persistent area or the transient area according to a directive.

Native program. A native program is a kind of a built-in predicate represented as C functions that are translated from a determinate predicate [27]. It is appropriate to a static predicate whose execution speed is strongly important, and one whose definition is rarely changed. Although the translation is automatic, its use is limited because the object binaries rely on the platform.

Incremental program. An incremental program is represented as a bytecode [2] generated by an incremental (non-optimizing) compiler invoked by `asserta/1` and `assertz/1`. It is appropriate to a dynamic predicate that is defined and executed dynamically. In such a case, the balance between the time required for each is important. The compilation is speeded up by the omission of the optimization while the execution is speeded up by the omission of the logical database update [19].

Interpretive program. An interpretive program is represented as a term that is interpreted by the Prolog interpreter. It is appropriate to a dynamic predicate which is defined and executed dynamically in the manner of an incremental program, but the compilation has little effect on execution time. In the case of a unit clause composed of ground terms, the same effect as that of structure copying [28] can be expected because terms are shared without being copied to the global stack. For example, it is appropriate to clinical information on drug-drug interactions [21,22] and engineering information regarding product catalogues [29] because they can be represented as a set of unit clauses composed of ground terms.

2.3   Optimization by Instruction Rewriting

On the execution of a predicate, the symbol table is repeatedly referred to in order to determine the program code associated with a predicate name. The time required for referring to the table once is very short, but the cumulative time is not negligible if the same predicate is executed repeatedly. Therefore, predicate

---

[2] It also has a term representation for `clause/2`.

call instructions, such as `call` and `execute`, are optimized by rewriting these instructions according to the type of a program code being called. For example, if a predicate being called is a static program stored in the persistent area, a predicate call instruction `call` to this predicate is rewritten as a direct call instruction `call_direct` with an absolute address because the location of a static program is fixed in the persistent area. Likewise, a call instruction to a native program is rewritten as `call_native`, and others as `call_indirect` that refers to the symbol table. Thus, instructions that refer to the symbol table are limited to only a few instructions such as `call_indirect`.

3   Multi-thread Extension for Enterprise Applications

This section describes a multi-thread extension of Inside Prolog for expanding its application domains to enterprise applications.

3.1   Multi-threading Prolog

Several approaches are known to realize multi-threading in Prolog. The first is to realize scheduling and context switching in a Prolog abstract machine by itself

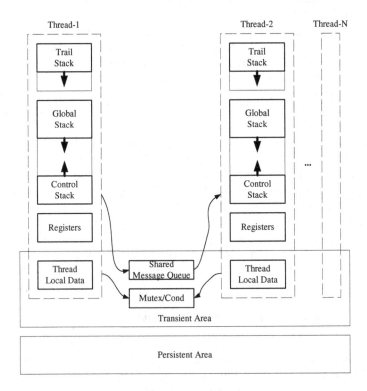

Fig. 2. Execution model of multi-threaded Inside Prolog

[7,30]. The second is to utilize a standard multi-thread library for scheduling and context switching [9,8]. In the case of Java-based implementation, the third is to create multiple single-threaded Prolog engines, and run them in multiple Java threads [10,31]. The first approach is a kind of user-level thread model, and has an advantage in performance because kernel resources are not consumed, and context switching and synchronization can be simplified. It is, however, difficult to utilize the multiple processors of an SMP system [32]. The second approach has disadvantages in regard to the costs of context switching and synchronization. However, the throughput can be improved by parallel processing on an SMP system. The third approach has advantages in parallel processing over other approaches, but it is inadequate for a large knowledge base because the data area cannot be shared between threads.

Inside Prolog adopts the second approach so that it can deal with a large knowledge base, and has advantages in throughput improvement on an SMP system. The POSIX thread library of Unix and Linux, and the Windows thread library can be used as the multi-thread library.

3.2 Execution Model

Figure 2 illustrates the execution model of multi-threaded Inside Prolog [3].

Shared variables. Shared variables between threads require major changes of the abstract machine TOAM regarding the handling of backtracking and its organization [8]. Therefore, communication mechanisms using shared variables between threads are omitted.

Communication. Shared message queues created in the transient area are used for communication between threads. The shared message queue is capable of sending and receiving messages in multi-thread safety. It is also possible to send an interrupt message as an exception from one thread to another.

Synchronization. Mutual exclusion object (mutex), condition variable (cond), and read/write mutex based on POSIX threads are provided for the basic synchronization mechanism. Mutex, cond, and read/write mutex are created in the transient area, and are shared between threads.

Thread-local data. Globally shared data that should not be reclaimed on backtracking are usually kept in the data area by associating them with the symbol table using `asserta/1`, `assertz/1` and so on. However, the risk of contention exists because the symbol table is shared by all threads. The thread-local data is provided for managing shared data specific to a thread.

3.3 Extension of Prolog Abstract Machine

Major changes of TOAM for realizing the multi-thread feature include the introduction of thread control data and synchronization [4]. The thread control

---

[3] Hereinafter, a multi-threaded version of Inside Prolog is also called Inside Prolog only when there is no possibility of confusion.

[4] Built-in predicates that access the symbol table and the data area also must incorporate synchronization.

data manages the state of multi-threaded TOAM per thread, such as stacks and registers; in single-threaded TOAM these are managed using global variables. Thread control data can be implemented using the thread local storage [5] of a standard multi-thread library. On the other hand, even though synchronization is unavoidable when accessing the symbol table and the data area, heavy use of synchronization may cause significant performance degradation, and multiple processors of an SMP system cannot be utilized effectively if the length of mutual exclusion is long.

There are three cases that require synchronization in TOAM. That is, the handling of catch/3 and throw/1 that deal with exceptions saved in the transient area; the rewriting of predicate call instructions such as call; and the handling of predicate call instructions that refer to the symbol table, such as call_indirect. The first case does not affect usual inference performance and parallelism because it happens only when exceptions are thrown. The influence of the second case must be negligibly small because synchronization is required only once for each instruction occurrence. On the other hand, the third case invokes a program stored in the transient area, and this invocation procedure consists of several inseparable steps. Therefore, synchronization is generally required so that the definition and execution of a predicate can be performed safely under a multi-threaded environment, though synchronization seriously affects inference performance and parallelism. In case the definition and execution of a predicate are performed in parallel, it is customary to ensure the consistency of a predicate definition using explicit synchronization by an application program itself, as described in Fig. 3 of Sect. 3.4. Consequently, the omission of synchronization by TOAM is less likely to become a practical issue.

Therefore, synchronization regarding static programs and incremental programs is omitted by TOAM in order to give priority to inference performance and parallelism. In contrast, interpretive programs are synchronized by clause/2, assertz/1 and so on for ensuring the consistency of hash tables for clause indexing and preserving the logical database update. This allows the choice of the most suitable representation of a program code according to its role and scene from the viewpoint of inference performance and parallelism, and the consistency of a predicate definition.

3.4   Examples of Multi-thread Programming

Figure 3 shows a programming example of the producer-consumer problem written in Inside Prolog. A condition variable is created by cond_create/1 for suspension and resumption of threads, and a mutual exclusion object is created by mutex_create/1. Consumer and producer threads that execute consumer/2 and producer/2 predicates, respectively, are created by thread_create/3. A buffer shared by these two threads is represented by buffer/1, and its contents are updated by assertz/1 and retract/1 with synchronization using

---

[5] For example, it is provided by pthread_getspecific() and its family of POSIX threads and TlsGetValue() and its family of Windows.

```
producer_consumer :-
    cond_create(Cond),        % Create a condition variable
    mutex_create(Mutex),      % Create a mutual exclusion object
    %% Create a producer thread, and call producer/2.
    thread_create(Producer, producer(Cond, Mutex), []),
    %% Create a consumer thread, and call consumer/2.
    thread_create(Consumer, consumer(Cond, Mutex), []).

producer(Cond, Mutex) :-
    repeat,
    produce_item(Item),
    with_mutex_lock(Mutex,
      (%% Wait until the buffer has a vacant.
       (buffer(Items0), length(Items0, 100) ->
        cond_wait(Cond, Mutex) ; true),
       %% Add an item to the buffer.
       retract(buffer(Items)),
       append(Items, [Item], Items1),
       assertz(buffer(Items1)),
       %% Notify a consumer when the buffer becomes non-emtpy.
       (Items1 == [Item] -> cond_signal(Cond) ; true)
      )),
    fail.

consumer(Cond, Mutex) :-
    repeat,
    with_mutex_lock(Mutex,
      (%% Wait until the buffer becomes non-empty.
       (buffer([]) -> cond_wait(Cond, Mutex) ; true),
       %% Take out an item from the buffer.
       retract(buffer([Item | Items])),
       assertz(buffer(Items)),
       %% Notify a producer when the buffer has a vacant.
       (length(Items, 99) -> cond_signal(Cond) ; true)
      )),
    consume_item(Item),
    fail.

%% An initial value of the buffer is empty.
buffer([]).
```

Fig. 3. Programming example of the producer-consumer problem

with_mutex_lock/2. Threads are suspended by cond_wait/2 when the buffer is
empty or full, and are resumed by cond_signal/1 when the state of the buffer
is changed.

4   Knowledge Processing Server

The knowledge processing server is a framework for operating a knowledge-based system written in Inside Prolog with an enterprise application, and for providing inference services to an enterprise application using a knowledge base. It is independent of any enterprise application and any knowledge-based system, and is realized by combining Inside Prolog and Java. The server improves interoperability with various enterprise applications due to its adaptation to distributed object technology, such as RMI, SOAP, and CORBA, using Java. The server also makes it easier to incorporate a knowledge-based system into a transaction system by allowing a knowledge-based system to inherit the transactions of an enterprise application in the J2EE environment.

Figure 4 illustrates a simplified system configuration of the server that applies a knowledge-based clinical decision support system to the hospital information system CAFE in a J2EE environment. The clinical knowledge base stores medical inference rules used for clinical decision support such as the validation of contraindications and proposals of appropriate administration conditions, while the clinical database consistently stores patient records such as the disease names and medication orders of patients. The EJB client provides clinical support functions to health care professionals using an application which handles workflow in a hospital, and the clinical decision support system. The session bean is a service interface to clinical decision support functions provided by the knowledge processing server. The inference engine for clinical decision support is a knowledge-based system written in Prolog. The knowledge base adaptor is a Prolog program that fits data types and data structures used in a service

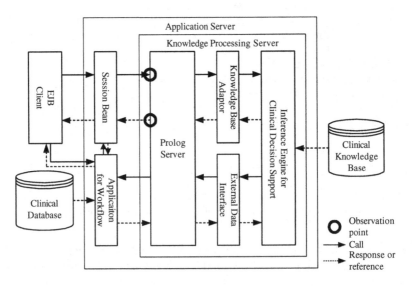

Fig. 4. System configuration of the knowledge processing server applied to a J2EE-based hospital information system

interface into an inference engine and a knowledge base, and vice versa. The external data interface is used to access external data, such as patient records in the clinical database, from the inference engine via EJB/JNDI services. The Prolog server is a generalized mechanism that mediates communications between a service interface written in Java and a knowledge-based system written in Prolog.

5   Performance Evaluation

This section presents the evaluation results for the multi-thread feature and parallelism of Inside Prolog, and the scalability of the knowledge processing server.

5.1   Overhead Costs of the Multi-thread Extension

In order to evaluate the overhead of the multi-thread extension, the elapsed times of single- and multi-threaded versions were compared using benchmark programs boyer, 8 queens, qsort, and takeuchi. Interpretive, incremental, and static program code representations were applied. Static programs were stored in the persistent area and executed once to obtain normal performance by forcing the instructions to be rewritten before the measurement. Sun V880 with 1 CPU was used in this experiment.

Figure 5 shows the elapsed time ratios of the multi-threaded to the single-threaded version. The results indicate that the overhead costs of the multi-thread extension are about 20 % at its maximum. These costs are due to synchronization and representation changes of the TOAM state from global variables to pointer accesses through the thread control data, as in SWI-Prolog [9].

5.2   Parallelism on SMP Systems

In order to evaluate the parallelism of each program code representation on an SMP system, the elapsed times of the benchmark programs were measured using

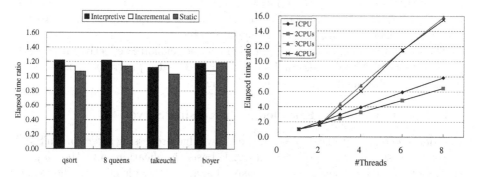

Fig. 5. Elapsed time ratios of multi-threaded version to single threaded version   **Fig. 6.** Elapsed time ratios of the interpretive program of the 8-queens benchmark

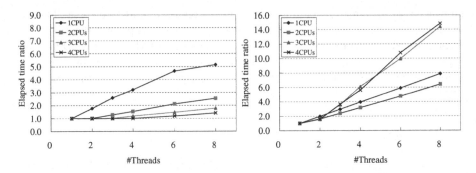

Fig. 7. Elapsed time ratios of the static program of the 8-queens benchmark

Fig. 8. Elapsed time ratios of the interpretive program of the boyer benchmark

a Sun V880 with various CPU configurations. Each of the benchmark programs was executed in parallel. The number of CPUs varied from 1 to 4, and the number of threads that execute the programs in parallel varied from 1 to 8.

Figures 6 and 7 show the results of the interpretive and static programs of 8 queens. Elapsed times are normalized by the elapsed time in the case of one thread for each CPU configuration. The elapsed times of the interpretive program were increased as the number of threads increased. Elapsed times were also increased if the number of CPUs was greater than two. This is because an interpretive program requires synchronization of the transient area as described in Sect. 3.3. In contrast, the elapsed times of the static program decreased as the number of CPUs increased when the numbers of threads were the same. Especially, when the number of threads was equal to or smaller than that of CPUs, the elapsed times did not increase even if the number of threads increased. This is because synchronization is unnecessary for a static program after the instruction rewriting. Results similar to those of a static program were obtained for an incremental program except for real elapsed times due to optimization differences. The results of qsort and takeuchi were almost the same.

On the other hand, the results of all program codes of boyer were similar to those of the interpretive program of 8 queens as shown in Figs. 8 and 9. This is because parallelism is decreased due to the synchronization caused by the heavy use of `functor/3` which accesses the symbol table.

These results indicate that the multi-thread extension is effective in parallel processing on SMP systems for incremental and static programs if predicates including synchronization are not used frequently.

5.3 Scalability of the Knowledge Processing Server

In order to evaluate the scalability of the knowledge processing server on an SMP system, the server was applied to a J2EE-based application, and the elapsed times of the inference service were measured against multiple clients. The experimental application was modeled upon the hospital information system CAFE, and its system configuration was similar to that shown in Fig. 4 except for an

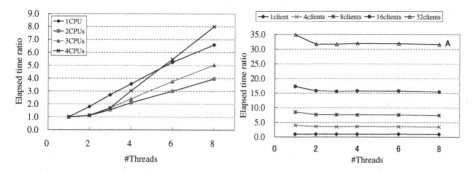

Fig. 9. Elapsed time ratios of the static program of the boyer benchmark

Fig. 10. Elapsed time ratios of the session bean of the knowledge processing server on 1 CPU machine

EJB client, the inference rules in the clinical knowledge base, and the entities stored in the clinical database.

Initially, a client creates twenty entity beans, whose class is defined for this experiment and has about ten fields, using an application server. A client then invokes the inference rules stored in the knowledge base through a session bean. The inference rules search for twenty entity beans that meet query conditions, and refer to the values of their fields.

The application server was deployed in a Sun V880 with from 1 CPU to 4 CPUs, and a database management system was deployed in a Sun Ultra60 with 2 CPUs. The number of threads that execute the inference engine was varied from 1 to 8. The number of clients varied from 1 to 32, and they were run on a maximum of eight machines. Elapsed times were measured at the point where a session bean invoked a method of the Prolog server (indicated as circles in Fig. 4).

Figures 10, 11, and 12 show elapsed times normalized by the elapsed time (about 0.027 seconds) in the case of one thread against one client. These results indicate that the elapsed times increased as the number of clients increased, but throughput speed was improved by increasing the number of threads and CPUs. For example, in the cases of 32 clients and 8 threads, the elapsed times of 2 and 4 CPUs cases were improved 0.51-fold (B in Fig. 11) and 0.28-fold (C in Fig. 12) over that of 1 CPU case (A in Fig. 10). The improvement ratios, however, did not reach the points estimated based on the number of CPUs, and they slowed down by degrees. Both the inference engine and the inference rules used in this experiment are represented as static programs [6], and the synchronization caused by these code representations is not included. Consequently, one reason for bounding scalability is the synchronization included in both the inference engine and the Java interface of Inside Prolog. However, it seems that this effect is sufficiently small because the elapsed times are not increased even on an SMP system of up to 4 CPUs, unlike boyer.

---

[6] Inference rules are represented as incremental programs in a development phase and static programs in an operation phase.

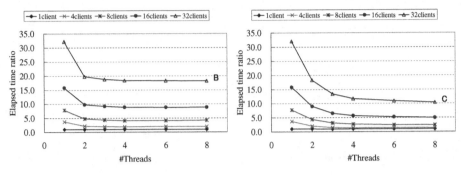

Fig. 11. Elapsed time ratios of the session bean of the knowledge processing server on 2 CPUs machine

Fig. 12. Elapsed time ratios of the session bean of the knowledge processing server on 4 CPUs machine

6   Conclusion

This paper describes a newly implemented multi-threaded Prolog system that evolves single-threaded Inside Prolog. It is intended as a means to apply a knowledge-based system written in Inside Prolog to an enterprise application. It provides several representations of a program code, and allows the choice of the most suitable one according to its role and scene in an application. This allows the realization of a high degree of parallelism on an SMP system by minimizing mutual exclusion in the Prolog abstract machine TOAM. Also briefly introduced is the knowledge processing server which is a framework for operating a knowledge-based system written in Inside Prolog with an enterprise application.

The results of experiments using benchmark programs indicated that the overhead cost of the multi-thread extension was about 20 % at its maximum, and predicates represented as a bytecode could achieve a high degree of parallelism on an SMP system. The results of experiments regarding the knowledge processing server also indicated that the extension was effective for the improvement of throughput speed on an SMP system, and the server could obtain scalability on it.

The knowledge processing server has been practically applied to clinical decision support in the hospital information system CAFE. It processes about a thousand prescription orders per day, and contraindications on one order are validated within about a second. The server has been problem-free for over a year. This indicates that Inside Prolog and the server are sufficiently robust for use in an enterprise application.

Because the application for the workflow of the hospital information system CAFE became too large to run in a 32 bits version of Java VM, a 64 bits version for workflow and a 32 bits version for the knowledge processing server were combined irregularly. It is necessary for Inside Prolog to support a 64 bits architecture in order to cope with large enterprise applications.

References

1. Kaplan, B.: Evaluating informatics applications – clinical decision support systems literature review. International Journal of Medical Informatics **64** (2001) 15–37
2. Toussaint, A.: Java rule engine api. JSR-94 (2003)
3. YASU   Technologies   http://yasutech.com/products/quickrulesse/index.htm: QuickRules. (2005)
4. ILOG, Inc http://www.ilog.com /products/jrules: ILOG JRules. (2006)
5. Drools Project http://drools.org: Drools. (2006)
6. Kobayashi, S.: Production system. Journal of Information Processing Society of Japan **26** (1985) 1487–1496
7. Eskilson, J., Carlsson, M.: SICStus MT – a multithreaded execution environment for SICStus prolog. In: Principles of Declarative Programming: 10th International Symposium. Volume 1490 of Lecture Notes in Computer Science., Springer-Verlag GmbH (1998) 36–53
8. Carro, M., Hermenegildo, M.: Concurrency in prolog using threads and a shared database. In: International Conference on Logic Programming. (1999) 320–334
9. Wielemaker, J.: Native preemptive threads in SWI-Prolog. In: Logic Programming. Volume 2916 of Lecture Notes in Computer Science., Springer-Verlag GmbH (2003) 331–345
10. Denti, E., Omicini, A., Ricci, A.: tuProlog: A light-weight prolog for internet applications and infrastructures. In: Practical Aspects of Declarative Languages. Third International Symposium, PADL 2001. Proceedings. Volume 1990 of Lecture Notes in Computer Science., Springer-Verlag GmbH (2001) 184–198
11. Tarau, P.: Jinni: Intelligent mobile agent programming at the intersection of java and prolog. In: Proceedings of the Fourth International Conference on the Practical Applications of Intelligent Agents and Multi-agent Technology. (1999) 109–124
12. Katamine, K., Umeda, M., Nagasawa, I., Hashimoto, M.: Integrated development environment for knowledge-based systems and its practical application. IEICE Transactions on Information and Systems **E87-D** (2004) 877–885
13. Tegoshi, Y., Nagasawa, I., Maeda, J., Makino, M.: An information processing technique for a searching problem of an architectural design. Journal of Architecture, Planning and Environmental Engineering (1989)
14. Nagasawa, I., Maeda, J., Tegoshi, Y., Makino, M.: A programming technique for some combination problems in a design support system using the method of generate-and-test. Journal of Structural and Construction Engineering (1990)
15. Umeda, M., Nagasawa, I., Higuchi, T.: The elements of programming style in design calculations. In: Proceedings of the Ninth International Conference on Industrial and Engineering Applications of Artificial Intelligence and Expert Systems. (1996) 77–86
16. Furukawa, Y., Ueno, M., Nagasawa, I.: A health care support system. Japan Journal of Medical Informatics **10** (1990) 121–132
17. Furukawa, Y., Nagasawa, I., Ueno, M.: HCS: A health care support system. Journal of Information Processing Society of Japan **34** (1993) 88–95
18. Umeda, M., Nagasawa, I.: Project structure and development methodology toward the IT revolution – lesson from practice –. In: Proceedings of the Fourth Joint Conference on Knowledge-Based Software Engineering. (2000) 1–8
19. ISO/IEC: 13211-1 Information technology – Programming Languages – Prolog – Part 1: General core. (1995)

20. Umeda, M., Nagasawa, I., Ohno, K., Katamine, K., Takata, O.: Knowledge base development environment and J2EE-compliant inference engine for clinical decision support. In: The Proceedings of The 8th World Multi-Conference on Systemics, Cybernetics and Informatics. Volume 1. (2004) 43–48

21. Ohno, K., Umeda, M., Nagase, K., Nagasawa, I.: Knowledge base programming for medical decision support. In: The Proceedings of the 14th International Conference on Applications of Prolog. (2001) 202–210

22. Ohno, K., Nagasawa, I., Umeda, M., Nagase, K., Takada, A., Igarashi, T.: Development of medical knowledge base for clinical decision support. In: The Proceedings of The 8th World Multi-Conference on Systemics, Cybernetics and Informatics. Volume 7. (2004) 193–198

23. Nagase, K., Takada, A., Igarashi, T., Ouchi, T., Amino, T., Ohno, K.: Development and implementation of J2EE based physician order entry system with clinical decision support function. In: The Proceedings of the 23rd Joint Conference on Medical Informatics. (2003) 1–G–2–2

24. Takada, A., Nagase, K., Ouchi, T., Amino, T., Igarashi, T.: Enhanced communication realized with UML utilization in the development of hospital information system. In: The Proceedings of the 23rd Joint Conference on Medical Informatics. (2003) O–3–2

25. Ait-Kaci, H.: Warren's Abstract Machine. The MIT Press (1991)

26. Neng-Fa, Z.: Global optimizations in a prolog compiler for the TOAM. J. Logic Programming (1993) 265–294

27. Katamine, K., Hirota, T., Zhou, N.F., Nagasawa, I.: On the translation of prolog program to c. Transactions of Information Processing Society of Japan **37** (1996) 1130–1137

28. Li, X.: A new term representation method for prolog. The Journal of Logic Programming **34** (1998) 43–57

29. Umeda, M., Nagasawa, I., Ito, M.: Knowledge representation model for engineering information circulation of standard parts. Transactions of Information Processing Society of Japan **38** (1997) 1905–1918

30. Clark, K., Robinson, P., Hagen, R.: Multi-threading and message communication in Qu-Prolog. Theory and Practice of Logic Programming **1** (2001) 283–301

31. IF Computer http://www. ifcomputer .co.jp/MINERVA: MINERVA. (2005)

32. Fukuda, A.: Parallel operating systems. Journal of Information Processing Society of Japan **34** (1993) 1139–1149

A Meta-logical Approach for Multi-agent Communication of Semantic Web Information

Visit Hirankitti and Vuong Tran Xuan

Intelligent Communication and Transportation Laboratory,
Department of Computer Engineering, Faculty of Engineering,
King Mongkut's Institute of Technology Ladkrabang, Bangkok, Thailand
v_hirankitti@yahoo.com, txvuong@yahoo.com

Abstract. The success of the semantic web would be determined by how easy and uniform to access to and exchange of the semantic information among computers. In this paper we have developed a framework of multi-agent communication of the Semantic Web information. The agent and the communication between agents are characterized in meta-logic. One single agent, understood as a meta-logical system, adopts a demo(.) predicate as its inference engine and meta-programs—transformed from some Semantic Web ontologies—as its assumptions. Such an agent can reason with its assumptions as well as other agent's assumptions. With this ability, when several agents are created by using this framework, the community of these agents can uniformly communicate the Semantic Web information between each other on the Internet.

1 Introduction

The success of the Semantic Web (or briefly "SW") would be similar to that of the web in that its success is mainly due to the easy and uniform way to access to and exchange of information among the computers on the Internet. Due to this significance, in this paper we shall propose a model of communication of semantic information among multiple agents using meta-logic.

Some previous works on an agent system related to SW are: Zou et. al. [4] used SW languages, as the languages for expressing agent's messages and knowledge base, to specify and publish common ontologies; [5] presented a multi-agent based scheduling application in which data sources are described by SW languages and encapsulated in the agents. In [6], an agent is built to perform scheduling with distributed ontologies about events, e.g. conferences, classes, published on the SW.

Those approaches are mainly related to applying the SW technology in a multi-agent system. However in SW there exist a large number of available distributed but linked ontologies, hence based on our previous work [2] in this paper we are concerned with multi-agent communication and reasoning with distributed ontologies.

The rest of this paper is organized as follows. Next we give an overview of our framework. Section 3 presents our meta-representation of SW ontologies and 4 describes our single agent architecture. Section 5 describes the meta-interpreter which is the agent's inference engine, and 6 introduces multi-agent communication. Section 7

M. Umeda et al. (Eds.): INAP 2005, LNAI 4369, pp. 215–228, 2006.

shows how to query and reason with SW ontologies by multi-agent communication. Finally, we discuss about some other related works and conclude this paper.

2 Our Framework

In our previous work [2] we applied meta-logic to develop a meta-logical system behaving as an agent, and in this paper such an agent framework has been extended to work as a web browser, a web server, or even a web-service provider, in order to communicate with each other in a multi-agent communication fashion.

The meta-logical system for one single agent consists of three main parts: meta-programs for multiple ontologies, a meta-interpreter, and the communication facility. Each of the meta-programs contains meta-level descriptions of ontologies from SW. That is, the ontologies expressed in their native form, e.g. in RDF, RDFS, and OWL languages, are transformed into a meta-logical representation. (RDF, or Resource Description Framework, is a language for representing information about resources on the World Wide Web, while RDFS, or RDF Schema, is a language to describe RDF vocabularies on the web. OWL is a Web Ontology Language. It builds on RDF and RDFS and adds more vocabulary for describing properties and classes.) Some elements in one ontology may be related to some elements in another ontology. The meta-interpreter is the system's inference engine which is used to infer implicit information from the multiple ontologies. The communication facility supports the communication among the individual agents. One block in Fig. 1. illustrates one agent.

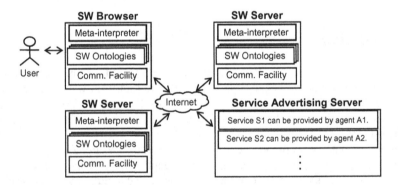

Fig. 1. Our multi-agent communication system

When several agents of this kind are formed as an agent community, the way the multi-agent system works can be explained as follows. Initially the user queries an SW browser to get answers from an SW ontology on SW. The browser can perform two alternative ways. Firstly, it may retrieve this ontology from SW, transform it into a meta-program, and finally reason with the meta-program to infer the answers; if some elements in this ontology are related to some elements of another ontology, the interpreter will try to reason with that ontology in itself (by retrieving it first), or request reasoning of that ontology in an SW server and obtain the answers from that server, and this scenario may repeat itself. Alternatively, the browser passes the query to an SW sever to answer and gets the answers back for the user. The server infers those answers based on its inferential results which sometimes also require support of the inferential results derived from other servers. In case the browser does not know which SW server can answer that query, it will consult the Service Advertising Server which gathers information telling which SW server can provide what service. The browser then uses this information to communicate with the selected server directly.

3 The Meta-languages and the Meta-programs

In this section we develop two meta-languages of an SW ontology by mapping the language elements of RDF, RDFS, and OWL into meta-language terms.

3.1 Language Elements of the Semantic Web Ontology

The language elements of an SW ontology are classes, properties, class instances, and relationships between and among them described in the object level and the meta-level as illustrated in Fig. 2. At the object level, an instance can be an individual or a literal of a domain; and a property is a relationship between individuals, or is an individual's attribute. At the meta-level, a meta-instance can be an individual, property, class, and object-level statement; and a meta-property is a property to describe a relationship between and among meta-instances, or is a meta-instance's attribute. Next we define meta-logical terms to express these elements of the object and meta levels.

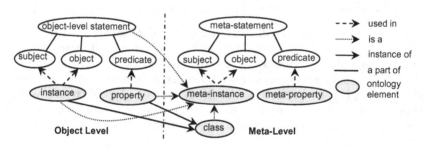

Fig. 2. The elements of an SW ontology at the object level and meta-level

3.2 Meta-languages of the Semantic Web Ontology

In our meta-logical framework, for an SW ontology we distinguish between its object and meta levels, and similarly its object and meta languages. Consequently, we have formulated two meta-languages: one discusses mainly about instances and their relationships, we call it "meta-language for the object level (**ML**)", and the other, called "meta-language for the meta-level (**MML**)", discusses mainly about classes, class instances, properties, and their relationships. Due to some connection between the object and meta levels, **ML** and **MML** are slightly overlapped.

- **A meta-language for the object level (ML)**

Instances and their relationships at the object level as well as some provability and references at the meta-level are specified in an SW ontology and this information is expressed at the meta-level by the elements below. (Note that the linguistic elements of provability are a part of **AgentML** (see section 5) and the linguistic elements expressing references are a part of **MML**.)

Meta-constant specifies a name of an instance and a literal, e.g. `john`, including a reference, e.g. a namespace, an ontology name. The latter is a meta-constant of **MML**. This means that **ML** and **MML** are not entirely separated.

Meta-variable stands for a different meta-constant at a different time, e.g. Person.

Meta-function symbol stands for the name of a relation between instances, or of an instance's property—i.e. an object-level predicate name, such as `fatherOf`, `name`— and also stand for other meta-level function symbol, e.g. `←`, `∧`, `:`, including the name of provability predicate, i.e. demo.

Meta-term is either a meta-constant or a meta-variable or a meta-function symbol (probably labeled with a name prefix) applied to a tuple of terms, such as `f`:`M1` where `:` is meta-function symbol and `f` is signified to be a namespace of `M1`.

To express an object-level predicate, it has the form: **P(S, O)** where **P** is an object-level predicate name, **S** and **O** are meta-constants or meta-variables (we presume all meta-variables appearing in the tuple are universally quantified), e.g.

```
`f`:`fatherOf`(`f`:`M2`,`f`:`M1`).//`M2`is the father of `M1`.
```

To express a provability predicate, it has the form: **demo(A, T, P(S, O))**, e.g. demo(a, o, `f`:`fatherOf`(`f`:`M2`, `f`:`M1`)). It means the sentence **P(S, O)** can be derived from an ontology (or a theory) **T** by an agent **A**.

The meta-term expressing an *object-level sentence* (sometimes with some provability) is a term **P(S, O)** or **demo(A, T, P(S, O))** or a logical-connective function symbol applied to the tuple of these terms. We presume all meta-variables appearing in the object-level sentence are universally quantified. One form of the sentence is a Horn-clause, e.g.

```
`f`:`fatherOf`(F,Ch) `←`        //F is Ch's father if b can
   demo(b,T,`p`:`parentOf`(F,Ch)) `∧`  //prove F is Ch's parent
   demo(c,T,`m`:`male`(F)).        //and c can prove F is a male.
```

Meta-statement for the object level reflects an object-level sentence to its existence at the meta-level. It has the form: **statement(T, S)**, where **T** is an ontology name and **S** is an object-level sentence, e.g.

```
statement(T, `f`:`fatherOf`(F, Ch) `←`
   demo(b, T, `p`:`parentOf`(F, Ch)) `∧`
   demo(c, T, `m`:`male`(F))).
```

In the above example, `'f'`:`'fatherOf'`(F, Ch) `'←'` demo(b, T, `'p'`:` parentOf'`(F, Ch)) `'∧'` demo(c, T, `'m'`:`'male'`(F)) is a rule expressing an object-level sentence which becomes a meta-representation (meta-term) to be manipulated at the meta-level by a meta-interpreter.

- **A meta-language for the meta-level (MML)**

Additionally, an SW ontology defines classes, properties, and their relationships, and also describes class-instance relations. This information is precisely *meta-information of the object level*. Here we express this information by **MML** which includes:

Meta-constant specifying a name of an agent, a resource location, a namespace, an ontology, an instance, a property, a class, and a literal.

Meta-variable standing for a different meta-constant at a different time.

Meta-function symbol standing for a logical connective, e.g. `'←'`, `'∧'`; or `':'` (for namespace labeling); or naming a function, e.g. # (a meta-function symbol for ontology name labelling); or a name of set operators applied on classes such as union, intersection, and complement; or a meta-predicate name being a name of a relation between entities, or being a name of characteristic of a property, which may fall into one of the following categories:

Class-class relations: subclass of, equivalent class of, disjoint with, etc.

Class-instance relations: instance of, class of, etc.

Property-property relations: sub property of, inverse of, etc.

Relations between literals and instances/classes/ properties. We can see these relations as attributes of instances, of classes, or of properties, e.g. comment etc.

Characteristics of properties: symmetric, transitive, functional, etc.

Meta-term being either a meta-constant or a meta-variable or a meta-function symbol applied to a tuple of terms, e.g. `'ontology'`#`'namespace'`.

In our framework, a name of a class, a property, etc., can be referenced by a meta-term in these three forms: uniqueName or namespace:name or ontology-Name#namespace:name, e.g. `'owl'`:`'inverseOf'`, `'o'`#`'f'`:`'fatherOf'`.

When a meta-term expresses a meta-level predicate stating a relation between entities it has the form of **Pred(Sub, Obj)**, and when it expresses a meta-level predicate stating a characteristic of a property it has the form of **Pred(Prop)**, where **Pred** is a meta-predicate name, **Sub**, **Obj**, and **Prop** are meta-constants or meta-variables.

The meta-term expressing a *meta-level sentence* is a term **Pred(Sub, Obj)** or **Pred(Prop)** or a logical-connective function symbol applied to the tuple of these terms. Let all meta-variables appearing in the meta-level sentence be universally quantified. One form of the sentence is a Horn-clause **meta-rule**, e.g.

```
'owl':'equivalentClass'(C, EC) '←'
   'owl':'equivalentClass'(C, EC1) '∧'
   'owl':'equivalentClass'(EC1, EC).
```

Meta-statement being a meta-representation of a meta-level sentence accessible by our meta-interpreter. It has two forms: **meta_statement(T, S)** and **axiom(T, S)**, where **T** is an ontology name and **s** is a meta-level sentence; the latter form represents a rule for a mathematical axiom. Here are some examples of the meta-statements:

```
meta_statement(T, 'rdfs':'subPropertyOf'(
  'f':'hasBrother', 'f':'hasSibling') '←' true).
axiom(T, 'owl':'equivalentClass'(C, EC) '←'
  'owl':'equivalentClass'(C, EC1) '∧'
  'owl':'equivalentClass'(EC1, EC)).
```

3.3 Meta-programs of the Semantic Web Ontology

Each ontology is transformed into a meta-program containing a (sub-)meta-program expressed in **ML**, called "**MP**", and/or a (sub-)meta-program expressed in **MML**, called "**MMP**". Another meta-program expresses some mathematical axioms, called "**AMP**". The inference engine often requires **AMP** to reason with **MP** and **MMP**.

- **The meta-program for the object level (MP)**
MP contains information of instances and their relationships in terms of meta-statements for the object level having the form of `statement(T, P(S, O) '←' true)` and `statement(T, P(S, O) '←' Body)`, where `Body` expresses a conjunction of object-level predicates and some provabilities; the latter is its Horn-clause form. Notice that we put `T` as the first argument in `statement(T, meta-statement)` to signify that `meta-statement` belongs to the ontology (or theory) `T`.

- **The meta-program for the meta-level (MMP)**
MMP contains description of classes, properties, their relations, and class-instance relationships in terms of meta-rules. Here are some typical elements of an **MMP**:

Some meta-statements discussing about classes and their relationships:

// The class C is sub-class of the class SC.
```
meta_statement(T, 'rdfs':'subClassOf'(C, SC) '←' true).
```
// Classes C & EC are equivalent.
```
meta_statement(T, 'owl':'equivalentClass'(C, EC) '←' true).
```
// Classes C & DC are disjoint.
```
meta_statement(T, 'owl':'disjointWith'(C, DC) '←' true).
```
// The class C is union of classes in Cs.
```
meta_statement(T, 'owl':'unionOf'(C, Cs) '←' true).
```
// The class C is intersection of classes in Cs.
```
meta_statement(T, 'owl':'intersectionOf'(C, Cs) '←' true).
```
// The class C is complement of the class CC.
```
meta_statement(T, 'owl':'complementOf'(C, CC) '←' true).
```
// The instance I is an instance of the class C.
```
meta_statement(T, 'rdf':'type'(I, C) '←' true).
```

Some meta-statements discussing about properties and their relationships:

// *The property P is sub-property of the property SP.*

```
meta_statement(T, 'rdfs':'subPropertyOf'(P, SP) '←' true).
```

// *Properties P & EP are equivalent.*

```
meta_statement(T,'owl':'equivalentProperty'(P, EP) '←' true).
```

// *The property P is symmetric.*

```
meta_statement(T, 'owl':'symmetric'(P) '←' true).
```

// *The property P is transitive.*

```
meta_statement(T, 'owl':'transitive'(P) '←' true).
```

// *The property P is functional.*

```
meta_statement(T, 'owl':'functional'(P) '←' true).
```

// *The property P is inverse functional.*

```
meta_statement(T, 'owl':'inverseFunctional'(P) '←' true).
```

// *The property P is inversion of the property IP.*

```
meta_statement(T, 'owl':'inverseOf'(P, IP) '←' true).
```

// *The domain of the property P is D.*

```
meta_statement(T, 'rdfs':'domain'(P, D) '←' true).
```

// *The range of the property P is R.*

```
meta_statement(T, 'rdfs':'range'(P, R) '←' true).
```

- **The meta-program for the axioms (AMP)**

AMP contains axioms for classes and properties. They are expressed in the meta-rule form. Here are some typical elements of the **AMP**.

// *The following relations of classes and properties are transitive.*

```
axiom(T, 'owl':'equivalentClass'(C, EC) '←'
  'owl':'equivalentClass'(C, EC1) '∧'
  'owl':'equivalentClass'(EC1, EC)).
axiom(T, 'rdfs':'subClassOf'(C, SC) '←'
  'rdfs':'subClassOf'(C, SC1) '∧'
  'rdfs':'subClassOf'(SC1, SC)).
axiom(T, 'owl':'equivalentProperty'(P, EP) '←'
  'owl':'equivalentProperty'(P, EP1) '∧'
  'owl':'equivalentProperty'(EP1, EP)).
axiom(T, 'rdfs':'subPropertyOf'(P, SP) '←'
  'rdfs':'subPropertyOf'(P, SP1)) '∧'
  'rdfs':'subPropertyOf'(SP1, SP)).
axiom(T, 'owl':'sameAs'(I, SI) '←'
  'owl':'sameAs'(I, SI1) '∧' 'owl':'sameAs'(SI1, SI)).
...
```

// *The following relations of classes and properties are symmetric.*

```
axiom(T, 'owl':'equivalentClass'(C, EC) '←'
    'owl':'equivalentClass'(EC, C)).
axiom(T, 'owl':'disjointWith'(C, DC) '←'
    'owl':'disjointWith'(DC, C)).
axiom(T, 'owl':'equivalentProperty'(P, EP) '←'
    'owl':'equivalentProperty'(EP, P)).
axiom(T, 'owl':'inverseOf'(P, IP) '←'
    'owl':'inverseOf'(IP, P)).
axiom(T, 'owl':'sameAs'(I, SI) '←' 'owl':'sameAs'(SI, I)).
axiom(T, 'owl':'differentFrom'(I, DI) '←'
    'owl':'differentFrom'(DI, I)).
...
```

// *inheritance axiom: an instance of a subclass is also an instance of its super class.*

```
axiom(T, 'rdf':'type'(I, C) '←'
    'rdfs':'subClassOf'(SC, C) '∧' 'rdf':'type'(I, SC)).
...
```

// *Some axioms are related to characteristics of a property.*

```
axiom(T, P(S, O) '←' 'owl':'inverseOf'(P, IP) '∧' IP(O, S)).
axiom(T, P(S, O) '←'
    'rdfs':'subPropertyOf'(SP, P) '∧' SP(S, O)).
axiom(T, P(S, O) '←'
    'owl':'equivalentProperty'(P, EP) '∧' EP(S, O)).
axiom(T, P(S, O) '←'
    'owl':'transitive'(P) ∧ P(S, O1) '∧' P(O1, O)).
axiom(T, P(S, O) '←' 'owl':'symmetric'(P) '∧' P(O, S)).
...
```

4   Single SW Agent Architecture

An agent in our framework is denoted by <**Meta-interpreter, Knowledge Base, Communication, Historical Memory, Transformation**> whose components are depicted in Fig. 3 and can be described as follows.

The Transformation module transforms ontologies obtained from SW into **MPs** and **MMPs**. The Knowledge base already stores **AMPs** and is later added with the transformed **MPs** and **MMPs**. The Meta-interpreter reasons with the three kinds of meta-programs in order to answer a query posed by the user, and communicates with other agents to get ontologies or answers for a query. Historical memory stores information required for advance reasoning by the meta-interpreter, such as backtracking between alternative answers derived from several agents. Communication module facilitates communication with other agents.

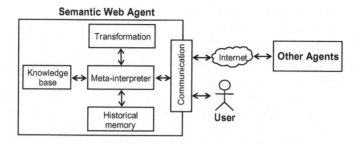

Fig. 3. Single SW Agent Architecture

5 Definition of a Communicative Demo

This meta-interpreter is an extension of the one proposed in [2]. The definition of demo/2 in [2] has been extended to demo/3. For demo(Agent, T, A), it means an answer A can be inferred from a theory T by an agent Agent. Here the Vanilla meta-interpreter [1] is adapted for reasoning with multiple ontologies on SW where we identified three kinds of meta-level statements, (1) statement(T, A '←' B), (2) meta_statement(T, A '←' B) for the meta-level of an ontology, and (3) the mathematical axioms axiom(T, A '←' B). The definition of demo/3 is as follows.

```
demo(_, empty, true).                                    (true)

demo(Agent, T, demo(Agent', T, A)) ←                     (ref)
   demo(Agent', T, A).

demo(Agent, T1∪T2, A) ←                                  (ost)
   statement(T1, A '←' B) ∧ demo(Agent, T2, B).

demo(Agent, T1∪T2, A) ←                                  (mst)
   meta_statement(T1, A '←' B) ∧ demo(Agent, T2, B).


demo(Agent, T1∪T2, A) ←                                  (ast)
   axiom(T1, A '←' B) ∧ demo(Agent, T2, B).

demo(Agent, T1∪T2, A '∧' B) ←                            (conj)
   demo(Agent, T1, A) ∧ demo(Agent, T2, B).
```

The clauses (true), (ost), and (conj) form the Vanilla meta-interpreter. The clause (ref) states that when the meta-interpreter tries to prove demo(Agent, T, demo(Agent', T, A)), it will prove demo(Agent', T, A) by a reflection.

For distributed ontologies, some of them may be referred to in other ontologies. In this case while demo() is reasoning with an ontology to derive an answer, this may require it to reason with another unavailable ontology. Therefore, we should add another demo() clause to allow demo() to retrieve that ontology which is sharable from its location on the web, then transform it into **MP** and **MMP**, and can finally reason with it to complete all the inference steps so that it can derive the answer.

```
demo(Agent, T, demo(Agent', T, A)) ←                    (retr)
   unavailable(T) ∧ myName(Agent') ∧ retrieve(O, location(T)) ∧
   transform(O, P) ∧ demo(Agent', P, A).
```

Here to prove demo(Agent', T, A) this clause first ensures that ontology T is not possessed by the agent with unavailable(T), and that Agent' is the agent's name with myName(Agent'). If these hold, the agent retrieves T from its location on the web and transforms it to a meta-program to be reasoned by demo(Agent', P, A). With this new clause, demo() can now work analogously to a browser.

Additionally, suppose that each server storing an ontology is equipped with this demo() definition. Now for the demo (at the client) to derive an answer from an unavailable ontology; this can be done easily by that the demo() at the client sends the query (for an unavailable ontology) to the server, which has that ontology, to answer the query. For this to be done, we may add two more demo() clauses:

```
demo(Agent, T, demo(Agent', T, A)) ←       (certain-agent-comm)
   not myName(Agent') ∧ known(Agent') ∧ unavailable(T) ∧
   agentLocation(Agent', Location, Channel) ∧
   connect(Agent', Location, Channel, ConnectID) ∧
   communicate(ConnectID, demo(Agent', T, A)) ∧
   disconnect(ConnectID).

demo(Agent, T, demo(Agent', T, A)) ←    (applicable-agent-comm)
   unknown(Agent') ∧ unavailable(T) ∧
   findAgent(Agent', A) ∧ demo(Agent, T, demo(Agent', T, A).
```

For the demo clause (certain-agent-comm), demo() will ask another agent (not itself) Agent', which is already known, to answer question A from a theory possessed by Agent'. To communicate with Agent', demo() must find its location on the network. After the location is known, demo() establishes the connection to that location and asking Agent' for an answer for question A. If it successes demo() obtains the answers and finally terminate the communication with Agent'.

For the last demo clause (applicable-agent-comm), demo() tries to get an answer for question A from any agent who can answer it. In this case, demo() searches for an agent who can provide an answer (service) by consulting the Service Advertising Server which is another agent. This is done by the goal findAgent(Agent', A) which will ask the Service Advertising Server which agent can answer (or provide the service) A. When this agent is known, demo() will call itself so that the (certain-agent-comm) clause will be employed later.

Given all above demo clauses, an answer A can be inferred from demo() in different ways: firstly A may be inferred using one or more statement in one or many **MP**, and/or using meta-statements in **MMPs**, and/or using axioms in **AMP**. Alternatively, the inference may require demo() to retrieve some ontologies from different sources on SW or to send demo(Agent, T, A) to other servers to request for the answer.

- **Meta-language of the agent (AgentML)**

AgentML is a meta-language we use to formulate the agent <**Meta-interpreter, Knowledge Base, Communication, Historical Memory, Transformation**>. It discusses about the agent's components, such as the demo() definition, the agent name and resources, assumptions in ontologies (this part is connected with **MP** and **MMP**), communication methods and facilities, other agents and their ontologies, and so on.

- **Agent creation and the agent's life cycle**

To create and start a new agent, we perform the following steps: (1) assign a unique name to the new agent by asserting `myName(agentName)`; (2) set up its communication channels; (3) start the agent to do an endless observation-action cycle. This means that the agent will keep listening to the communication channels to get a request from the user or from other agents, and response to that request accordingly; when the response is done it returns back to the observation stage again.

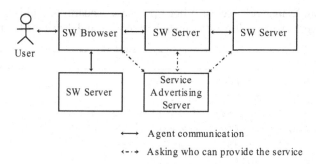

Fig. 4. Web-based multi-agent communication

6 Multi-agent Communication

An individual agent created by our agent framework can behave in two fashions. One is to work as an SW browser and the other is to work as an SW server. The only difference between them is that the former communicates with a human user and SW servers, whilst the latter communicates to SW browsers and other SW servers. To follow the way people have used web browsers so far, an SW browser is designed not to receive a query from an SW server or another SW browser although it can do that.

According to the present use of the current web, we expect that a multi-agent community of SW would consist of several SW browsers, SW servers, and a few Service Advertising Servers virtually linked together on the web, see Fig. 4.

- **Service Advertising Server**

This server maintains information telling which agent can provide which service in the form of `agentCapability(Agent, Service)`, where `Agent` is a name of a registered agent, and `Service` is a service provided by the agent in the form of `OntologyName#Namespace:PredicateName(…)`.

- **Backtracking among alternative answers**

Backtracking among alternative answers is an ability of query answering supported in our multi-agent framework. Suppose an agent A possesses this statement

```
statement(t, 'd':'bookInfo'(ISBN, Cover, Price) ←
    demo(b, _, 'b':'cover'(ISBN, Cover)) ∧
    demo(c, _, 'p':'price'(ISBN, Price))).
```

in its **MP**. The user may pose A a query `?demo(a, _, 'd':'bookInfo'(ISBN,
Cover, Price))` to find out the cover type and price of a book. Then to get the
answers, A will pose the query `?demo(b, _, 'b':'cover'(ISBN, Cover))` to
agent B and `?demo(c, _, 'p':'price'(ISBN, Price))` to agent C. The alternative answers inferred from B and C will be given to A one at a time, and A will
perform backtracking to all the possible answers. This is achieved by each agent em-
ploying a historical memory to keep trace of the possible answers.

7 Query Answering by Multi-agent Communication

To illustrate our framework, we use a book purchase scenario of multi-agent communication that works with multiple distributed ontologies and distributed reasoning.

Publish SW Server

PMP: *Meta-program for the publication ontology*
```
statement(pmp, 'pmp'#'p':'bPrice'(
  'pmp'#'p':'0262631857', '$40') '←' true).
statement(pmp, 'pmp'#'p':'bCover'(
  'pmp'#'p':'0262631857', 'hard') '←' true).
statement(pmp, 'pmp'#'p':'bPrice'(
  'pmp'#'p':'0262635828', '$27') '←' true).
statement(pmp, 'pmp'#'p':'bCover'(
  'pmp'#'p':'0262635828', 'paper') '←' true).
```

Bookshop SW Server

BMP: *Meta-program for the book ontology*
```
meta_statement(bmp, 'rdfs':'type'('Genetic Algorithm',
  'bmp'#'b':'GeneticProgramming') '←' true).
statement(dmp ∪ T, 'dmp'#'d':'bookInfo'(Title,Cover,Price) '←'
  demo(bookShopAgent, T,
    'dmp'#'d':'bookInfo'(Title, Cover, Price))).
```

DMP: *Meta-program for the documentation ontology*
```
statement(dmp, 'dmp'#'d':'bTitle'('pmp'#'p':'0262631857',
  'Genetic Algorithm') '←' true).
statement(dmp, 'dmp'#'d':'bTitle'('pmp'#'p':'0262635828',
  'Genetic Algorithm') '←' true).
statement(dmp ∪ mp,'dmp'#'d':'bookInfo'(Title,Cover,Price)'←'
  'dmp'#'d':'bTitle'(ISBN, Title) '∧'
  demo(_, pmp, 'pmp'#'p':'bCover'(ISBN, Cover)) '∧'
  demo(publisherAgent, pmp, 'pmp'#'p':'bPrice'(ISBN, Price))).
```

Service Advertising Server

```
agentCapability(publisherAgent,
  service(pmp, 'pmp'#'p':'bCover'(ISBN, Cover))).
```

Fig. 5. The MMP and MP programs for the demonstration

Suppose we have an online bookshop selling books supplied by some publishers. The bookshop and the publishers have their own SW servers which provide information about the books able to be supplied by them. This book information is described by some SW ontologies and there are differences between the ontologies in the SW servers of different book shops and different publishers.

An online book purchase begins with firstly a customer wants to buy some books from the bookshop. He then uses an SW browser to get some book information—i.e. title, short description about the book—(expressed in some ontologies) from the bookshop SW server. This information helps him decide which titles to buy. Sometimes, he may want to get more information of the interested titles, such as their publishers, book cover types (e.g. paperback, hardcover), and prices before placing an online order with the bookshop server. Suppose this information is not stored in the bookshop server, but the server can request it from some (probably unknown) publisher servers. In **Fig. 5**, we list only some small parts of the meta-programs, **MP** and **MMP**, possessed by a publisher server, the bookshop server, and service advertising information in the Service Advertising Server, respectively.

A demonstration of the query answering of the SW browser is shown in **Fig. 6**. To answer the first query, the SW browser reasons with its ontologies obtained from the bookshop server and derives the answer from the **BMP** ontology's first statement. However, for the second, the browser adopts **BMP**'s the second statement, and this requires it to pass this query to the bookshop server to answer. The bookshop server uses **DMP**'s third statement to infer the ISBN from the title; and it then queries an unknown publisher and the publisher `publisherAgent` for the cover type and price respectively. According to this example, since the `'Genetic Algorithm'` book has two editions, i.e. hardcover and paperback, the user may ask to get more answers after the first one has been derived and the browser then performs backtracking to get further answers with the similar reasoning steps of the previous one.

```
?-demo(browser, _,
     'rdfs':'type'(X, 'bmp'#'b':'GeneticProgramming')).
  X = 'Genetic Algorithm'
?-demo(browser, _,
     'dmp'#'d':'bookInfo'('Genetic Algorithm', Cover, Price)).
  Cover = 'hard', Price = '$40';
  Cover = 'paper', Price = '$27'
```

Fig. 6. Query answering with the multi-agent communication

8 Related Works

There are some works investigating a multi-agent system adopting SW ontologies. In [3], Serafini and Tamilin proposed a distributed reasoning architecture for SW which used Distributed Description Logic (DDL) to formulate multiple ontologies interconnected by semantic mappings and used a tableau method for performing inference in DDL. To compare it with our work, here we use meta-logic to represent SW ontologies, and a demo(.) predicate to perform inference. We also formalize the demo(.) predicate to perform multi-agent communication.

9 Conclusion

We have developed a meta-logical framework for multi-agent communication of SW information. The multiple ontologies represented by meta-programs are reasoned by individual agents using a demo(.) predicate. With this framework the ontologies and the information derived from them can be exchanged uniformly among the agents in their community.

References

1. Kowalski, R., A., and Kim, J., S. A Metalogic Programming Approach to Multi-agent Knowledge and Belief, *in AI and Mathematical Theory of Computation*, pp. 231-246, 1991.
2. Hirankitti, V., and Tran, X., V. Meta-reasoning with Multiple Distributed Ontologies on the Semantic Web. *In Proc. of the 8ᵗʰ International Conference on Intelligent Technologies*, Phuket, Thailand, pp. 301-309, 2005.
3. Serafinil, L., and Tamilin, A. DRAGO: Distributed Reasoning Architecture for the Semantic Web. *In Proc. of the 2ⁿᵈ European Semantic Web Conf.*. LNCS, Vol. 3532, Springer-Verlag, pp. 361-376, 2005.
4. Zou, Y., Finin, T., Ding, L., Chen, H., and Pan, R. Using Semantic Web technology in Multi-Agent systems: a case study in the TAGA Trading agent environment. *In Proc. of the 5ᵗʰ Int. Conf. on Electronic Commerce*. ACM Press, pp. 95-101, 2003.
5. Grimnes, G., A., Chalmers, S., Edwards, P., and Preece, A. GraniteNights - A Multi-agent Visit Scheduler Utilising Semantic Web Technology. *In Proc. of the 7ᵗʰ Cooperative Information Agents*. LNCS, Vol. 2782, Springer-Verlag, pp. 137-151, 2003.
6. Payne, T., R., Singh, R., and Sycara, K. Processing Schedules using Distributed Ontologies on the Semantic Web. *In Proc. of the Int. Workshop on Web Services, E-Business, and the Semantic Web*. LNCS, Vol. 2512, Springer-Verlag, pp. 203-212, 2002.

Author Index

Abreu, Salvador   38

Banbara, Mutsunori   1
Bartenstein, Oskar   190

Dignum, Virginia   175

Geske, Ulrich   117

Hashimoto, Masaaki   200
Higuchi, Tatsuji   148
Hirankitti, Visit   215
Hofstedt, Petra   12

Inoue, Katsumi   1

Katamine, Keiichi   200
Kitagawa, Yusuke   148
Kleemann, Thomas   135
Kosmatov, Nikolai   25
Krzikalla, Olaf   12

Mure, Yuji   161

Nagai, Tatsuichiro   148
Nagasawa, Isao   148, 161, 200

Nakashima, Yasuo   161
Nishidai, Yasuyuki   148
Nogueira, Vitor   38

Ogawa, Masuharu   161
Ohhashi, Masahito   148

Sakai, Hiroshi   48
Schrader, Gunnar   66, 88
Schutt, Andreas   66
Sinner, Alex   135

Takata, Osamu   148, 161, 200
Tamura, Naoyuki   1, 81
Tran, Vuong Xuan   215
Tsurusaki, Tsuyoshi   148

Umeda, Masanobu   148, 161, 200

Wolf, Armin   66, 88

Yamamoto, Akihiro   102

Lecture Notes in Artificial Intelligence (LNAI)

Vol. 4369: M. Umeda, A. Wolf, O. Bartenstein, U. Geske, D. Seipel, O. Takata (Eds.), Declarative Programming for Knowledge Management. X, 229 pages. 2006.

Vol. 4342: H. de Swart, E. Orłowska, G. Schmidt, M. Roubens (Eds.), Theory and Application of Relational Structures as Knowledge Instruments II. X, 373 pages. 2006.

Vol. 4333: U. Reimer, D. Karagiannis (Eds.), Practical Aspects of Knowledge Management. XII, 338 pages. 2006.

Vol. 4327: M. Baldoni, U. Endriss (Eds.), Declarative Agent Languages and Technologies IV. VIII, 257 pages. 2006.

Vol. 4304: A. Sattar, B.-h. Kang (Eds.), AI 2006: Advances in Artificial Intelligence. XXVII, 1303 pages. 2006.

Vol. 4303: A. Hoffmann, B.-h. Kang, D. Richards, S. Tsumoto (Eds.), Advances in Knowledge Acquisition and Management. XI, 259 pages. 2006.

Vol. 4293: A. Gelbukh, C.A. Reyes-Garcia (Eds.), MICAI 2006: Advances in Artificial Intelligence. XXVIII, 1232 pages. 2006.

Vol. 4289: M. Ackermann, B. Berendt, M. Grobelnik, A. Hotho, D. Mladenič, G. Semeraro, M. Spiliopoulou, G. Stumme, V. Svatek, M. van Someren (Eds.), Semantics, Web and Mining. X, 197 pages. 2006.

Vol. 4285: Y. Matsumoto, R. Sproat, K.-F. Wong, M. Zhang (Eds.), Computer Processing of Oriental Languages. XVII, 544 pages. 2006.

Vol. 4274: Q. Huo, B. Ma, E.-S. Chng, H. Li (Eds.), Chinese Spoken Language Processing. XXIV, 805 pages. 2006.

Vol. 4265: L. Todorovski, N. Lavrač, K.P. Jantke (Eds.), Discovery Science. XIV, 384 pages. 2006.

Vol. 4264: J.L. Balcázar, P.M. Long, F. Stephan (Eds.), Algorithmic Learning Theory. XIII, 393 pages. 2006.

Vol. 4259: S. Greco, Y. Hata, S. Hirano, M. Inuiguchi, S. Miyamoto, H.S. Nguyen, R. Słowiński (Eds.), Rough Sets and Current Trends in Computing. XXII, 951 pages. 2006.

Vol. 4253: B. Gabrys, R.J. Howlett, L.C. Jain (Eds.), Knowledge-Based Intelligent Information and Engineering Systems, Part III. XXXII, 1301 pages. 2006.

Vol. 4252: B. Gabrys, R.J. Howlett, L.C. Jain (Eds.), Knowledge-Based Intelligent Information and Engineering Systems, Part II. XXXIII, 1335 pages. 2006.

Vol. 4251: B. Gabrys, R.J. Howlett, L.C. Jain (Eds.), Knowledge-Based Intelligent Information and Engineering Systems, Part I. LXVI, 1297 pages. 2006.

Vol. 4248: S. Staab, V. Svátek (Eds.), Managing Knowledge in a World of Networks. XIV, 400 pages. 2006.

Vol. 4246: M. Hermann, A. Voronkov (Eds.), Logic for Programming, Artificial Intelligence, and Reasoning. XIII, 588 pages. 2006.

Vol. 4223: L. Wang, L. Jiao, G. Shi, X. Li, J. Liu (Eds.), Fuzzy Systems and Knowledge Discovery. XXVIII, 1335 pages. 2006.

Vol. 4213: J. Fürnkranz, T. Scheffer, M. Spiliopoulou (Eds.), Knowledge Discovery in Databases: PKDD 2006. XXII, 660 pages. 2006.

Vol. 4212: J. Fürnkranz, T. Scheffer, M. Spiliopoulou (Eds.), Machine Learning: ECML 2006. XXIII, 851 pages. 2006.

Vol. 4211: P. Vogt, Y. Sugita, E. Tuci, C.L. Nehaniv (Eds.), Symbol Grounding and Beyond. VIII, 237 pages. 2006.

Vol. 4203: F. Esposito, Z.W. Raś, D. Malerba, G. Semeraro (Eds.), Foundations of Intelligent Systems. XVIII, 767 pages. 2006.

Vol. 4201: Y. Sakakibara, S. Kobayashi, K. Sato, T. Nishino, E. Tomita (Eds.), Grammatical Inference: Algorithms and Applications. XII, 359 pages. 2006.

Vol. 4200: I.F.C. Smith (Ed.), Intelligent Computing in Engineering and Architecture. XIII, 692 pages. 2006.

Vol. 4198: O. Nasraoui, O. Zaïane, M. Spiliopoulou, B. Mobasher, B. Masand, P.S. Yu (Eds.), Advances in Web Mining and Web Usage Analysis. IX, 177 pages. 2006.

Vol. 4196: K. Fischer, I.J. Timm, E. André, N. Zhong (Eds.), Multiagent System Technologies. X, 185 pages. 2006.

Vol. 4188: P. Sojka, I. Kopeček, K. Pala (Eds.), Text, Speech and Dialogue. XV, 721 pages. 2006.

Vol. 4183: J. Euzenat, J. Domingue (Eds.), Artificial Intelligence: Methodology, Systems, and Applications. XIII, 291 pages. 2006.

Vol. 4180: M. Kohlhase, OMDoc – An Open Markup Format for Mathematical Documents [version 1.2]. XIX, 428 pages. 2006.

Vol. 4177: R. Marín, E. Onaindía, A. Bugarín, J. Santos (Eds.), Current Topics in Artificial Intelligence. XV, 482 pages. 2006.

Vol. 4160: M. Fisher, W. van der Hoek, B. Konev, A. Lisitsa (Eds.), Logics in Artificial Intelligence. XII, 516 pages. 2006.

Vol. 4155: O. Stock, M. Schaerf (Eds.), Reasoning, Action and Interaction in AI Theories and Systems. XVIII, 343 pages. 2006.

Vol. 4149: M. Klusch, M. Rovatsos, T.R. Payne (Eds.), Cooperative Information Agents X. XII, 477 pages. 2006.

Vol. 4140: J.S. Sichman, H. Coelho, S.O. Rezende (Eds.), Advances in Artificial Intelligence - IBERAMIA-SBIA 2006. XXIII, 635 pages. 2006.

Vol. 4139: T. Salakoski, F. Ginter, S. Pyysalo, T. Pahikkala (Eds.), Advances in Natural Language Processing. XVI, 771 pages. 2006.

Vol. 4133: J. Gratch, M. Young, R. Aylett, D. Ballin, P. Olivier (Eds.), Intelligent Virtual Agents. XIV, 472 pages. 2006.

Vol. 4130: U. Furbach, N. Shankar (Eds.), Automated Reasoning. XV, 680 pages. 2006.

Vol. 4120: J. Calmet, T. Ida, D. Wang (Eds.), Artificial Intelligence and Symbolic Computation. XIII, 269 pages. 2006.

Vol. 4118: Z. Despotovic, S. Joseph, C. Sartori (Eds.), Agents and Peer-to-Peer Computing. XIV, 173 pages. 2006.

Vol. 4114: D.-S. Huang, K. Li, G.W. Irwin (Eds.), Computational Intelligence, Part II. XXVII, 1337 pages. 2006.

Vol. 4108: J.M. Borwein, W.M. Farmer (Eds.), Mathematical Knowledge Management. VIII, 295 pages. 2006.

Vol. 4106: T.R. Roth-Berghofer, M.H. Göker, H.A. Güvenir (Eds.), Advances in Case-Based Reasoning. XIV, 566 pages. 2006.

Vol. 4099: Q. Yang, G. Webb (Eds.), PRICAI 2006: Trends in Artificial Intelligence. XXVIII, 1263 pages. 2006.

Vol. 4095: S. Nolfi, G. Baldassarre, R. Calabretta, J.C.T. Hallam, D. Marocco, J.-A. Meyer, O. Miglino, D. Parisi (Eds.), From Animals to Animats 9. XV, 869 pages. 2006.

Vol. 4093: X. Li, O.R. Zaïane, Z. Li (Eds.), Advanced Data Mining and Applications. XXI, 1110 pages. 2006.

Vol. 4092: J. Lang, F. Lin, J. Wang (Eds.), Knowledge Science, Engineering and Management. XV, 664 pages. 2006.

Vol. 4088: Z.-Z. Shi, R. Sadananda (Eds.), Agent Computing and Multi-Agent Systems. XVII, 827 pages. 2006.

Vol. 4087: F. Schwenker, S. Marinai (Eds.), Artificial Neural Networks in Pattern Recognition. IX, 299 pages. 2006.

Vol. 4068: H. Schärfe, P. Hitzler, P. Øhrstrøm (Eds.), Conceptual Structures: Inspiration and Application. XI, 455 pages. 2006.

Vol. 4065: P. Perner (Ed.), Advances in Data Mining. XI, 592 pages. 2006.

Vol. 4062: G.-Y. Wang, J.F. Peters, A. Skowron, Y. Yao (Eds.), Rough Sets and Knowledge Technology. XX, 810 pages. 2006.

Vol. 4049: S. Parsons, N. Maudet, P. Moraitis, I. Rahwan (Eds.), Argumentation in Multi-Agent Systems. XIV, 313 pages. 2006.

Vol. 4048: L. Goble, J.-J.C.. Meyer (Eds.), Deontic Logic and Artificial Normative Systems. X, 273 pages. 2006.

Vol. 4045: D. Barker-Plummer, R. Cox, N. Swoboda (Eds.), Diagrammatic Representation and Inference. XII, 301 pages. 2006.

Vol. 4031: M. Ali, R. Dapoigny (Eds.), Advances in Applied Artificial Intelligence. XXIII, 1353 pages. 2006.

Vol. 4029: L. Rutkowski, R. Tadeusiewicz, L.A. Zadeh, J.M. Zurada (Eds.), Artificial Intelligence and Soft Computing – ICAISC 2006. XXI, 1235 pages. 2006.

Vol. 4027: H.L. Larsen, G. Pasi, D. Ortiz-Arroyo, T. Andreasen, H. Christiansen (Eds.), Flexible Query Answering Systems. XVIII, 714 pages. 2006.

Vol. 4021: E. André, L. Dybkjær, W. Minker, H. Neumann, M. Weber (Eds.), Perception and Interactive Technologies. XI, 217 pages. 2006.

Vol. 4020: A. Bredenfeld, A. Jacoff, I. Noda, Y. Takahashi (Eds.), RoboCup 2005: Robot Soccer World Cup IX. XVII, 727 pages. 2006.

Vol. 4013: L. Lamontagne, M. Marchand (Eds.), Advances in Artificial Intelligence. XIII, 564 pages. 2006.

Vol. 4012: T. Washio, A. Sakurai, K. Nakajima, H. Takeda, S. Tojo, M. Yokoo (Eds.), New Frontiers in Artificial Intelligence. XIII, 484 pages. 2006.

Vol. 4008: J.C. Augusto, C.D. Nugent (Eds.), Designing Smart Homes. XI, 183 pages. 2006.

Vol. 4005: G. Lugosi, H.U. Simon (Eds.), Learning Theory. XI, 656 pages. 2006.

Vol. 4002: A. Yli-Jyrä, L. Karttunen, J. Karhumäki (Eds.), Finite-State Methods and Natural Language Processing. XIV, 312 pages. 2006.

Vol. 3978: B. Hnich, M. Carlsson, F. Fages, F. Rossi (Eds.), Recent Advances in Constraints. VIII, 179 pages. 2006.

Vol. 3963: O. Dikenelli, M.-P. Gleizes, A. Ricci (Eds.), Engineering Societies in the Agents World VI. XII, 303 pages. 2006.

Vol. 3960: R. Vieira, P. Quaresma, M.d.G.V. Nunes, N.J. Mamede, C. Oliveira, M.C. Dias (Eds.), Computational Processing of the Portuguese Language. XII, 274 pages. 2006.

Vol. 3955: G. Antoniou, G. Potamias, C. Spyropoulos, D. Plexousakis (Eds.), Advances in Artificial Intelligence. XVII, 611 pages. 2006.

Vol. 3949: F.A. Savacı (Ed.), Artificial Intelligence and Neural Networks. IX, 227 pages. 2006.

Vol. 3946: T.R. Roth-Berghofer, S. Schulz, D.B. Leake (Eds.), Modeling and Retrieval of Context. XI, 149 pages. 2006.

Vol. 3944: J. Quiñonero-Candela, I. Dagan, B. Magnini, F. d'Alché-Buc (Eds.), Machine Learning Challenges. XIII, 462 pages. 2006.

Vol. 3937: H. La Poutré, N.M. Sadeh, S. Janson (Eds.), Agent-Mediated Electronic Commerce. X, 227 pages. 2006.

Vol. 3932: B. Mobasher, O. Nasraoui, B. Liu, B. Masand (Eds.), Advances in Web Mining and Web Usage Analysis. X, 189 pages. 2006.

Vol. 3930: D.S. Yeung, Z.-Q. Liu, X.-Z. Wang, H. Yan (Eds.), Advances in Machine Learning and Cybernetics. XXI, 1110 pages. 2006.